Still Standing

From
debutante
to detox

Still Standing

From debutante to detox

Liz Jamieson-Hastings

HarperCollins*Publishers*

In this book some names and identifying details
have been changed.

National Library of New Zealand Cataloguing-in-Publication Data
Jamieson-Hastings, Liz.
Still standing : from debutante to detox / Liz Jamieson-Hastings.
ISBN 978-1-86950-701-5
1. Jamieson-Hastings, Liz. 2. Alcoholics—New Zealand—
Biography. 3. Women alcoholics—New Zealand—Biography.
4. Alcoholics—Rehabilitation—New Zealand. I. Title.
362.292092 dc—22

First published 2009
HarperCollins*Publishers (New Zealand) Limited*
P.O. Box 1, Shortland Street, Auckland 1140

ISBN 978 1 86950 701 5

Cover design by Louise McGeachie
Cover photograph by Charlie Smith

Typesetting by IslandBridge

Printed by Griffin Press, Australia

70gsm Classic used by HarperCollins*Publishers* is a natural,
recyclable product made from wood grown in sustainable forests.
The manufacturing processes conform to the environmental
regulations in the country of origin, Finland.

This book is dedicated to Ian, the love of my life — soul mate, husband, lover, friend and the greatest encourager to live life to the full whom I have ever met; and to Debbie, who in typing this manuscript has truly demonstrated the art of forgiveness.

What you have experienced,
no power on earth can take from you.

Viktor E. Frankl (1905–1997)

He who has a why to live
can bear with almost any how.

Friedrich Nietzche (1844–1900)

Contents

Foreword

I will never forget the first time I saw Liz Jamieson. She stood up to address a group of recovering alcoholics in a small church hall in Khyber Pass — dressed to the nines, red hair flaming in the dim hall, intense blue eyes holding the audience, powerful voice bellowing off the rafters . . . yet, at the same time, diminutive, vulnerable, almost insecure. It was a compelling performance, indeed inspiring in its emotional outpouring.

Emotions and verbalizing them are Liz Jamieson's trademark. She says things other people feel, and she expresses them dramatically, vividly and without fear.

Yet as I have grown to know her, that first impression remains as true today as it was when made thirty years ago. Liz is unique — a complex mix of power, hope and strength, on the one hand, matched by vulnerability, sensitivity and constant questioning, on the other.

Liz is never relaxing to be with. She is always on the go, pursuing intently a solution to the world's ills. It is her extraordinary energy, her unfailing diligence, her explosive vocabulary, and her instinctive shrewdness that have allowed her to survive emotional and social upheavals that would have killed a man twice her size.

She is quite simply the best speaker I have heard on addiction, on recovery, and on the disease of alcoholism. She says it the way it is — direct, honest and without frills. It is a subject she knows, because she has lived it and continues to battle elements of it despite being sober for almost forty years.

In America, she would have been a celebrity, and I still believe Oprah was lucky she was born the other side of the world. Liz was made to be a television talkback host.

Liz and I have had our moments when we attempted to educate New Zealand youth about the dangers in the use of drugs and alcohol. I would like to think we did make a difference, but not nearly enough.

Few people have been to either the depths or the heights that Liz has. Her story is an inspiration to all of us who battle our demons.

Murray Deaker

Preface

This is the story of what it was like, what happened, and what it is like now: a story I could never have imagined would be as difficult to write as it has been. Too much of my painful life could mean a sob story; too much of the spiritual lessons learnt would become a sermon; and too much of my achievements would be an ego trip. It is also far too easy to lay blame, too easy to vindicate behaviour, and too easy to character-assassinate in order to justify actions than to take responsibility. However, this does not mitigate arrogance, ignorance, stupidity, sadism or manipulative behaviour on the part of others. I would remind the reader that in many instances of the above, these observations were not mine alone.

I have not set out to deliberately hurt anybody, so there are areas in which I have needed to be non-specific; but at the same time, to ignore certain behaviours and attitudes besides my own would be to deny the unacceptable behaviour of others. I have also attempted to be as fair as I can, but taking an objective view of a subjective event can only be done in retrospect, and can never be accomplished one hundred per cent.

Finally, my wish is that in these pages I have given hope to those who feel bereft of it, encouragement to any who are on life's journey and feel they are journeying through Hell (as Winston Churchill put it: 'just keep going'), and a sense of purpose to those who have emerged on the other side. It is not what happens to us in life that is important so much as what we do with it.

> I shall pass through this world but once. Any good thing, therefore, that I can do, or any act of kindness that I can show to any human being, let me do it now. Let me not defer or neglect it, for I shall not pass this way again.

> Well-known saying among American Quakers

Acknowledgements

I am grateful for the telephone call from Roger Scherrer which prompted these pages to materialize; and to Judith White, Mike Johnson, Murray Deaker, and in particular the late Diane Haworth, authors themselves, for their encouragement and persistence in convincing me I could write this myself; to Ruth Hamilton, Don Waddell and all the wonderful women at HarperCollins, all with experience in the area of publishing; and finally to those people mentioned and unmentioned who have participated in my life, including family and friends, the hundreds of prison inmates and thousands of schoolchildren with whom I will continue to work for as long as I am wanted, and the millions of recovered alcoholics and addicts who by their recovery make their world and mine a better place in which to live.

Chapter 1

Sucking a silver spoon

'And who the fuck are you?'

Two coal-black, defiant, fearful eyes challenged mine as, seated on the swivel chair at the front of the room, I scanned the faces in front of me.

He must have been thirty-something. The coffee-coloured hands were pock-marked with old-fashioned tattoos — chains, 'love' and 'hate', a bird between the thumb and forefinger. Slouched in the chair, legs splayed, what caught my eye was the nerve twitching on his face below the left eye, and his right leg which appeared to suffer from St Vitus's dance. The body never lies unless the owner has a PhD in the art of super-intelligence espionage, and this one had no chance of that. The brown face, the tattoos, the fiery eyes had far from the desired effect on me. Kindly, sympathetically and compassionately, I held the gaze as I replied calmly: 'Well, if you stay here for the time they suggest, I will help you to discover who the fuck I am.' He blinked. This was *not* what he had expected from the mature, redheaded, confident, obviously well-educated woman from the other side of the tracks calmly relaxed in front of him — but then alcohol and drug treatment centres are always full of surprises.

How was *I* confidently able to deal with a brown-skinned ex-prison-inmate in a drug and alcohol treatment centre when my background was obviously one of white, upper-middle-class, well-educated debutante society? That's my story.

I lived in a suburb like any upmarket suburb in Auckland. Mine was where the men who had fought in World War II lived with their wives; the ones who had been the officers and had married the soft-petalled, delicate-skinned English girls and brought them proudly home, like trophies after a cricket match. How English these girls were. They seemed old to me, because I was so young and my mother was one of them. She had come 12,000 miles with a husband she barely knew. In the war, you see, they never knew how long anybody would live; particularly people like my father, a lieutenant on a destroyer in the Mediterranean. So they married, because 'nice' girls did not sleep with men out of wedlock in those days. These ladies arrived with all the accoutrements of an English country house upbringing. Their lives had been with nannies and governesses, cooks and servants. Meals appeared at appropriate times, and as children they had always eaten in the nursery, seeing their parents for twenty minutes or so before bedtime. When later in life I met my grandfather in England, I found him austere, authoritative and intimidating, even when I was aged twenty. My mother hardly ever talked about him.

New Zealand was an adventure for many of these women, and they arrived believing that the trappings of the life they had left behind would be available in the new 'colonies'. The culture shock for most of them must have been horrendous.

My mother had never boiled an egg, never ironed a shirt, and rarely made her own bed. War rationing had limited the menu and taken care of any possible idea of wastage. To the day she died, the remains of the evening meal went into the blender and either became soup or sauce. Sixty years later, I cannot break this habit I learnt from her.

I didn't meet my father until I was eighteen months old, as he was in Gibraltar when he received the message that he had a daughter, and on his return I would have nothing to do with him. He was a stranger; and this initial lack of emotional bonding was to influence my relationship with him for the rest of my life.

The twelve-week boat journey from Britain to New Zealand in

1945 must have been a nightmare for many of the war brides. Poor Mother was seasick for the entire journey; she was four months pregnant with my first sister, and travelling with a husband she barely knew, an English nanny who was coming with us ostensibly to look after me but who spent most of the journey confined to the cabin, sick as well, and a stroppy daughter. Father and I were the only two who did not succumb to the incessant rolling. My dislike of my father was so intense that most of the meals he tried desperately to feed me ended up adorning his head as I either threw or spat them at him. Perhaps the only ray of sunshine in his life during that period was that I learnt to walk on the rolling ship's deck. As a retired naval officer and sea-lover himself, it was probably hugely gratifying and more than likely a source of entertainment for the ship's crew.

All her life, Mother had a strong sense of duty which never left her, although I am sure she must have questioned it at times. To this day, she is for me a classic example of the indomitable British spirit that won wars and built an Empire which, for all its faults, must be the most influential the world has known. She knew no one on her arrival, and one can only imagine the culture shock that met her. Not only was New Zealand the end of the world, but she was one of many English brides whom the local New Zealand girls detested with a vengeance. For them, these women had stolen their potential husbands; even in 1946, there were still hate clubs in existence. These groups of vindictive women set out to ensure that the 'intruders' were made as miserable as possible. Scone-making competitions and jam bring-and-buys were held to ridicule the new arrivals, although Mother was fortunate to avoid being involved in most of these. City life was too busy, and a new baby and a two-year-old took up much of her time.

The English nanny was replaced by June, a Karitane nurse who was fresh out of school. I loved June. She took me swimming, and was a great builder of sand castles with me on St Heliers Bay beach. Best of all, we went shell collecting. The old toffee tin we kept them in remained with me for years after she had gone. The nostalgic memories that can arise from the simple activities of childhood are so precious in later life. I wonder today how many of our children have been deprived of these as a consequence of the technological and electronic age.

Exciting and dramatic memories of St Heliers are still with me, along with gentler ones. I remember threading daisy chains with Mother and Jenny, my sister, when the daisies were scattered like out-of-season snowflakes on the summer lawn. They became our pearl necklaces, which were only surrendered the following morning after meeting their deaths by suffocation in the bed overnight.

An old-fashioned volunteer fire siren stirs memories of the pine trees alight from the sparks of the incinerator, the neighbours and their children running to join us as the firemen turned their hoses not only on the fire but also on Mother's newly washed clothes on the line and the precious bed of roses that she had nurtured so lovingly. In true British style, she had become determined to adapt where needs be to the colonial lifestyle, realizing that nannies would not always be around.

Being lost at the age of four was a traumatic experience. I was sure that Mother had told me to start walking home from kindergarten and she would meet me. Somehow there was a misunderstanding, and I found myself wandering the streets of St Heliers Bay until I found familiar landmarks which guided me home. Father arrived to find me in a pool of tears on the front doorstep and the entire St Heliers Bay police force combing the streets, attempting to find an 'abducted child'!

Then there was the train. I have no idea why I wanted a wind-up train for my fourth birthday, but it became my pride and joy. No one but me was allowed to wind the engine with its enormous key, a big red ribbon attached to it so that it wouldn't get lost. The engine was green and black. It had a green coal truck that I used to fill with everything from sugar to flour to garden dirt, depending on the story I would be telling at the time about where it was going for its next adventure. Golden syrup 'for the bears in the woods' didn't go down very well with Mother, and after that its cargo became a tad limited for a while.

Jenny, my two-year-old sister, was mesmerized by the whole contraption and the adventures 'Clickity Clack' got into as it went around and around its oblong set of tracks. A lever would stop it at the station, where imaginary people would alight and board the two brown carriages behind the coal truck. Sometimes there were farmers, their sheep piled into the truck from the toy farm we played with at the same time. All the figures on this farm were painted metal, and it was a never-ending chore for me to stop Jenny grabbing them to chew. June said that Jenny would die if she did that: 'They will make her very sick and she will die.' I wasn't too sure what dying meant, but it didn't sound very nice. That train set stayed with me until I was thirty-eight years old and sold it in a garage sale. The little boy who chose it from the pile of nondescript items on the garage floor had a face lit up like a lighthouse beacon as he walked away. I just knew Clickity Clack would be well cared for.

Mother became pregnant again, not that I remember being particularly interested. I was more interested in the fact that we were moving house. The steps needing to be climbed from the garage at the bottom of the hill at 1 Auckland Road in St Heliers to the front door were too much for Mother. She had already struggled with baby Jenny up and down them, and simply could not face doing the same with another baby *plus* two children. We had to move. And where were most of their friends? Remuera!

What a difference there was. Just two steps to the front door, but best of all there were *trams*. Running up and down Victoria Avenue at the top of the street, clanging their bells, they were such a novelty for Jenny and me, *and* we rode on them to school, by ourselves; well, not quite — we had new school friends join us along the way.

Pam and Judy became my best friends at school. We lived within walking distance of each other in Victoria Avenue, and we loved to play, we loved to create; we were inseparable at times and screeching rivals at others. We were loyal and we were jealous, we were bossy and submissive, we were competitive and co-operative; but best of all, we shared a puckish sense of humour. I do not remember any of us ever being cruel; petulant and abrasive, yes, but never cruel. Perhaps that is why our friendship has survived. From our primary-school years at Hill Top, when it was in Khyber Pass next to the brewery, until the present day over sixty years later, we have never lost contact. The three of us attended primary and secondary schools together, were Auckland debutantes, and then each went her separate way in life, but we still come together to reminisce and laugh over the old times and old memories.

But back to Hill Top, where memories are of hard work in the classroom and creative experiences in the playground. Judy had seventy-two Derwent coloured pencils and was the envy of the class. It was hardly conceivable that there could be that number of colours in a box of colouring-in pencils, but somehow there were. Most of us had either twenty-four or thirty-six — but *seventy-two*. Forget the brand of our tennis racquets, or the label on our school bags: the pencils were *the* status symbol at ten years of age, the *ultimate* status symbol.

Pam was the scrapbook queen. We had to create these for Mrs Mackie's general knowledge lesson, and Pam would discover a piece of general knowledge in a label off a tin of soup. Judy would periodically allow her to use the seventy-two Derwent pencils, providing Pam helped her with her scrapbook. My contribution as the third member of the trio was to thread needles for each of them in our embroidery classes with Mrs Innes. Woe betide our mothers if they did not use our tea-showers, carefully appliquéd with cut-out organza flowers, for their tea parties or bridge sessions. My embroidery (a quaintly antiquated pastime in today's world) has carried me through many traumas, disappointments and difficult times over the years, calming me in a way that I suppose chemicals of one sort or another would do today. Not a school curriculum item now, and certainly of little practical use, embroidery demands patience and perseverance, and for me was a great teacher of both. How I long for many of our children today to keep skills such as this alive, for their own satisfaction as well as a way of encouraging them to find talents and supportive mechanisms to help them through life's vicissitudes.

A glass of warm milk revolts me even now — we had half a pint of free milk every day at school, warm from having been in the sun for an hour, and with a two-inch layer of cream at the top of the glass bottle. I found it disgusting, far preferring the dripping or spaghetti sandwiches I had for lunch (incredibly unhealthy, but *such* a treat!), and on *very* special occasions a meat pie. We would bolt our food down to enable someone in the class to rush out and grab a spot for us on the tennis court (which was never used for tennis) so that we could play rounders. Like baseball without the bat, we would hit a bowled tennis ball with our fist, and run as fast as we could from base to base before the ball was thrown and it hit us or the base guard. The 'best-fisted' were always chosen first when we picked our teams, and the games would continue for weeks until the first team reached 100 full runs. We would then dissolve the teams and pick again. Never at any stage do I remember that we cried boredom, either at school or at home. Pam, Judy, I and the girls with whom we associated in Remuera could easily make our own amusements.

After school, sister Jenny and I would have swimming lessons at the Parnell Baths with Mr Kraus, or tennis lessons, and on a Saturday morning we went for ballet lessons at a ballet school in Swanson Street in the city. Sunday was Sunday School, and church on special days such as Easter or Christmas. We were always in awe of Archdeacon Prebble at St Mark's Church, totally convinced that he would just *know* if we had done anything wrong during the week.

What Judy, Pam and I loved the best were our theatre and acting presentations to our three respective families, various brothers and sisters included. We spent hours learning our lines from a children's book of plays. My mother had the most wonderful dress-up trunk that we would raid for our costumes, and all three sets of parents would co-operate if necessary with current items of clothing — except for shoes. Teetering around in high heels, no matter how wedge-like they were, was a total no-no, much to our fury, as we needed them (as we understood the situation) to lend authenticity to Lady or Lord So-and-so. How I wish we had preserved more items from that trunk. The old purple parasol with its ivory handle, the dainty little evening bags made of velvet and embroidered with rhinestones, the peacock-blue taffeta skirt that rustled with richness when the wearer swept onto our home-made stage. Fortunately, over the years I rescued the ostrich feathers, the black and pink lace fans, and the elbow-length cream kid gloves with their mother-of-pearl buttons, but the lizard-skin handbags and the old fox furs found their way to charity, or hopefully perhaps to a theatre company.

Mother was an enthusiast for learning. Schooling was one thing; learning was something different, yet paradoxically the same. What we learnt in school was different to what we learnt at home. At home, we learnt social graces, which among other things incorporated the appropriate usage of words. Serviettes were napkins; drapes were curtains; the lounge was the sitting or drawing room; Mum and Dad were Mummy and Daddy; one had visitors, *never* 'company'. There was no such thing as 'partaking' — one *ate*; said 'goodbye' not 'bye bye', 'thank you' not 'ta', 'yes' not 'wouldn't mind if I do'; and woe betide anyone who used their knife like a spoon, did not tip their soup away from them when they drank (never *slurped*) it, cut their roll with a knife, did not put butter on the side of the plate before buttering, shook the salt over their food instead of placing it on the side of the plate, and — horror of horrors — stuck their little finger in the air whilst drinking tea or coffee! Mother was not a snob; she had simply been raised in a stratum of society which is now, sadly, one of the last areas of prejudice that needs to be erased. 'You can't make a race-horse out of a draught-horse,' she used to say. 'Perhaps a draught-horse out of a race-horse, but never vice versa.' She came from a family with titles and a history that stretched a long way into the Scottish highlands. For her, learning incorporated discipline along with information and knowledge; there were right and wrong ways of doing, just as there were good and bad. Some of her ways now appear quaint and outdated, while others have been wonderful foundation stones in my life. I would never be where I am today if it hadn't been for my mother's instilling of principles, values, and behaviours. The various nannies validated many of these, but Mother was the instigator; and play, or perhaps more appropriately *games*, were one of the avenues she used for teaching. 'Parlour games' she used to call them when we had our birthday parties.

These were held between the hours of 2 p.m. and 5.30 p.m. We would be dressed in our organza party dresses (which we disliked intensely until Mother found a way of stopping the material scratching under our arms), bows in our hair, white ankle socks and our special party shoes. Mine were pink with a little white bow on the front. Nannies were generally left behind, as mothers enjoyed these social outings with their daughters, which began to develop into a competition about whose child had the prettiest dress and how they were progressing in school. Mother was always proud of me: not only did I undemocratically end up as chief organizer of the group, but by the age of ten I was able (unsolicited) to recite Robert Browning's 'Pied Piper of Hamlin' in its entirety! Heaven help anyone interrupting the spiel.

We played musical chairs, and musical bumps (with cushions) if there were not enough chairs available. This entailed one less chair or cushion on the floor for the number of children present. Music would be played, and when it stopped the person who couldn't find a free chair or cushion was out of the game. This progressed until the last two were left with one cushion or one chair. The final claimant won. This game was guaranteed to find the spoilt 'Mummy's child', bad loser or most aggressive child in the group. It often ended in tears or a fight, so was generally placed immediately before the birthday tea or — ultimately — erased from the list of games! Years later I saw a group of adults play this, with completely different outcomes!

Pass the parcel was fairer. We sat in a circle with a large parcel made of layers and layers of newspaper, and passed it around until the music stopped. The person holding the parcel would then unwrap a layer, the music would start again, and the exercise would continue until the last layer had been unwrapped to reveal the 'prize' that had been won: a bar of chocolate, a small china ornament, or some colouring pencils.

Tea was the highlight of the party. Every place at the table had a name tag telling us where we were to sit. There were party hats and crackers. Sandwiches, bread with butter and hundreds and thousands on it, and pikelets. Sausage rolls were a real treat, as were baby chipolatas and bright red cheerios. This first course was then followed by Sally Lunn cake, miniature sponges with pink icing and a cherry on top, chocolate biscuits, and jelly and ice-cream; and finally the birthday cake was brought in with all the candles, and blown out to the singing of 'Happy Birthday'. Most of the time we were beautifully mannered: 'Please may I have . . .' and 'Thank you' floated around the table unless there appeared to be a shortage (particularly of chocolate) — then the 'I wants' would start and, horror of horrors, there would be the occasional grab followed by a smacked hand, tears, and a forced retreat from the room, leaving the rest of us like stunned mullets. The offender would be allowed back only if accompanied by an apology; looking back, this must have taken a good deal of courage.

When there were cherries or other stonefruit, we would recite 'tinker, tailor, soldier, sailor; rich man, poor man, beggar man, thief; silk, satin, cotton, rags; big house, little house, pigsty, barn; Rolls, Jag, Ford, Chevy' as we went through the stones on the plates. This often ended in tears as well, when someone ended up a sailor dressed in rags living in a barn as a thief driving a Chevy! No amount of emphasis on the fact that it was 'only a game' seemed to make the slightest bit of difference to the contender's conviction that that was to be his/her fate in life.

Although seldom present at birthday parties, nannies always took charge once we returned home. Their sole purpose was to instil discipline, but unfortunately they stifled spontaneity at the same time. I thrived on the exhilarating periods between nannies, as it meant a certain freedom from their discipline.

Some left of their own accord, like the German woman whom Jenny and I shut out on the flat roof of the house while she was hanging laundry out to dry. We reckoned we were doing our part to compensate for World War II. How she got back into the house, I will never know. I now suspect she was a Jewish refugee, poor woman, but I never found out. Then there was Miss Marney. She was small and mean. She used to pinch me and pull Jenny's hair. Several months after she left — she was sacked — great excitement occurred when the police discovered that it was she who had forced the French windows of the drawing room and stolen Mother's housekeeping money from her writing desk. Noeleen followed; she used to steal Mother's stockings, and wore Mother's clothes when our parents went to Sydney for a week's holiday. Every night she would crawl into bed with me so that 'the bogey men can't find me'. She had disappeared one day when we arrived home from school.

Then Miss Crocker arrived. She was every child's worst nightmare. My introduction to her was being hauled upstairs into bed, with the curtains drawn and bread and water for dinner. I had asked Jenny to tell Mother I was going to play with a friend on the way home after school and would be back by 4.30 p.m. I didn't even see Mother. This *apparition* met me in the hall and marched me off to my room, dictating rules and regulations along the way. The first one I had apparently broken was not to ask for permission to stop off to play. How dared I just assume I could do so! In future, I was to make prior arrangements with both my family and that of the friend. This was to cause enormous confusion in my life, as spontaneity and impulsiveness became a blurred grey mist. It took me years to differentiate between the two.

Miss Crocker was from a long line of English nannies. I was seven years old when she arrived, and she was to remain with us for the next four years. Both my sisters and I believe that she is responsible for my youngest sister's stutter, which fortunately has declined with age. Poor Georgina (the third in our line of girls) was pounced on whenever a 'baby' word was uttered in Miss Crocker's presence. There was no such thing as a 'woof woof'; it was a dog. A 'moo cow' was a cow. Jenny had the hardest time of the three of us. She was always losing things: ribbons, shoes, socks. She spilt raspberry drink down her pink cardigan, and refused to wear the bright yellow embroidered braces on her trousers to keep them up. She tore her dresses and muddied her shoes. She was the one caught reading *School Friend* and *Girls' Crystal* when homework was on the agenda. She was always in trouble.

I found it easier to be agreeable. Much of the discipline I found irritating, such as making my bed with hospital corners, but I went along with it anyway (why waste energy?). The exceptions came when there was an issue over what I could and could not read. The only totally ballistic, scratching, biting, screaming, out-of-control tantrum I ever had with Miss Crocker (that I remember) was over reading. Miss Crocker was a Jane Austen, Charlotte Brontë, Rudyard Kipling, *Wind in the Willows*, and *Alice in Wonderland* promoter. In my estimation, these stories were either pathetic or just plain stupid — who wanted to chase white rabbits or read about lonely women trudging over English moors, when there were the Famous Five, Bulldog Drummond and that exciting English rake the Scarlet Pimpernel with whom to go adventuring? And what about Proserpina and Pluto and Echo and Narcissus from Ancient Greece, and then Rider Haggard and King Solomon's Mines? For once, Mother came to my rescue. I could read whatever

I chose, providing I consulted with her; and so began my lifelong love affair with books and reading. I grew up into the Austens, the Brontës, the Thackerays and the Eliots, and many more. Some became compulsory as I moved through my schooling, but I will be eternally grateful to a mother who encouraged my curiosity with books rather than compelling me to read certain publications as part of my education in what some termed 'the classics'.

However, nobody is ever without some mitigating characteristics; and one of Miss Crocker's was her organizing ability. I believe that in her own way (never to be admitted by her), she was extremely fond of the entire family. Our parents were never in any doubt that she would abdicate or abuse her role of nanny in any way. During the six weeks they once spent in England with Georgina, Miss Crocker became a good deal gentler and, I believe, genuinely attempted to ensure that we enjoyed the days despite the separation from our parents. Excursions to the zoo on several occasions, with or without school friends, were always a thrill, especially when we could have an elephant ride and watch the chimpanzees' tea party. She took us for walks through the bush in the Domain and educational afternoons in the Museum. Sometimes there was tea at the kiosk on One Tree Hill, where we always felt *so* grown up!

The highlight of our parents' six-week absence had to be the fancy-dress party Miss Crocker organized for us. Jenny and I were each allowed to ask eleven of our school friends, who had to attend dressed as a character or title from a book. What a day that was, plus the excitement building up to it. Miss Crocker made my outfit when I decided to go as a Georgette Heyer character — The Grand Sophy. My high-waisted dress was pink with cream lace around the neckline. The cap, pink as well, sported two ostrich feathers set at rakish angles, one pale blue and the other a deep burgundy red, which looked stunning in contrast to the pink dress. Finally, there were the long, cream, above-the-elbow mittens. I looked the perfect lady hostess; I felt the ultimate lady hostess; I was in my element! All my mother's aristocratic English genes rose to the surface, and I *knew* that one day the world would see me as a lady. I would have a title somehow, and my parents would be proud of me — such girlish dreams.

We had a magician, we had a Punch and Judy show, we played games — and *no one* misbehaved at the table. Why? Because no mothers had been allowed to attend. Miss Crocker was in charge, and the afternoon ran like clockwork. There is a box amongst my silk embroidery skeins, which if opened contains, within layers of tissue paper, two ostrich feathers: one blue, one burgundy red.

On our parents' return, Miss Crocker went on holiday; and despite the excellent six weeks we had had alone with her, it was a relief. She left when we broke up at the end of the school term. We drove for a whole day to our grandparents' holiday home at Mourea on the Ohau Channel between Lakes Rotorua and Rotoiti. Here there was a freedom for all of us; well, perhaps not so much for Mother, although I believe she grew to enjoy the rather basic life dictated by a water tank and septic tank system. Drinking water had to be boiled, washing was done in an old copper with a hand-turned wringer, and such ironing as I did (for sixpence an hour) was with a heavy metal iron that had to be heated on the stove. The only way to discover if it was hot enough was to sprinkle water on it. If the water spat off the metal, that was it and I ironed furiously until the iron became too cold. Sprinkling water became too slow in the end, so I resorted to spitting — if the spittle curled into a ball, the iron was ready. Miss Crocker would never have approved, but then she was not there.

We loved our times at Mourea, especially the days we spent with Nellie, a young Maori girl from the local marae who came twice a week to help Mother. She must have been about fifteen or sixteen, and Jenny and I adored her. Nellie would take us down to the Channel and help us catch whitebait. Koura would be turned up from under stones in the lake (often too small in the shallows, so we were *never* allowed to take them home), or we would fish for them in the Channel waters. Mushrooms, blackberries and fir cones were to be had from the fields behind the house, but the place we liked best was the marae. The greatest fun there was learning to ride the sheep, hanging onto their fleeces for dear life and timing who could stay on the longest. Helping the women wash the clothes in the Channel was fun, too, especially when they would sing to us and slap the washing in time to the rhythm. Sometimes when we went trolling for trout in the early hours of the morning with Father, we would catch enough to take some to the marae. We taught Nellie's mother to make pikelets, and she wove a kete (flax bag) each for Jenny and me, with tiny little pieces of shell decorating the outside. Somehow in all our travels the kete got lost, but for a long time mushrooms found a temporary home in them when we raided the fields.

Although they owned the house, Gaga and Papa (I could never get my child's tongue around 'Grandma' and 'Grandpa') never came to stay. Gaga enjoyed her Auckland life too much, and Papa had the family business to manage. I adored my grandmother, and now in retrospect can see that I inherited many of her character traits.

Gaga Merritt (McLaren as she was born) was Scottish to the core. The daughter of a ploughman from Stirling, she had made her way south to Birmingham by the early 1900s and met my grandfather who was working in the hardware, carpet and linoleum business. Birth and marriage certificates, gained years later when I was in London, turned up some interesting facts. Gaga was obviously pregnant with my eldest uncle at the marriage ceremony, and not a blushing young bride (as she would always have us believe) but a woman of thirty-two, eight years older than my grandfather, when they arrived in Auckland in 1911. Amazingly, they held back their Golden Wedding celebrations for one year so that the family would not know their secret. We never discovered why they had decided on the arduous trip to New Zealand. Was my grandfather my uncle's natural father, or had he felt sorry for my grandmother who was pregnant by someone else, and offered the adventure of a life in the colonies? We will never know.

Gaga was no shrinking violet. She bore three more sons and was the driving force in establishing H.T. Merritt Ltd. Their home 'Dilkusha' was one of the original houses in Papatoetoe, and its orchard, vegetable garden, rose garden and tennis court, along with a horse and a car (the latter a luxury), a housekeeper and a gardener, soon established the Merritt family in Auckland. Not on the same scale as the Fletchers, Kerridges or the Seabrooks, of course, but Auckland society knew who the Merritts were. This was both a plus and a minus for me in the years ahead.

Gaga took us to tea at the Lyceum Club at Smith and Caughey's, bought us our party dresses, and insisted that Jenny and I had lessons in floral arrangement at the Constance Spry school in Auckland, and at the Cordon Bleu cooking school. More than anyone, she encouraged me to continue with my silk embroidery, and she would have loved to have seen me as a piano player in my later years — a skill I have never been able to master, much to my chagrin. She was determined that I would be the lady she had fought so hard to become, so far from her own background.

Papa I ultimately attempted to avoid, without being able to explain the reason for this to anyone. I cannot remember the precise age I was when he persuaded me to visit him in his potting shed each weekend when we drove out for Sunday lunch. He would lift me up on the bench, amongst the tulip bulbs of which he was so proud, pull my skirt up and get me to pull my panties down. All he ever did was look — until one fateful evening when I was sitting on his knee in an armchair in the study. The others had just left for the dining room when his hand crept up my leg and his fingers were inside me. To this day I can remember the revulsion, the sense of betrayal, and the fear that was established by that one act. How much more terrifying, bewildering, shaming and damaging it would be for a woman — let alone a child — when rape or any other non-consensual sexual act is performed on her.

Over the years I have discovered that literally hundreds of men and women in the upper social strata of society have had similar (or more traumatic) experiences to mine from family members. Women *and* men, some of whom still carry the scars that have affected relationships, marriages, jobs and careers. Too frightened, too ashamed, to do anything except try to bury the memories and the feelings. I have never met *anyone* who has managed to erase memories such as these. Anaesthetized them with alcohol or prescription chemicals, yes. Transferred and projected their anger onto individuals and society in general, yes. Repeated and perpetuated the behaviour in their own families, yes. But *erased* the memories — never.

What I *have* done, and seen others have the courage to do, is to deal with these memories and the resulting feelings so that they do not continue to cripple the individual for the rest of their lives and perpetuate the harm that they do to people around them. No one buries memories or feelings dead — we bury them alive. It is what we do with those memories and feelings that is important. Memories are our reference books in life. They are never erased; they can be used. The associated emotions are what we deal with, and we learn the art of forgiveness; we are truly fortunate if we can couple this with acquiring compassion and understanding.

As my life unfolded, I learnt what I needed to do, I did what I needed to do, and now I share with others what I did. The process of forgiveness is a choice that relieves us of past burdens. Memories can be used; it is up to us to find our own reasons for them. Today, that childhood experience is one of life's scars that I carry. Perhaps, when I talk about mine today, I can help someone else with theirs. For even God cannot change the past.

Chapter 2

Grooming to become a socialite

Boarding-school years began in the chaos of emotional pain and ended in the turmoil of confusion. A whole day was spent travelling by bus from Auckland to Havelock North in Hawke's Bay, to the 'school on top of the hill' — Woodford House. We were led to believe, and *did* believe, that we were the élite of the élite. Iona, Nga Tawa and St Matthew's jockeyed for a poor second place.

Preparations for this phase of my life were exciting. Judy and Pam were coming, too, so it was like the Three Musketeers embarking on an adventure. Mother had been sent a list of the uniform requirements, and she and I sat for hours sewing on Cash's name tapes that had been ordered from England. These were white strips of cotton cloth stitched with my name, so that each item could be identified for the school laundry and, of course, in case we left any clothing around once at school. I was to discover that was not a good idea: the item went into the school 'pound', and our meagre pocket-money was used to extract it. I never discovered where the 'pound' money went — who knows?

Among the requirements, the list informed us, were two pairs of grey lisle stockings made of fine, smooth cotton thread (at least they were not woollen, although they were nearly as bad), one pair of black lace-up shoes, one grey worsted suit, two long-sleeved white blouses, one maroon-and-white striped tie, and a grey felt hat that had to be worn with the brim turned down all the way around. *That* was our best winter outfit. Our summer best dresses were grey linen, buttoned to the neck with small white collars, grey socks, and black shoes with a strap and buckle. The hat was white panama, again with the brim turned down. All skirts had to be worn below the knee. One item of clothing that has been with me ever since my first day at Woodford — somehow never having been lost, stolen or sold during the ensuing years with all their dramas — is my grey worsted cloak. When I left school, I had it dyed black and a red satin lining installed. Today it is much coveted, but no one needs too much imagination to realize that, in the depths of a Hawke's Bay winter when over a hundred of us marched (in step!) to church in these grey cloaks, often with the hoods up in the rain, we looked like a crocodile of novitiates!

I was miserable my first two terms (we had three-term years in those days), and thank heaven for two people who helped me through that time. One helped me academically; the other, emotionally.

Miss Garnett was our English teacher, from England; and from the first day I met her I hung on her every word. She was articulate, with an amazing command of the English language; not just vocabulary, but *language*. For her, it was mandatory to learn 100 lines of poetry, write at least three book reviews, a series of limericks and several poems a term. We had spelling tests, and vocabulary tests. Our poetry had to be of different stanzas, and similes, acronyms and alliterations were terms that were to become part of our written and spoken vocabulary. As a thirteen- or fourteen-year-old schoolgirl, I worshipped the ground she walked on, and will be eternally grateful that she replaced my mother in this area of my life for the time that she did.

Janey, along with Pam, sat with me for a whole morning on my second day at school as I was unbelievably homesick. Janey was in the room next to me in the sleeping house and had listened to my muffled, pillowed sobs for the two previous nights. She was the eldest daughter of a farming family of six children and had spent a good deal of her life taking care of younger siblings, so was well practised when I came along.

Today, I believe that it was an incredible sense of loneliness, fear, abandonment, anger, bewilderment and exhaustion that overwhelmed me. Intellectually I knew, because my parents' enthusiasm had conveyed as much, that I was being given an amazing opportunity in life. I believe the fear was due to the fact that I had no idea how I was going to live up to their expectations; the bewilderment to not knowing what these expectations were; and the anger to expectations having been placed on me in the first place; all mixed with a continuing sense of abandonment, separation and loss. Not only had I experienced this mentally over the years of nannies, but now, physically, it would be approximately three months before I would see any of my family again.

For my parents, it was the most natural thing in the world for me to attend boarding school. In his teens, Father had gone from Auckland to Clifton College in England to board; Mother had been born in Sri Lanka (Ceylon as it was then) and, like most English girls, after her early years with nannies and governesses had completed her final school years as a boarder in England. For them, there was no reason why I should not follow the same road. In the higher echelons of society, boarding school was unquestionably the natural way to complete education. Most of us emerged as highly educated but socially inept women — and into the world of the 'sixties *not* the 'thirties.

Janey was to become my best friend at school. She was quiet, almost withdrawn, a compassionate, understanding and sympathetic listener; and at thirteen had a mothering quality far beyond her years. She took me under her wing until I was able to find my feet, which slowly but surely I did. Within a month I was class captain — I was to be a captain in a variety of areas throughout my school days.

As the months and terms progressed into my teenage years, boarding school became more of a haven to me. In hindsight, I can see how naïve some of us were, which was both a minus and a plus for me. We were extremely closeted. On only three days a term were we allowed out (other than for organized school excursions), and all three days were Sundays. Two Sundays were from 11 a.m. to 8 p.m., and one Sunday from 8 a.m. to 8 p.m. Those of us who did not live within a few hours' driving distance of the school relied on the local girls to ask us home for the day. Many of us were fearful that no one would ask and we would be left all alone at school. This never happened to me, but it remained a constant fear. (A sense of impending abandonment again? Who knows.)

Although I was popular and so was often elected as captain of various groups (the tennis team, basketball team and class), I was fundamentally shy, reserved, awkward and insecure, and always felt different. There was never at any stage a sense of belonging. It was almost as though I had been dumped on the wrong planet and one day someone would arrive in my life to say 'Sorry, Liz — wrong place. Come with me.' This sense of being an 'alien' was even more marked during the school holidays. As the various holiday parties grew more sophisticated and were eventually interspersed with dances, so my shyness and insecurity increased. I was slightly overweight (the result of boarding-school food!), and had red hair, teenage acne, and two broken and protruding front teeth (broken from a fall off my tricycle when I was nine, and protruding as a result of thumb-sucking as a baby). I believed that all I needed was a pair of glasses — which thankfully never happened — and I would be the epitome of the gangling, ugly schoolgirl. Eventually I got braces, which at least corrected the protruding teeth but added to my misery at the time.

In later years, when we participated in the annual dance with the boys from Lindisfarne College in Hastings, I spent the weeks before the dance in fear and trepidation, dreading the whole prospect of being a 'wallflower' for the night. I was painfully self-conscious; and when grey stockings, black shoes and a linen dress buttoned to the neck were added to my image, any form of participating in life out of school — but in uniform — was agony.

At least I never thought of myself as dumb. I had too many school prizes to contemplate that, but I had no idea how to relate to boys. Outwardly, I appeared to have no problem in coping with whatever life dealt me, but my insides told a different story. With no brothers, an autocratic Victorian (although in his own way probably very loving) father and those *other* memories of a grandfather, I was horribly ignorant of how to even begin a relationship. When Kings College boy Jimmy Johnson entered my life, I couldn't have been more fortunate. He was totally undemanding, and, with all due respect to him, I barely remember our first kiss. This only occurred after Pam had told me emphatically that it would *not* make me pregnant. My God — this was at *sixteen!* The closeted life I led!

Jimmy and I started writing 'love' letters to each other. How I wish I had kept some of them, but, when moving around the world as much as I was to do, letters such as those seldom accompanied me. Writing (and receiving) letters at Woodford, other than those to or from my parents or immediate family, had to be vetted. There would be a queue outside Headmistress Lucy Hogg's door on a Sunday evening, all of us holding letters that needed to be approved and would be left with her for posting. In those days, there was no other way for them to reach the mail. I remember Pam holding her breath as one of her letters to John Lyttelton, son of the then Governor General, Lord Cobham, was passed. Miss Hogg rarely held a letter back, but Pam's contained a couple of photos of herself, requested by John for his 'rogue's gallery', as he called it! Later, when I would exchange letters with Janey's brother Paul at Hereworth — the boys' school in Havelock North whose pupils also frequented the local church — we would do it surreptitiously when no staff members were watching. Wonderfully exciting!

School rules were strictly enforced, and punishments ranged from 'hard labour' dished out at anywhere from half an hour to two, to cancellation of visiting days. 'Hard labour' consisted of demerit points for your sports house, and tasks such as sweeping the cloisters (no wonder we were thought of as novitiates!), weeding the grouting between the bricks in the quadrangles, or — the least onerous — cleaning the prefects' 'squat' (sitting room). There were random cleanliness checks after breakfast when we would be inspected by Miss King, the Deputy Headmistress, to ensure our fingernails were cut and clean, shoes polished, gym tunics ironed, and no repairs needed to any clothing. Woe betide a culprit. *More* demerit points for your house!

In the sleeping houses, where almost all of the rooms were single, there was no talking or whispering after lights out, no entering another's room, only seven items were allowed on the dressing table, nothing on the walls, and every morning our two drawers, clothes cupboard and stripped-back bed were inspected by the prefect in charge of the corridor. Any forbidden items, such as transistor radios, were confiscated and held until term's end. For the two years before I became a prefect, I hid my transistor radio by strapping it under my towel on the towel rail — it was never discovered.

We could congregate in the common room, and could talk to each other at our bedroom doorways, although we were never allowed into each other's rooms, but the time I remember best was our E2 Radio Session. E2 was a room number, the one occupied by Judy Blathwayt (now Fyfe), who would hold radio sessions outside her doorway in the middle of the corridor. It was a hilarious one-woman show. Judy progressed in later years to become part of the *Fair Go* team with Brian Edwards.

I acted in school plays, led my house debating team, captained the tennis and basketball teams, gained School Certificate, and was one of the few girls who became a school prefect without having a year as a sub-prefect. In my year in the Lower Sixth Form, I was the only prefect. But when I asked my father if I could apply for accreditation for my University Entrance because of the added workload, his answer was a cryptic, emphatic and unhesitating 'No'. So far as he was concerned, accreditation was a ridiculous modern invention. I would sit the exams. I did, and passed. I was seventeen years of age and, as far as those around me were concerned, more than adequately equipped to enter the world of the 'sixties. The year was 1961. Lucy Hogg had written a glowing testimonial for me, which included the commendation that 'Elizabeth takes the ups and downs in life calmly'. No one, least of all me, could have anticipated the next ten years of my life.

Chapter 3

Silent rebellion

My final term at school brought with it a vast amount of confusion as it dawned on me that I was about to enter the period in my life that would set the scene for my future in the outside world. Somehow, I had been led to believe that my aim and object in life was to find a husband, settle down and produce grandchildren. Preferably, to marry into one of the well-known professional or merchant families of Auckland. A Fletcher, Caughey or Horton would be ideal. The Richwhite and Fenwick boys were too young. But then, to marry an Englishman would be even better! Interestingly enough, the whole career/marriage situation was never actually *discussed*. I suppose I drew conclusions from insinuations.

What did *I* want to do? Attend university, gain an English and History degree, and teach. The idea of a possible 'bluestocking' in the family sent shudders through my father: 'No daughter of mine will end up teaching!' His fear was that in such an environment, particularly in the girls' school where he anticipated I would end up, I would be left a spinster and a disgruntled old maid. Later, I was to discover that the 'sixties in fact saw a total upheaval in vast areas of people's lives. From the change in sexual values (the contraceptive pill making its entrance) to the women's movement (bras were burnt with great enthusiasm and Germaine Greer arrived on the world stage), to changes in the place of women in the workforce. There were some in my era who managed to kick off the traces and end up at university, but few (if any) whom I can remember from my circle in Auckland.

One goal I had set for myself before I left school was to lose weight. If I could not control what happened to me in the next phase of my life, then at least I could control my food intake. So in the final term I regimented myself to a strict diet of a piece of toast for breakfast, no potatoes or pudding for lunch, pieces of cheese and honey for dinner, and nothing in between. To remain in the senior tennis team, I practised for an hour to an hour and a half each day. I had to lose a stone (just over 6 kg), and I had to lose it before I went home.

I was holding the classic entrance visa to anorexia nervosa: I was seventeen years old, uncertain as to what the future held, self-conscious, and had tended to be a loner through my secondary school days. I had never belonged to a group, or 'gang' as we used to call them at school; Janey had been my only close friend. I now realize that even then I had an inability — or simply did not know how — to form intimate relationships. I had learnt to shut off my emotions at sixteen after being told by Father to 'Turn the water tap off: you are too old to cry.' I discovered later that my father was an extremely emotional man, and as a result probably found it unsettling when emotions were expressed openly. So I learnt what to do with them: bury them. The trouble was that in burying them I buried them alive, not dead. They were to fester for years. Two unhealthy lessons had been learnt: do not talk and do not feel.

I had become very self-conscious about the shape of my hips and thighs over a period of several years. A chance remark by my sister Jenny had remained with me since I was fourteen. We had been racing each other along the road to see who could reach the front gate first, and as I overtook her she said — and I could still hear her voice three years later — 'You're winning, but your legs wobble!' A childish, thoughtless remark, born out of frustration, that any sister could have made and soon forgotten, but it latched onto my memory bank like a limpet.

So there I was, lonely, insecure and confused, feeling totally out of control of my life. I was to go to Auckland Business School to gain a secretarial diploma, and Father would pay for a trip to England. My life was still being mapped out for me. But I could take charge of how I ate, if nothing else. By my eighteenth birthday, I looked and acted the model of an Auckland upper-middle-class, marriageable young woman, except that that was *not* what I was. The cover of the book looked appealing, but its contents were a seething volcano.

I enrolled in the secretarial college and at the University of Auckland: Father had at least conceded that I could take one subject there, English. It would add to my secretarial qualifications, so he thought. What he had not foreseen was my enthusiasm for and involvement in campus life. I joined the debating society and the ski club (where we double-booked the hut with Victoria University one weekend, and I spent two nights trying to sleep sitting up with the overpowering stench of wet socks around me), and was voted Miss University in the pin-up contest. I spent more time on my English assignments than on my secretarial course work. I hated the latter with a vengeance.

At the year's end I faced a dilemma: my English and secretarial exam dates clashed. Professor Musgrove kindly wrote a letter acknowledging my work in English for the year, as I was forced to choose the secretarial exams. I failed my typing and barely passed my Pitman's shorthand. By this time I was dangerously thin — emaciated would probably have been more correct — and my behaviour had become bizarre. I was obsessed with food, weight and exercise. My parents, particularly Mother, were extremely concerned, and massive arguments about food were now a regular occurrence, along with threats and cajoling. The entire family was focused on me and how to solve my eating problem. My focus was also on eating — but on how to avoid it and remain in control of my weight. Along with the food obsession came a fascination with it as well. I knew I had to eat *something*, but how much and what type of thing was a daily preoccupation. I bought slimming magazines, I bought books for counting calories, I ripped pages out of magazines that had charts of height-to-weight ratios, and I learnt what foods contained what vitamins and minerals.

I would have a cup of coffee for breakfast, take an apple and some celery or carrots for lunch, and then tell Mother on my return that I had also had more for lunch with a friend. Sometimes I would deliberately arrive home at 7.30 or 8 p.m., (well after dinner time), having told her I was staying in town, again to eat with a friend — anything to avoid ingesting food.

Exercising now became a secondary obsession. I was still living in Remuera, a two-hour walk from the city, and would walk home every day. The reason I gave was that I needed to save my money for my forthcoming trip to England. The underlying reason, of course, was to burn calories and lose more weight.

I soon discovered Mother's hiding place for the bathroom scales, which I used at any and every opportunity, and I gained a bizarre satisfaction from the numbers on the dial gradually receding down the scale. I would then take stock of my outline in the full-length mirror and breathe a sigh of satisfaction to see my pubic bones becoming more prominent as the months progressed. My perception of my body was becoming more and more distorted as I entered into a peculiar competition with it to see how thin I could become. I had disengaged myself from reality, and on a daily basis my entire focus was centred on my bodyweight.

Simultaneously with my perverted thinking, changes were taking place physiologically and socially in my life. Menstruation had ceased; my skin was dry and flaking, particularly on my hands and feet; soft, downy hair (lanugo) started to grow on my spine and face (obviously trying to keep me warm as my blood pressure and body temperature dropped). My hair started to thin out, although fortunately I was blessed with quite a thick head of it, and my teeth began to loosen. As my hair thinned, my eyebrows disappeared (now I have to pencil them in every day, as they never grew back); a result, I believe, of damage to my thyroid. I was nearly always cold and had difficulty with bowel movements, going for days without eliminating anything — so began my support of the laxative industry. My social life was zilch by the end of my first year out of school, primarily because I had a fear of having to eat if I was around others who were eating, but also because physically

I had started to look like a concentration-camp victim and could not have appeared less sexually attractive.

Life at the beginning of that year had not always been so isolating. For the first six months it was a hive of social activities for all of us as the socially prominent families of Auckland attempted to intermarry their offspring. There was round after round of cocktail parties, during which competition was high for the girls to outdo each other. I had a magnificent royal blue chiffon dress with a full skirt, and when Mother loaned me her three-string choker pearl necklace and matching earrings I felt a good deal more confident in facing the evenings. Alcohol was of little interest to me. I had discovered that it carried a high number of calories, so it was not on my list of acceptable substances to consume. It would be a few years before I would discover what it could do for me.

My parents attempted not to show too much interest in who took me to and from the various tennis parties, sailing outings, dinner parties and drinks parties, but I knew they and their contemporaries talked amongst themselves. Mother later acknowledged that she could never sleep properly until she heard my key turn in the front door lock, and Father never settled until he had heard the car pull away from the front gate. I was encouraged to have coffee at home with whomever I happened to be with at the time; there were few nightclubs and coffee bars in those days. Our greatest excitement was going to either the Montmartre nightclub in Lorne Street or a ball at the Peter Pan Ballroom. No alcohol was allowed to be brought into the ballroom, so the girls all wore long dresses under which we hid the bottles. Very risqué at the time, but unbelievably tame by today's standards.

Mother was wonderfully thoughtful, in that she would leave a tray in the kitchen set with her best Crown Derby china, silver cream jug and sugar basin containing lump sugar, and a pair of sugar tongs. A plate of home-made shortbread and ginger crunch was covered with a table napkin, and the kettle was always full of water. The sitting room was dark and cosy, but there was *always* a problem: sooner or later the third stair on the bottom flight of stairs would creak — Father coming down to ask when whoever was with me was going home. Sometimes this didn't happen until two-thirty in the morning, but it did inevitably happen. 'Heavy petting', as we called any sexual foreplay then, was as far as it ever progressed on those evenings (or any others). Father's interruptions were both a curse and a salvation. More than likely a salvation for me with those memories of my grandfather lurking in the shadows, but at least my reputation remained intact during this time. Not too far in the future it was to be processed through the shredding machine.

The early 1960s saw the last of the debutante balls in Auckland, which in retrospect were wonderful dress-up occasions. At some of these we would have little printed notebooks itemizing each dance. Attached was a pencil on a red ribbon, sufficient to tie the notebook to our wrists. The men would ask us to reserve certain dances for them, but none mattered as much as the last one. The last waltz was generally accompanied by the lights being switched off to announce the end of the evening. If this dance had not been reserved in the notebook, then it was preferable to have escaped to the loo rather than be engulfed in a slimy, slug-like embrace by an undesirable.

The drawing room at home for *my* debutante dance was turned into a spectacle worthy of a London Season ball. The carpet was taken up, the floorboards sprinkled with white 'French' chalk so that shoes would not slip while dancing, and the two chandeliers were cleaned until the light from the candle-shaped bulbs sent a cascade of rainbows through each string of glass. Gold paint was meticulously applied to the carving around the enormous mirror above the fireplace. The French doors into the dining room were tied back with white and gold ribbon, and the dining table covered in an enormous white, floor-length, linen tablecloth on which were set an assortment of Mother's silver trays. Polished until they winked as you walked by, and the family crest in the centre of each one daring you to ignore it. A white marquee was erected on the back terrace, the poles festooned with more white and gold ribbons, and large trestle tables ensconced for the supper at ten o'clock. Fairy lights twinkled across the canvas ceiling as dusk fell, and the six-piece band arrived at the same moment as the birthday cake. It was the night of my eighteenth birthday. The whole scene was probably more appropriate for a wedding reception, which is what many of these balls resembled.

At seven-fifteen the guests started to arrive. The invitation had nominated seven o'clock, but in those days it was totally unfashionable to arrive on time — and certainly never *before* seven, which would definitely show the side of the tracks on which you had been born! Men were in dinner jackets, and a few of my father's contemporaries in tails (always a black tie with dinner jackets and a white tie with tails — *never* vice versa!), the girls in long dresses, many of them white with crinoline skirts, and elbow-length white gloves. The wine, beer and champagne flowed, although I drank very little as I disliked the taste and was more intent on playing hostess. Shy and insecure though I was, it was 'my' evening, so the attention paid to me meant it was much easier for me to feel a sense of belonging.

The band played the waltz, the foxtrot and the occasional cha-cha. There was not enough room on the dance floor for a quick-step, although at the Dorchester and Mandalay — large dance halls where some girls held their balls — there would be the opportunity for a few of us to demonstrate our prowess. Once supper was over, however, black ties were flung aside, top shirt buttons unbuttoned and sleeves rolled up, the girls hitched up their skirts, and the rock 'n' roll would start. Some of us had learnt the twist, which was creeping onto the dance scene, and the floor would clear for those who could demonstrate it. I *loved* to dance; I was exceptionally talented, felt supremely confident on the dance floor, and the twist and rock 'n' roll were my all-time favourites. The floor cleared for me as the birthday girl, probably the only time at this stage of my life when I had a sense of acceptance in a world in which I felt desperately different.

My parents were so proud of me. I was three months into my first year out of school, and this was my official launch into society and the adult world. What hopes and dreams were theirs on that night as they stood beside me while I cut my cake. The pain and heartache to come for them were nowhere in sight. I remember feeling so grateful for the evening, telling them so and really, really meaning it.

'You will have a psychological as well as a physical problem on your hands if you prevent her from going' was Dr Lloyd Richwhite's statement as my second year out of school began and my promised trip to England loomed on the horizon. Mother was extremely concerned, as my weight had now dropped to barely six stone. However, at Lloyd's insistence she agreed that I should go, and so it was that Anna Caughey and I boarded the New Zealand Shipping Company's boat *Rangitoto* to share a cabin for the start of our big OE (overseas experience).

I could not have been more naïve in the ways of the world. Our first port of call was Papeete, known in the 'sixties as the 'Hell Hole of the South Pacific', and the first evening ashore was spent in one of the bars with a contingent of the ship's officers. I had no idea that bestiality even existed, let alone that it could be indulged in publicly. Thankfully, there were others in the group who must have felt as sick as I did, but I will never forget that night — Quinn's Bar must have been the Hell Hole in the Hell Hole. I certainly was not willing to explore any more, despite the fact that I was on what I had imagined was a South Sea island paradise.

Just how many girls lost their virginity on the Pacific Ocean will remain a mystery. I strongly believe that some power, force, God or angel has watched over me in life, and even in the vastness of the South Sea I was taken care of. He was kind and gentle; perhaps he also felt compassion for the waif that I was, for as a medical man there may have been an instinct that told him I was lonely and afraid. My initiation into womanhood was fraught with uncertainty and anxiety which lasted for the remainder of the voyage, but I believe I was fortunate: it was not an experience I regretted.

We met up again on several occasions when he was in London, but lost contact after a while. He was Polish. As I came to discover more of the history of the Polish people over the years, I suspect that perhaps he had known fear and loneliness, too. I will never know, but I am grateful to him.

Chapter 4

Total confusion

The following two years until my parents arrived with sister Jenny were years controlled by anorexia. I was interested in little except food, with my behaviour becoming steadily stranger as the months went past. At this stage I had progressed into bulimia, a state I now understand often occurs with anorexics. Later in the 1960s this came to be known as bulimarexia, and today is a recognized disorder. At the time I slipped into it, not only was there no name for the behaviour, but the majority of the medical profession knew nothing about it.

Bulimia (self-induced vomiting) was a discovery made after an evening with my uncle in London. He had taken me to dinner at his favourite restaurant and had insisted that I eat the food we had ordered. There were lengthy periods between the various courses — soup, entrée and main course — and I was feeling exceptionally bloated. My stomach had shrunk so it now became distended, my heart was racing, I was starting to hyperventilate, and I could feel the food stuck in my gullet. All I could think about was eliminating everything I had eaten. I began to panic, and excused myself to go to the bathroom where I vomited up the entire meal.

The relief was indescribable as the panic abated, but I had learnt another sick lesson: I had found a way of pacifying my critics and eliminating the constant nagging of family and friends to eat. I became cunning, deceitful, evasive and even more of a confusion to all with whom I came in contact. I had not only lost the ability to enjoy food, but now had crossed a line and could not control it any longer, for once I started eating I found I could not stop. Oh,

I could eat (and keep down) half a banana, an apple, or a carrot, or even at times a boiled egg, but that was barely eating — it was sustenance to at least give me a modicum of energy. My relationship with food became grotesque, and it *was* a relationship. It comforted me. I could forget my loneliness, my sense of isolation, the feeling of being different, of being born on the wrong planet at the wrong time amongst the wrong people. Now when I was eating, I forgot the regrets of yesterday and the fears of tomorrow. At whatever time of the day or night my eating frenzies took place, they were my total focus and complete obsession. And the majority of them were planned.

Those around me, friends (or rather acquaintances, as I had no friends because I trusted no one and led a life of deceit anyway) and relations began to visibly breathe sighs of relief. I was not only eating, I was stuffing myself with food whenever I went out or spent weekends away with relations. Little did they realize that there were peculiar rituals around my so-called 'recovery'. These rituals depended on the circumstances and were carefully planned. A weekend away was the most difficult, particularly when no grocery shops were in the vicinity or there were servants in the house.

Many of my cousins and my uncle, Mother's brother, had cooks and maids, which should have been a delight for me to experience as a way of life in English country houses. Instead, they were a frustration and an inconvenience to me. First, I could not raid the kitchen for more food; secondly, I had nowhere to buy more, so I had to smuggle it in in my suitcase; thirdly, I had to make sure the maid did not unpack my bag.

Bananas, cheese and yoghurt would be packed. They would be eaten first to line my stomach. The first lot of food to go in was the last lot to be vomited out, and if I was not able to empty my stomach, then at least the early intake contained healthy calories. Bread and cake were also included, for if I had not finished my eating binge I could always top up with those in my bedroom and they would be the first to be vomited up. During the whole ritual, water was important as that would liquefy the stomach's contents and I would be able to eliminate it all without too much straining of my chest and throat.

Timing was also crucial. Two hours was the maximum before I excused myself, either to go to the bathroom or to bed for the night so I could stick my fingers down my throat. It was not long before I had trained the reflex action in my stomach, chest and throat to regurgitate the food without the necessity of fingers, and also to conduct the whole ghastly ritual silently. If time and opportunity permitted, copious amounts of water would then be consumed in an attempt to wash the last of the contents out of my system, and I would rinse my mouth with Listerine before returning, if necessary, to the dinner table or the social environment. I was perfectly aware that my breath would not have been entirely salubrious!

People soon came to realize that something was amiss. While my food intake was unusual, I did not seem to be gaining weight, and my trips to the bathroom were becoming noticeable. Then, for my part, I was forced to change tactics slightly: I had to drink more water with my meal, try to avoid any starches (bread, potatoes, pasta, sauces) and any foods which were high in calories, and extend the length of time between the end of the meal and the trips to the bathroom. The 'game' became one of outwitting and out-manoeuvring those around me. Not only was my behaviour completely baffling for those who watched it on a regular basis, but without being aware of it many of them were hooked into either trying to understand it or else trying to control it.

People truly tried to help. I had the experience of a Commem Ball at Oxford University being arranged for me, with a Canadian Rhodes Scholar as my partner — a unique experience for anyone even within the university fraternity itself, let alone a colonial girl from the bottom of the world. My aunt hoped that I would meet a 'nice man' there. The whole establishment filled me with awe and with memories that I still hold today. The old stone buildings with their lead-light windows, the cloisters, the surprise of emerging through the archways to find lawns and walkways in the embrace of architecture that had been the seat of learning for hundreds of years. Inexplicably, of all the universities I have entered for one reason or another since, Oxford has been the one that somehow touched what I now believe is my soul and sparked a deep-seated hunger for learning. The feeling was fleeting; the significance of it not to come for years.

I wore my white debutante dress and long white gloves, I gorged myself on chicken (a delicacy in the 1960s) and salmon, strawberries and cream, and in the early hours of the morning we went punting on the river. It was like a scene from a Jane Austen or Georgette Heyer novel, and in retrospect I had no idea how to appreciate the entire experience. I knew that sooner or later more than heavy petting would be demanded of me, and I spent a large portion of the evening in a constant state of anxiety. Finally, as the rest of the city awoke to the working day I was able to escape to my aunt and her car. Sadly, I failed to appreciate how unique the experience was and how truly fortunate I had been to be a part of the ritual.

So many people wanted to help me, including my godmother who offered to have me stay with her in London. She was secretary to the Spanish ambassador, speaking fluent Spanish, and was determined that I needed a change of environment and to stop wasting my energies in temporary secretarial work (which I hated anyway). A family she knew in Madrid were looking for a nanny/ governess for their three older children, the eldest of whom was due to return to the United States to enter college. His father was extremely concerned that his son's command of Spanish was far superior to that of his English, so he wanted someone to teach English to all of the children. A total change and a trip abroad was the immediate and extended family's united prescription for me to recover.

Spanish Customs was the pits. In nearly fifty years of international travel, the Spanish border is the only place where I have ever had the entire contents of my suitcase up-ended and then shoved to the end of the conveyer belt. I was travelling on a British passport, and often wonder whether some ancient grudge was being enacted on me!

During the four months that I spent with the two boys and one girl, I felt a sense of freedom and delight that I had not known in years. The Spanish amah who took care of the eighteen-month-old boy took an immediate dislike to me, which was mutual. She was as sour as a Meyer lemon and had a tongue that could peel a pineapple.

I learnt Spanish by ear (not to write or read) within the first three weeks of my arrival, as with university-level French, English, Latin and a sprinkling of German under my belt it was not difficult to pick up. Retaliating one day with a rather expletive remark which she was totally not expecting, I seldom heard or saw her again except at meal times.

Eight-year-old Elizabeth adored me. Her mother was American, the Spanish editor for an international women's magazine, and, like Winston Churchill's description of *his* mother, she 'shone like the evening star, but at a distance'. Every morning at about nine-thirty we would all traipse into her room for her to spend time — about ten minutes — with the children, and again in the evening after she had dressed for dinner. Beautiful, elegant and cold, to Elizabeth she appeared like an ethereal goddess. I was real, and after the first two days Elizabeth would leave my side only when necessary.

In 'school time' we read Mark Twain and Jack London, *The Wind in the Willows*, *Alice in Wonderland* and Rider Haggard. Story-time at night was with Enid Blyton's Famous Five, and the threat of not having the Five to go to bed on kept disobedience down to a minimum each day. Poetry was learnt by heart and recited to their father, Tennyson being the most popular, with 'The Highwayman' acted out with great gusto! My pet hurdle was to eradicate double negatives: 'I don't know nothing about it' would bring twenty, forty, sixty lines of the correct expression to be written out. Good old-fashioned rote, but it worked!

I taught Elizabeth to swim and the boys to play knuckle-bones. We had ten wonderful days in Comillas, a seaside resort on the Atlantic Coast, where we visited the caves of Altamira with their thousand-year-old rock paintings, virtually closed to the public now because of the damage people's breath is doing to the art. I found a meaning in life with the children, and a sense of achievement in contributing to their lives. I was teaching, not only academically but also helping them to discover their talents and attributes.

My eating pattern was still erratic and my bulimia an ever-present threat, but both had been modified. I was still desperately thin, but eating with the children meant there was no one around me whom I felt threatened by with a disapproving look or attitude. The amah couldn't have cared less about me. She now tolerated my presence only because she had no choice.

The long, balmy Spanish evenings were a delight. Shops and offices closed in the middle of the day for the universal siesta and, for the majority, dinner was taken at around ten in the evening. I made friends with an English girl at the British Embassy, and would often meet with her after the children were in bed. We spent time in many little bistros around the city; she introduced me to Sangria (red wine and lemonade mixed) and KOOL cigarettes, a menthol brand that rasped my throat and spun my head. *How* I enjoyed that wine-and-lemonade mixture, the latter erasing the acidic bite of the former. I enjoyed the concoction more and more over the next few months, until during the final weeks of my stay I threw out the lemonade — for I had discovered that the wine started to fill the hole in my soul that I had lived with all my life. I had found the answer to *all* my problems. My inside started to match other people's outsides. No more was I on the wrong planet at the wrong time with the wrong people. The wine did for me what I could not do for myself: it helped me gain a modicum of a sense of belonging in the world, and I started to look forward to the evenings with Christine and our 'dinner' of wine, cigarettes and a shared paella (with her eating most of it). I felt self-confident, sophisticated and at long last a member of the human race.

Elizabeth was devastated and hysterical at the airport when I left. Fortunately her mother was not there, but it was embarrassing enough for her father, who made a valiant attempt to disguise his concern. He was profusely grateful for all I had done for and with the children, and begged me not to remain in contact with Elizabeth. I could see he was disturbed by the whole incident, and have often wondered since then what traumas Elizabeth might have been through in life as a result of the obvious distancing from her mother. How little we know even today of parenting skills and the effects, some of which can be devastating, on a developing child.

We came to the conclusion that it must have been the contractors working on the scaffolding, but of course could never prove it. I was now living with my 'Spanish' godmother, and she had arrived home to find the lock on the door of the apartment jemmied and all my jewellery in the neat little box in the top drawer of my dressing table gone; for her, it was a string of pearls and matching earrings. Why does the tidy person always seem to be a victim? Godmother Denyse was a drinker, a Scotch drinker, and that was how she decided we should commiserate our losses. 'Hold your nose,' she said, 'and take a gulp.' It was neat red-label Johnnie Walker. No water, no ice, no lemonade! Nothing except the raw whisky. It burnt my throat, it made my eyes water, I coughed and spluttered — but I kept it down and Christmas and Guy Fawke's Night came all at once. Not only was I no longer an alien born into the wrong family, but I was now confident, effusive, articulate and funny. I had made another life-changing discovery: spirits. They got me 'there' faster, higher, with only one swallow and perfectly legitimately: my father always drank whisky. When he sat with his glasses of whisky before dinner, I knew it always helped him unwind after a day at the office; I *saw* what it did to him. Now I discovered what it could do for me. So Denyse and I commiserated over our losses; me with one more whisky and water (for I did not want the jolt of the first one to be repeated), and she with almost two-thirds of the bottle. I remember being intriguingly surprised at the fact that she did not seem too affected by the amount she consumed. I know now that heavy drinkers seldom are. It is the alcoholic who has the personality change with alcohol. More often than not they will consume less than the heavy drinker, but the problem is not how much they drink but what the alcohol does to them when they drink it.

I now entered a new phase in my ever-more bewildering life-style: I added alcohol and nicotine to my anorexia and bulimia. The alcohol was by no means a problem at this stage of my life, although I was developing a preoccupation with it on certain weekends. When Denyse was away and I had decided to stay in London, I would plan a ritualistic night. There would be a bottle of spirits and my 'banquet' all set up. The latter would consist of something like the following:

> 2 large loaves of sliced white bread
> 1 packet of butter
> 1 jar of jam
> 2 lbs of cheese
> 6 eggs
> 2 pints of milk
> 4 containers of yoghurt
> 2 fruit cakes
> 2 packets of crumpets
> ½ lb sliced luncheon sausage
> 2 large bags of potato chips
> Packets of various assorted biscuits
> 2 pints of ice-cream.

I would either turn on the radio or play Strauss waltz music on my portable gramophone, and then the evening would start. I would drink my alcohol slowly while I scrambled the eggs (they would line my stomach), then I would stand at the kitchen bench and start to eat: scrambled eggs followed by yoghurt and cheese until my stomach became distended and I would have to vomit. I would then rest for maybe thirty minutes, and start the binge all over again until I became drained and exhausted and fell into bed having barely undressed.

The next morning I would feel light-headed, lethargic and totally uninterested in anything except sleeping most of the day away in bed. Often the kitchen needed to be rescued from the night before, as my lack of energy had had me collapsing into bed with no concern for the mess.

These weekends on my own in London started to become more frequent. I had developed a raft of fictitious friends with whom I informed Denyse I spent my time. The truth was that they did not exist except in my imagination. If I genuinely spent a weekend out of the city, it was always with relations and often with cousins who had house parties. I had discovered that a little alcohol made me less inhibited and my excursions to the bathroom were less noticeable. In retrospect, it was a sad and pathetic existence.

My twenty-first birthday party, held at the Royal Thames Yacht Club in Knightsbridge, competed in grandeur with my debutante ball. My parents had arrived with Jenny, and the evening was planned to accommodate a series of occasions. Primarily, my 'coming of age'; secondly, for the extended family to meet Jenny; and thirdly, for my parents (Mother in particular) to see all the relations at once. Ninety-five per cent of the people present were people to whom I was related. The others were acquaintances of mine whom I had dredged up somewhere from brief encounters. March is still cold in England, and because of the lack of flesh on my bones I felt the cold even more than most people. The emerald-green, long-sleeved dress disguised my poor child-like body, although I saw the embarrassment in the many eyes that watched me as I cut the cake, a replica of the North and South Islands of New Zealand provided by my godmother, the bewilderment and sadness apparent on my parents' faces, and a combination of pity and indifference emanating from the others.

I got drunk on champagne that night. After all, it *was* my twenty-first. I was officially an adult and deemed a responsible member of society. Nothing could have been further from the truth. I was a lonely, bewildered, angry, frightened little girl who saw no meaning in life and who had failed to accomplish what her trip to England was supposed to have done: find a husband and have children. I was not just angry, I was seething; I could not escape into food, so I escaped into champagne.

The following tour of Scotland and then Europe by car should have been an exciting and unforgettable adventure. Mother had always been a walking history-book (learning the dates of the reigns of the Kings and Queens of England by heart as a child), but had never fulfilled her dream of a university degree. The war had intervened; she had married Father and been sucked into the role of wife and mother in 'the colonies'. I later learnt that some of my anger had arisen because, although I knew she supported my ambition for a university life, she had not fought hard enough for me to have what she had yearned for. I felt betrayed. Hindsight is a great awakener.

Drinking was not a problem as we explored museums, cathedrals and art galleries in various countries over the following weeks. Father insisted that we find a licensed pub to stay in, or if it had to be a bed and breakfast then a bottle of whisky would always be produced for his regular imbibing prior to dinner. There would be nights when arguments would start; Mother rarely drank except on special occasions, but Father soon realized he had a drinking companion in me. I found a new hobby along the way — collecting miniature bottles of booze from which now and again I would have a swig before we went to the bar. A sherry before dinner and maybe wine at dinner was the rule imposed on me. That was 'ladylike', and acceptable to all except me. My tolerance to alcohol was rising, and so the odd slug from a miniature bottle of rum, gin, vodka or brandy helped me gain the effect I wanted. The bottle was always filled up with water, just in case its being empty was discovered and questions asked. Deceit had started around my consumption.

We had scarlet Cunningham dress-tartan kilts made in Edinburgh (Mother's grandmother's tartan); we climbed the Leaning Tower of Pisa, when it was still leaning; saw glass-blowing in Venice; and were awestruck by the Coliseum. Versailles and Fontainebleau were so opulent that I could understand and have absolute sympathy for the revolutionaries in 1789; I had never realized that the Mona Lisa painting was so small.

My bulimia was spasmodic, my anorexia still evident, and my drinking becoming more of an escape.

Then Mother and I hit Harley Street, that world-renowned and most expensive street of medical practitioners in England. A waste of time and I have no idea how much money. I had no intention of stopping my eating and purging, the reason we were sitting in an expensive psychiatrist's office. The whole situation was like a red rag to a bull. In front of me was a pompous, arrogant, grey-haired *man* (every subconscious reaction to controlling men leapt at me) who talked *at* me and wanted me to talk *to* him. My mother — obviously on his side, which meant that she had betrayed me — was sitting between him and me. The fact that she was beside herself as to what to do for and with me, that she was there to support me and try to gain help for me and her, that she was heart-broken, bewildered, frightened, guilty (where had she gone wrong?) and going out of her mind with despair because she was watching her eldest child commit slow suicide, never occurred to the self-centred creature I had become. I just refused to speak. *He* was being paid. *He* could do the work.

Years later I wrote a letter to my mother, attempting to put into words — which still seem so inadequate — how desperately sorry I was for the pain and grief I had caused her. After she died, we found a box tied with pink ribbon in a drawer by her bedside. Among the tiny pile of letters that she had stored over the years was that one, written on pink paper in my handwriting. Watermarks had blurred a few words. Mother always read her mail over a cup of tea; these were not tea stains. In all my life, I had never seen my mother cry.

Chapter 5

Introduction to the funny farm

The six weeks in first class on the P&O ship *Oronsay* back to New Zealand were one long party. There was another ship's doctor, more food at the buffets than anyone could possibly eat and, better still, there was every reason to drink from eleven in the morning to all hours into the night. So long as I had alcohol inside me, I *loved* the parties. I found what alcohol could do for me — it was my connection, my lifeline, my liquid bridge; it plugged me into the human race. I started to discover that in my longing for and yet terror of intimacy, booze tore the walls down and beckoned me through. Because we were travelling first class, there were few young, single attractive women in this area of the boat, the area that the officers had a 'duty' to entertain. I was the life and soul of the social occasions. I drank as much as, sometimes more than, most; I was witty, funny, brazen, shocking; I would volunteer for any game that was being played, and challenge others to be more outrageous at whatever was being suggested. A couple of gins next morning from my bottle in the cabin would take care of the guilts and the headache, which were the only withdrawal symptoms I had at this stage. More and different were to come.

A storm off the coast of Miami was not a pleasant experience, and, as I groaned with genuine seasickness in the medical centre that evening, Roger the doctor (my shipboard romance) suggested that I drink less and eat more for the next couple of days. The latter I could adhere to, as I ate nothing but lettuce and fruit; the former simply meant I put fruit juice in the drinks and threw out the ice.

As we headed for the Pacific Ocean, my drinking pattern was changing progressively and subtly. Not only was I spending more time drinking socially during each twenty-four-hour period, but sneaking drinks in my cabin became more frequent because most of the time other people were not drinking fast enough for me. I adopted a strategy of appearing to be drinking moderately, holding a glass of wine for some time before graduating to the harder spirits — but this was because the effects of my cabin gin had taken hold and I was mindful that the wine would stabilize my poor brain for a while.

Unbeknown to me, alcohol had now become a necessity. There was an urgency associated with the first drink, wherever it was consumed, and as my tolerance increased it needed to be stronger, larger and taken more quickly. It had become necessary for me, as it relieved the tension that was now consciously a part of everyday life. I had discovered a comparison: how I felt without alcohol (inadequate, insecure and a phoney), and how I felt *with* alcohol (confident, funny, intelligent and with my insides now matching other people's outsides). My drinking pattern and general behaviour seemed no different to those of others around me. However, the life and environment on board a ship, as I came to discover with a jolt, are far from their equivalents in the real world.

The night I arrived back in Auckland, Chris Innes (who was such a gentleman and who had even flown to England at one point to ask me to marry him) arrived at the house to take me to a welcome-home party, given by an old school friend. I never made the party. Chris walked in the front door to find me babbling drunk, sitting on the front hall staircase. An ambulance was called when I passed out. Not remembering any of this, I awoke the following morning to find Dr Gilmore, a surgeon at Auckland Hospital, sitting on the end of my bed. 'We took your packet of cigarettes, Elizabeth, because we had to test them for drugs. It seems it was just the alcohol. You really will need to watch your drinking.' That was it.

I was scared. It hadn't happened like that before — there had been incidents during the travel around Europe and on the boat, but I had never lost a complete eighteen hours before. Although I didn't know this, one of the many signs of alcoholism is that alcoholics seldom complain about hangovers. The alcoholic suffers in silence. The non-alcoholic moans and groans about their head the following day. They don't care who knows how they feel. They may feel sick, but they rarely feel the guilt and the crippling shame. They will exaggerate; I always minimized: 'I only had two.' Most people think that means two gin and tonics, two brandies and ginger ale. That was what I wanted them to think; and in my mind I was telling the truth, distorted as it was. My 'only two' were glasses of neat gin — forget the tonic — or in the end two bottles of wine or sherry. As my consumption increased, so did my tolerance, which meant I needed more and more to gain the effect I craved.

Dr Gilmore's remark about needing to watch my drinking, however, struck a spark of conscience in me. Maybe there *was* something wrong with my drinking. Maybe people *didn't* lose consciousness like I had just done. I felt there was perhaps some way in which I could secretly find out if there was something wrong, and, as I have always done when possible, I sought out and bought a book. Titled *Alcoholism*, by Neil Kessel and Henry Walton, this book remains with me today. *That's me*, my brain kept telling me — but I needed someone to validate my discoveries, and for some unknown reason I chose to show it to my father one evening. He took one look at the cover and literally threw the book back across the room at me, along with the statement 'No daughter of mine can be an alcoholic.' That was my licence to drink: I had been pardoned and absolved of ever having a problem with liquor.

My trip to Auckland Hospital was only the beginning of the

hospitalization saga; Brightside, Lavington and Selwyn followed. Over the following nine months, life was a series of hospitals, doctors and nightmares for my parents. At one stage, I became a member of the Girls' Club of the Navy League — where my drinking antics became almost too much for them. I was asked to temper my consumption.

Then there was the night, and it must have been a horror movie for my parents, when I displayed how sick I had become — to almost the entire upper strata of Auckland society. Dinner parties were all the rage in the 'sixties, and in true English aristocratic fashion Mother always returned hospitality and had become a superb cook. On this particular night, I decided I needed a party myself; as the drawing room was underneath my bedroom, I could hear the laughter and clink of crystal glasses and what must have been coffee cups as well. Everyone had adjourned to the drawing room when this *apparition* appeared, like Bette Davis as Baby Jane Hudson. The dressing gown was pink candlewick, old brown vomit stains trying to hide themselves in shame down the front lapels, and I swept into the room through the double glass doors, weaving my way towards the silver drink tray with its Waterford crystal decanters of whisky and brandy.

A vibrating silence descended over the room as the eyes of the cream of Auckland society were riveted on the scene. Eyes belonging to the Caughey family, the Richwhites, the Hortons, the Benjamins, the Gressons, the Manchesters, the Fenwicks. I didn't pick up a glass and fill it to toast them all; I picked up the brandy decanter, turned to this gathering of the élite of Auckland, and raised the decanter with a 'Cheers'.

The spectacle must have kept tongues wagging for the next five years. You see, I was virtually naked. I had the hideous pink dressing gown on, of course, but by the time I'd reached the brandy it was flapping around like a spinnaker that had lost its ropes. No one could have been left in any doubt that I was a natural redhead!

The first to move was my father, to grab the decanter, then

my mother, to wrap my dressing gown around me, and thirdly our family doctor, Lloyd Richwhite. I was whisked from the room, protesting loudly, and bundled upstairs. Two days later, I was admitted to Oakley Psychiatric Hospital for the first time. I had run out of all other options.

The tragedy of alcoholism is in the number of lives it affects. It was not only about me and my drinking; it brought years of stress, fear, shame, embarrassment, hurt, anger, and most of all bewilderment to my family, and in particular to my parents. When they visited me in Oakley two days later, I remember my father walking towards me with tears in his eyes. 'Why, Elizabeth, why?' Then he turned and walked back again down the long hall, his shoulders stooped and his head down. It was one of the few times I ever saw my father cry. His eldest daughter, of whom he had been so proud five years previously, was now a 21-year-old, 5½ stone (35 kg), anorexic, bulimic, nicotine-consuming alcoholic in a mental institution.

Today, I realize that my father taught me about drinking, although he was never the actual cause: I chose to drink. But every night that I can remember, except perhaps when he was sick in bed, he drank. There was a ritual to the evening. He would arrive home from the office, spend time with Mother in the kitchen, have a bath, change, have his two to three whiskies before dinner, read the newspaper, eat dinner, finish the newspaper, go to sleep in the chair and then go to bed. As the years progressed, the whiskies became stronger, the evening discussions became monologues, and now and again he would stagger to the dinner table. Years later I discovered I had an alcoholic uncle — he had to be Father's brother, but nobody ever talked about him in any way other than as a no-hoper who had been damaged on the beaches at Dunkirk. Society, even now, so often sees alcoholism as a moral issue that is simply a matter of self-control: if we find reasons why people drink, then they can stop; we can help the alcoholic control his drinking — about as senseless as asking someone to control diarrhoea! Perhaps Father was living out his own internal pain through me; perhaps he, too, had learnt to live with the secrets of alcoholism.

Oakley was not the end of the road. It was not even the *beginning* of the end of the road. But it was the end of the beginning. Like many psychiatric hospitals in the middle of the 1960s, Oakley Hospital was a haven for some, but an unmitigated nightmare for others. Perhaps even the original haven became a nightmare; who knows. For me it was terrifying, but my parents and long-suffering Dr Richwhite had run out of options.

As my guardians, my parents were determined to keep my condition and behaviour as secret as possible. Queen Mary Hospital at Hanmer Springs was the ideal place for me, but there was the risk that people, Remuera society in particular, would get to know. Roger Culpan, a psychiatrist at the Bexley Clinic who was also on the board of Oakley, decided after consultation with my parents and Dr Richwhite that Oakley would be the best place for me. For the family, there was the added advantage that there would also be less risk of anyone discovering me there. In Hanmer, there could be people who knew me who would disclose my presence and embarrass the family.

Every piece of clothing in Oakley had to have a name tag sewn on, as stealing was rampant. I was housed in the Observation Ward for obvious reasons — I had to be observed! There were no separate rooms; I was in a dormitory with beds lining both sides of the room. Every few days a large machine was wheeled into the room and selected patients were strapped to their beds while the others were ushered from the room. Months later, I discovered that they were being subjected to ECT (electrical current therapy) treatment behind the closed doors.

One day the door was left open as a nurse left the room, and I was able to see, with mounting horror, a scene that totally terrified me. Bodies that had been strapped to beds appeared sedated, as there did not seem to be any movement in them. Halfway down the room was the large machine and a man holding what appeared to be earphones. As I watched, he placed these on a woman's head and then stood to one side. Nothing happened. The members of the team just stood waiting and talking amongst themselves. One of them glanced up, saw me and strode across the room to slam the door. I was shaking both inside and out, silently calling out to a God that I did not comprehend to keep me safe. 'Please don't let them mess with my brain. Please, please, please, no. Not my brain. Oh God no . . .' My stomach was knotted, my heart racing; I could feel the perspiration under my arms — and thank God for my embroidery.

Through all the years of turmoil I have found solace and respite in a needle and thread. I have four Royal School of Needlework embroidered samplers hanging on my bedroom wall today, each with a story to tell if they could only speak: each has seen my tears of anger, frustration, bewilderment, sadness, loneliness, desperation and despair, and heard my eternally silent, pitiful cries for help. I took out the purple thread and began to embroider a Scottish thistle. How insignificant are so many of our actions until we see them in retrospect. The Scottish blood in me mingled with the purple thread as the needle pricked my finger on its journey through the linen. I have never washed that piece of cloth, and today it rests behind glass on my wall. A fleeting second in time, a sliver of steel guided by an unseen hand. Perhaps God does look after drunks and fools. Mercifully, I was spared ECT.

The pills prescribed for me I hid under my tongue and eventually spat down the handbasin. The blue and black ones and the creamy yellow ones were tranquillizers or antidepressants. I was so pleased I had inherited Mother's attitude towards pills, which was one of abhorrence even for a headache. The only exception I ever remember her making was the occasional antibiotic when she could not find a natural remedy. Had I not inherited her aversion to them, I would simply have added another problem to my chaotic life: a pill addiction. Many of the women at Oakley, and possibly the other 'funny farms' around the country (let alone around the world), must have been fed these 'answers' — Mother's Little Helpers, as they were known then and over ensuing years. Today we have a billion-dollar drug industry, yet I am convinced that, then and now, many of those with stress-related disorders could have been and can be helped without the necessity for such medications. Too often they simply anaesthetize the individual, thus stymieing the whole process of enabling that person, with the help of a trained listener and guide, to work through whatever situation or incident has triggered the stress in the first place. Dependency on the medication may result: after the individual stops taking the pills, they are then left with not only the original problem but also withdrawal symptoms from the chemicals — which sends them back to the original medication to deal with the withdrawal symptoms. A ghastly, vicious cycle that fortunately I was spared, probably out of a healthy fear which overrode my curiosity.

That first trip to Oakley was long enough for me to swear I would never return; I was bored to death every single day. Perhaps the Little Helpers were designed to take care of that, but they didn't for me because they couldn't — they were out there somewhere making their way to the Waitemata Harbour. I also had another problem: how to get out of the place. I was determined to keep my wits about me, aware that swallowing pills would mean that I would no longer have control over my own mind, no mental resistance against the void that would suck me in and ensure I was powerless to disassociate my mental and emotional being from my physical body. In that environment, I learnt to trust nobody and nothing except myself. The final nail had been hammered into the coffin — any emotional connection to my parents was slashed; I was totally alone.

The night I silently sobbed myself to sleep should have brought recurring nightmares, but fortunately whatever guardian angel I have took care of me over those horrendous weeks and spared me this.

The dance had *sounded* like a good idea, and appealed initially as a form of escape, not only from the ward but also from the need to be constantly on the alert in order to survive. An opportunity to go dancing lifted my spirits, and I felt sure that the whole occasion would be scrupulously supervised because of the normal male and female segregation. That assumption was completely erroneous. The event was like a scene from *One Flew Over the Cuckoo's Nest*. If there were any other undrugged inmates in that ballroom, then I never found them. I was mauled, slobbered over, grabbed and humiliated beyond belief. I am convinced that the only staff who ever agreed to police such evenings were voyeurs and sadists. There was no escaping. Compliant inmate that I had to become in order to survive and hopefully gain an early discharge, I was compelled to remain for the entire horror movie. I had, after all, volunteered to go, and no one was prepared to take a specific 'loony' back to the ward until the allotted time, compassion being totally foreign to these staff members.

During a staff shortage one morning, I volunteered to help clean out the geriatric ward; the machine in the Observation Ward had terrified me into becoming a model patient, compliant and helpful. *Never* volunteer to clean a geriatric ward in a psych hospital! The place was a pigsty. The smell of urine and faeces emanated from under the door even before it was opened; there were half-dressed, babbling elderly women draped over beds and chairs, incoherently murmuring as they rocked themselves, examined each other's heads or stared blankly into space. How long it had been since the ward had been cleaned I had no idea. I stood rigid at the door, then my stomach heaved and I projectile-vomited halfway across the room, adding to the filth and stench. The nurse in front of me received vomit over her stockings and shoes. As she turned and raised her hand as if about to hit me, she must have thought better of it and instead shoved me back into the corridor, yelling at the nurse behind me to take me back to my ward. How many years has it taken for some of these appalling conditions to be recognized?

I made no 'friends' there in Oakley. I complied with everything that was expected of me, including eating (promptly regurgitating the food, which was disgusting anyway). I attended occupational therapy, persuading the naïve young therapist to let me continue with my embroidery rather than the inane practice of making cane baskets. I duped medical staff into believing I was taking my medication; I had decided it might be prudent to keep my wits about me, considering the catatonic state of many of my fellow inmates. I was the model patient for Dr Needham, my psychiatrist, whom I immediately labelled as a pathetic wimp, but who in retrospect was probably an overworked, gentle, caring man. By this stage I was into the blame game, because I realized that everyone trying to stop me drinking wanted to know *why* I drank. If I couldn't find something or someone responsible for making me drink, then there was only one other choice! I was to continue blaming outside influences until finally confronted with the fact that I drank because I had no idea how *not* to drink; this was not a realization I came to sitting in front of Dr Needham, however.

It wasn't long before I was discharged. I would really try to do things differently, I told Dr Needham. I certainly swore I'd never set foot in Oakley again. However, I had now become an arch-manipulator, one of the classic skills that alcoholics develop as a defence mechanism. When my parents decided to 'have a talk' with me about my drinking, it wasn't long before I manipulated Mother into defending me and shifting a large portion of the reason for my consumption to the example set by my father. I was also becoming skilled at guilt trips: *If you hadn't done that, then I wouldn't need to do this . . .*

Conversations that were along the lines of the following:

'I wish you wouldn't drink so much, Daddy.'

'Why should I stop drinking when it is not my problem? I have hard days at the office and it helps me to relax.'

'But, Roy, you know that often you drink more than you should and become quite belligerent with it.'

'But I only have a couple of whiskies before dinner.'

'And sometimes one afterwards.'

'Only very occasionally.'

'Roy, that's what makes you so argumentative. I cannot hold a conversation with you when you are like that.'

'I find it hard to talk to you, too, Daddy, and that's often why I go to bed [to sneak more booze in my room], because there is not much point in staying up and listening to you and Mummy arguing.'

'We're not here to talk about my drinking, Elizabeth — we are here to talk about yours.'

'Yes, but if you didn't drink so much then I probably wouldn't either.'

And so the conversation would continue, ending with Father's slammed-door departure from the room. I became adept at the blame game; the family was now caught up in the alcoholic dance with me.

My job at Russell and Somers, a travel agency, had been held open for me on the basis that I was on emergency sick leave, although I knew that many of the staff thought there was something 'not quite right' with me. They were polite, including me in their conversations during the morning and afternoon tea breaks, but there was an underlying current that instinctively told me they were treading on eggshells when I was around. I knew I had to leave, but there would be two more incidents before this happened.

One was on Queen's Birthday weekend. A group of us had travelled north by bus to tour Russell, visit Cape Reinga, experience the kauri forest, and walk part of Ninety Mile Beach. My entire focus the preceding week was how to ensure I would have enough alcohol for the three days. I knew that each night there would be alcohol around, as the men would drink beer, but the problem was guaranteeing that I would not run out. Two small bottles of vodka would suffice; one was in my voluminous handbag that never left my side, and the second was decanted into a series of miniature plastic travelling make-up bottles. All went well until the last evening, on Ninety Mile Beach, where everything nearly ended for me. We bussed out there on the Sunday night to watch the sunset. I saw no sunset, no beach; just a vast amount of salt water. I decided to paddle, with my shoes on, fully clothed and clutching the inevitable handbag slung across my chest. I was not tipsy, I was drunk — and the waves of the Tasman Sea spare no one. Walking a straight line over the sand to reach the water's edge had not been successful, and when the wave knocked me over I was totally unprepared. The rip was relentless as I was hauled out to sea. I can swim, I can float, I can tread water — but not with a skinful of vodka and a handbag full of sea. I didn't sober up so much as come to, choking on seawater and gasping for air. Thank God for the bus driver and the two rugby players in the group who hauled me ashore. I was not concerned for the shoe I had lost, the clothes I had ruined, or my waterlogged watch. My one and only thought was for the half-full bottle of vodka; mercifully for me, still in the bag.

I stopped drinking. I had a mouth like a piece of sandpaper, a head with a steel band around it, and hands that found it difficult to hold the copious cups of coffee I drank that night and the following day. But I stopped drinking. I didn't stop *thinking* about drinking. I didn't plan never to drink again. I just decided I had better stop for a while so that I could prove to everyone I *could* stop. In retrospect, I've come to understand the full scope of alcoholism — normal drinkers do not set out to prove they can stop drinking. It never occurs to them. Why would they need to prove it? They can take it or leave it, and also take it *and* leave it: sitting on the table, the mantelpiece (what a waste!).

I set out to convince everyone, including myself, that alcohol was no problem — sure, there were other problems in my life, but alcohol was not one of them and I was certainly not alcoholic. Dr Richwhite had told me several months prior to the Ninety Mile Beach incident that I was an alcoholic (strange how I remembered that), and, like Mike Gilmore, he had warned me about my consumption. I now chose to prove to him and others that I was not.

My definition of 'alcoholic' had been instilled in me by a society that had, and to a degree still has, its own, totally erroneous definition. For me, this was a problem for the middle-aged and underprivileged. I was too young, too smart, too well-educated; there were no such people as *alcoholics* in my area in society, and certainly not women. Alcoholics were men in long overcoats, with brown paper bags hiding a bottle in their coat pockets. For me, drinking was a bad habit at best, and at worst I was weak-willed, and I would prove I could control both of those. Alcoholics drank every day, consumed large amounts of alcohol and drank before breakfast. They did not have jobs, they lived on the streets and rummaged through rubbish bins. Little did I realize that this was the end of the road, not the beginning or even the middle. Those street people *were* the middle-aged and underprivileged; about 5 per cent of alcoholics. The other 95 per cent were out there working their way towards that predicament. Although I did not realize it, I was following the typical progression of the disease. Every alcoholic can stop drinking, for days, weeks, months or even years — but cannot *stay* stopped and lead an alcohol-free life, which means being comfortable each day without it, including not *thinking* about it. I was not drinking, but I had certainly not lost my obsession with it.

The non-drinking lasted approximately two weeks before the rationalizations and justifications commenced as to why I could start again; I was yet to discover that, no matter how bad things are, continued drinking makes them worse. I was smart; I simply had to practise control, I thought. The truth was that it was not that I *wanted* to drink, but that I *needed* to drink. I had rid myself of alcohol, but that was not really the problem. Drinking was my only answer to the disease inside me. I still felt out of step with the world; an alien. I had excruciating feelings of insecurity and inadequacy, and was still plagued by nameless fears. I lacked confidence and self-esteem, and was easily hurt by the slightest hint of criticism. I was shy, sensitive, emotional, and found social situations impossible to handle (let alone being able to enjoy them).

The walls between me and the world had started to build again, and my bizarre eating patterns returned with a vengeance. Excessive consumption and purging became more frequent, at times up to three times daily. I would visit two eateries on my way to work, gorging on pies, chips, sandwiches and other junk washed down with Coca-Cola and Fanta (an orange fizzy drink), sometimes adding milkshakes as well. Several trips to the bathroom later, I would be able to attempt to work; my head would be spinning, probably due to low potassium and a lack of the other minerals that had been depleted by the vomiting. But I *was* controlling my drinking. My parents were helping with that. I would sit at night while Father drank his (now limited) two whiskies, and I had my two glasses of sherry. It was *agony* for me. 'Give me none or the bottle!' my head screamed. 'Don't torture me — I need more, more. Two aren't working.' Inevitably, I had to buy the bottle to hide under the mattress. I could not stand the mental torture any longer. At least I could sleep, although 'pass out' was probably the more accurate term.

Six o'clock closing and no opening of liquor stores on a weekend were horror times for people like me. On a Saturday morning, my first thought on waking was the bottle I had hidden under the bed the night before — or *thought* I had hidden under the bed. That was where they went now, for easy access, until Mother discovered them when vacuuming. This morning, there was no bottle there. Like a shot of cold water having been thrown at me, my mind became crystal clear. Where else could it be? I searched the pockets of my coats in the wardrobe, my drawers, under my chest of drawers, behind the books in the bookcase, behind the curtains, in the shoe boxes, under the mattress; and then the vacuum cleaner caught my eye. I had taken to cleaning my own room. Vague flashes of incidents the night before led me to open the dust-collecting part of the machine, as my heart raced with anticipation. There was the bottle. My overwhelming sense of relief soon turned to heart-palpitating panic, however: there was barely enough liquid for two mouthfuls.

How in the name of Heaven was I to survive the weekend? There were no bottle stores open, and would not be until Monday. The wine shop, twenty minutes away, was hopeless as I had to open the bottles with a corkscrew and then ran the risk that they would leak if I didn't replace the cork properly. It was a long way from Remuera to Gleeson's, the sly-grog place in the city where they sold liquor illegally over weekends, and I would never be able to smuggle it back to the house — Mother would be suspicious if I was away for too long, and the walk there and back would take a couple of hours. Father had not only locked his liquor cabinet with a padlock (I had picked the original lock open), but on discovering I had found his back-up supply and raided that, he now also had *all* liquor in the house under lock and key.

I contemplated my options on the front doorstep, accompanied by a brain-jolting cup of coffee. The wine shop won. I planned it to the last detail. The money went into the sole of my shoe, three paper drinking straws were secreted up the arms of my sweater (to poke in the tops of the bottles so I did not need to move them), my cigarettes and lighter were in my trouser pocket, and I clutched five dollars in my hand, a reasonable amount in the 'sixties just after decimal currency had been introduced. Father was at golf. His ritual every Saturday was Middlemore Golf Club for an all-day round of golf, followed by gins and tonic at the nineteenth hole. He should have been pleased that there were no breathalysers back then as he and his compatriots weaved their Jaguars home.

I announced to Mother that I was off for a walk. See — only

cigarettes, lighter and five dollars for more cigarettes and some chewing gum. (Cigarettes were not even three dollars for twenty, then.) The plan worked perfectly. One bottle found a home amongst the shrubs around the church hall at the top of our street, one in the neighbour's hedge by the footpath, and one behind the hydrangeas in our front garden, all with straws sticking out for easy access. As the weeks progressed I even managed to dig bottles into the garden, developing an interest in weeding that was unexplained until Mother discovered a half-empty bottle of gin submerged under her bed of violets. The games alcoholics play. I swear to this day: sober us up and we would be able to train the detectives in the police force!

Finally, the inevitable happened; although the dreadful episodes occurred unexpectedly and were unpredictably different, they were always worse than before.

The US Navy had arrived in town, and as a still-functioning member of the Girls' Club of the Navy League it was my 'duty' to help entertain the visiting personnel. The Town Hall had been booked for a large dinner-dance on the Friday night. At the end of the working day at Russell and Somers (the last time I would tread their carpet), I emerged from their bathroom in my stunning Indian silk, off-the-shoulder, figure-hugging ball gown. I had my old school cloak (now black with its red lining) around my shoulders, my evening purse primed with two plastic bottles full of neat gin, my long, white gloves clutched in my hand, and a skinful of the remaining gin from the half-bottle under my belt. I chewed peppermints as one of the staff drove me to the Town Hall. I needed the large glass of Coca-Cola (the first thing I drank) just to put out the fire! The gin had burned all the way from my lips to my stomach and needed watering down — just a little.

I remember only fragments of what happened up until I looked at my watch: it was 5.30 at night on *Saturday*. I had no idea where

I was, who I had been with, or what had occurred in the lost hours. What had I done? What had been done to me? I had not meant to get drunk; I had just wanted to have a good time. Somehow, getting drunk had just happened. I have no idea how long I lay frozen on that bed, terrified to move. I thought I would go mad. Mad from the guilt, fear and remorse of what must have occurred during the night, and the dread of what the future might disclose. I lay there with me, and I had no idea who 'me' was. There was a wall six inches thick between me and the world, behind which I was dying. I had no friends, and instinctively I knew I had no job.

I had to do *something*, so I got out of bed and searched the room. My bag was there with everything intact, my gloves, shoes, underclothes; everything. I found the telephone book and discovered that I was in the Great Northern Hotel at the bottom of Queen Street. (No longer a hotel, today it is a series of offices above upmarket shops such as Mont Blanc.) Then I saw the card tucked into the mirror with US$50 behind it: *Lieutenant Commander* ___, *United States Navy*. I kept that note, a large amount in those days, for years. Somehow I could not bring myself to exchange it for other currency. It was finally cashed years later, when I realized it was a part of my past that had to be abandoned.

For some inexplicable reason I said a little thank-you prayer, then gathered my belongings, wrapped my cloak around me, walked brazenly out of the hotel and made my way to the wine shop at the Downtown bus terminal. Half a bottle of sherry in the ladies' toilet, and I was on my way. Of course I was not mad. I was perfectly aware of what I was doing as I walked up Queen Street clutching my bottle of sherry in one hand and keeping my black cloak wrapped around me with the other. At least that hid my evening dress. I was going somewhere; I had no idea where, but it's possible I was walking home.

Somewhere in the vicinity of the Peter Pan Dance Hall was a restaurant (if this eatery could be called that), and I was hungry. Two pies and a cup of coffee laced with sherry later, I was in a car — with whom and going where I had no idea. The next thing I knew was waking up in the back seat of the car with a rug over me. I was alone. My knee throbbed and my stomach ached, but I knew I had to get out of that car.

It's a long way on foot from Newmarket to Victoria Avenue in Remuera, particularly when it's necessary to take the longest route possible, hiding in gardens and behind garages on the way. Today it seems nothing short of miraculous that I survived that Saturday night and early Sunday morning. My gloves were gone and the strap on one of my shoes was broken, but the handle of my bag was knotted around my wrist and two tiny plastic bottles, one still half full of gin, were inside. Today I would probably not be alive, or I would be on a list of missing persons.

My parents were at church as I crept through the back door and up the stairs to repair myself. By the time they arrived home, I was in the garden with coffee and cigarettes — and two large slugs of Father's whisky inside me. He had inadvertently left the bottle out from the night before. I had also filled a large glass with whisky, pouring water up to the original level in the bottle, and the glass was in my dressing-table drawer. My father confronted my inscrutable, granite-like face with the usual questions, for which I had the usual answers. Where had I been? Nowhere. What had I been doing? Nothing. Who had I been with? No one. I could see his fury rising with every reply I stoically threw at him. Then I attacked, without a shred of conscience. 'In a hotel, with a US naval officer, *and* he was black *and* he paid me.' Perhaps the only mitigating factor that this knifing included was the word 'officer'. The whisky gave me false courage, guilt induced me to lash out, and fear prompted me to attack. I spat like a cornered animal as I strove to subdue the rising panic and terror gnawing my insides. Mother stood pale and tight-lipped as I flounced inside to spend the remainder of the day in my bedroom.

By evening I was drunk again. The contents from the plastic bottles in my evening bag had been consumed, the vodka from nail polish remover bottles followed; then the liquid from the hot-water bottle disappeared down my throat, and the glass of whisky followed suit. It was probably fortunate that I had no way to attack the gin in the turpentine bottle in the garage, or there is a distinct possibility I would have overdosed.

I came to on Monday morning; *late* Monday morning; too late to go to work on Monday morning. Mother, in her well-meaning but (oblivious to her) enabling way, had rung work to advise them I was ill and unable to go in. She learnt in that telephone call that I was to lose my job. Hardly surprising, as in retrospect I admire Russell and Somers for giving me all the chances that they did.

That was not all I faced that morning. I opened my bedroom door to find that the carpet in the hallway and on the stairs had been removed. I always had a bath before I went to bed. Well, nearly always, the exception being when it was too much trouble to make it into the bath and I could not guarantee I would make it out again. (On those times I would lie on the bed, and have this strange sensation of the bed moving under me and of my body being elevated. Not quite passed out, but anticipating that I soon would be.) Mother's grey, granite face informed me there was something amiss, and instinctively I knew that the something had to do with me. Sure enough, I was the culprit. Mother's auditory sense had always been phenomenal; she could hear a tap dripping at the far end of the house, *underneath* the house. She had heard the bath running for my nocturnal cleansing ritual; running and running and running, but then there had been a change in the water's tone. In fact, there had been two different tones to the water, which necessitated an investigation. Halfway up the stairs she had met the results of the strange sound. Water was merrily on its way down, having a great time like a Slinky toy as it slithered from stair to stair. I was nowhere to be seen. I had passed out on my bedroom floor.

Chapter 6

A social embarrassment

Two doctors and two distraught, exhausted parents now convened to find a more promising solution. Perhaps if they could *really* find out why I drank, that would help. The prescribed pills did not appear to be very effective (of course not — the ones Mother watched me take at home were travelling the same route as those in Oakley), so a new course of action was agreed upon. Bexley Clinic, Roger Culpan's clinic, was administering a truth drug to specific patients in the hope that, under its influence, an individual's natural guard would be removed and they would not feel inhibited to discuss anxieties, problems or the causes of their behaviours.

The experience did me far more harm than good, and in fact simply precipitated the bizarre behaviours of both my drinking and my eating. For a start, I did not *know* why I got drunk at certain times — it just happened. This statement is totally understandable to any alcoholic, and totally incomprehensible to anyone else. That *was* the truth but no one believed me, so of course I had to find reasons to satisfy clinicians who were convinced that there had to be a cause for every behaviour.

I have no idea what I said in that chemically induced state, but I certainly remember the experience. I was lying on a raised bed much like those found in doctors' surgeries. There was a stranger, a man whose voice I did not recognize on the side of the bed near the end, asking questions. An extension of me, not me, appeared to be talking, rambling, talking, talking, talking. I wanted to sit up, but could not move. It was as though I was tied to the bed with invisible ropes — so that when his hand and fingers made their way up my calves and thighs to between my legs, I felt paralysed. I could not move. My whole body was fighting, screaming to somehow back away. I wanted to kick and kick and kick with all the power I could muster, yet I couldn't move a muscle. I was helpless and could only lie there, inert and silently whimpering. Defenceless, broken and completely isolated in a world in which I did not belong. I had no one I could turn to. No friends in whom I could confide, parents who were frightened and bewildered with my whole life, and doctors who would totally discount anything I had to say. I was powerless, helpless, humiliated and alone. Alone and desperately, desperately lonely.

Mother collected me from the clinic and took me home, still in my dressing gown. I so much wanted to tell her what had happened, but knew I would never be believed. It would simply be one more lie, as she would see it, to be added to the myriad I had told over the years. What could she do even if she *had* known? Accuse the clinic of sexual violation of her daughter by one of their staff, the accusation emanating from a drug-induced patient? It would have been a useless exercise, and I knew it. The whole incident became just one more layer of pain and horror that I added to the accumulation I already carried.

My eating patterns became even more incomprehensible; my drinking episodes attaining socially unacceptable levels of recognition.

The Chilean Navy training ship *Esmeralda* was hosting a cocktail party for members of the Navy League, and my behaviour that night forced League President Joe Wilson to quietly have a word with my father and suggest I attend no more functions. Sir Douglas Robb (Chancellor of the University of Auckland) had to ensure that his daughter Sally, who had invited me to their party, deposited me at home safely; to the utter embarrassment of my mother, who opened the door. I was the hot topic at the Northern Club and Middlemore Golf Club, and even flatting for a while with long-suffering and caring Di Milne (of Milne and Choyce) could not alter my behaviour. Incident after incident would emerge at unexpected and inappropriate times.

I didn't drink every day, nor did I binge and purge every day. However, often when I drank I also binge-ate, would not remember that I had eaten, and would wake up next day feeling sick, bloated, lethargic and miserable. Perhaps in a strange way those episodes kept me alive, in the sense that I was gaining *some* nourishment and increasing my weight. Because of this, although the manner in which I consumed food was abhorrent, at least I appeared to be getting heavier.

I had to be put somewhere — again. But what now? Father had become uncommunicative and could barely bring himself to enter the doors of the Northern Club, let alone walk the greens of Middlemore Golf Course. Mother was in her own living Hell. I had become a total stranger to her, a hideous nightmare that would not disappear. She had reached the end of her emotional tether, and one Friday evening had been the last straw. As I was fumbling to open the door with my key, she opened it for me, and stood aside while I attempted *not* to trip over the doorstep. The liquid sloshed ominously in my copious handbag, and as she pulled at the bag and I staggered to keep my balance she gained possession of it. Without even asking, she reached in and pulled out the bottle. Years later, she told me that the look of sheer, utter hatred on my face was worse than if I had cut her incessantly with a machete. Her eldest daughter, of whom she had been so proud, whom she had loved so much as she had breast-fed her during those dark days living with the Battle of Britain overhead, and whom she had just known would *do* things with her life, was weaving in front of her, drunk, friendless and with a look of sheer hatred on her face, ready to attack her own mother for a bottle. She turned and climbed the stairs to her bedroom, and I heard the lock turn in the door. I did not care. All I could care about was the bottle: my friend, my lover, my answer, the only companion I had in the world had been snatched from me. I had become some hideous, nameless creature who walked over everything and everybody, oblivious to the human debris I left in my wake.

This time it took *four* doctors to decide what to do. Dr Richwhite, Dr Culpan, Dr Needham, and now the Superintendent of Oakley Hospital, Dr Pat Savage.

The year of 1967 saw Pat Savage looking to explore a new treatment for altering an individual's drinking patterns, in fact to instil in them an aversion to liquor. Great idea, but absolutely ineffective in my case and those of the thousands of others who have the three-fold disease of alcoholism with its physical, mental and emotional/spiritual components. If all I had to do was not drink, I would have 'got well' months ago. I was intelligent and smart. According to my health records, I was 'of above average intelligence, well educated, with an engaging personality but unable to accept and adjust to a rigid and upper class family background and up-bringing'. I was 'a social embarrassment to the family', who were 'determined to prevent any information leaking out in case this would affect their position in the Remuera [read Knightsbridge/Vaucluse/New York] social scene'!

I knew everything about alcohol and the alcoholic, and would describe the latter in such a way that I did not fit the description. I knew *nothing* about alcoholism, the disease that is progressive, relentless and fatal; that it creates chaos, not only in the drinker's life, but also in the lives of those around her. That was what was happening. I was like a tornado tearing through other people's lives, leaving them shocked, embarrassed and bewildered, while I was totally insensitive to the mayhem I was causing.

I was either to enter Oakley voluntarily, or I would be committed under a Government Act; that was the choice. I was cornered. Indescribable panic gripped me as memories of the last visit engulfed me. The dormitory with its total lack of privacy, and the ECT machine hovering around the beds ghoulishly waiting to attach its octopus tentacles to the next unsuspecting victim. I convinced myself that this time I was in line for its hideous fingers. (I discovered later that, had I been committed, my consent for ECT would not have been necessary; I would have had no say in the matter.) My fellow inmates who had scared me witless as they paced the corridor or sat in chairs staring into oblivion, distressed, drugged, unpredictable and murmuring incomprehensibly to themselves, would still be there. As would the pathetic patients who cleaned the skirting boards in the hallways with toothbrushes; the stench and filth of the geriatric ward; the nurses who provoked patients, threatening them with paraldehyde, other injections or ECT if they did not conform; the dribbling, scratching, coughing and uncontrollable muscle spasms that provided bizarre entertainment for some and could light a fire of violence in others.

I begged, I pleaded, I promised I would never drink again; all to no avail. Kicking, screaming and throwing a tantrum would only end up with a needle sticking in me, and so I went quietly, seething like a cauldron inside. I had now abdicated all my rights and was at the mercy of a medical system that would experiment with me like some guinea pig in a laboratory. Nobody believed me any more, even when I told the truth. Why should they? For so long they had not been able to differentiate truth from fiction. I had no idea what was going to happen to me, but I was still willing to fight — if for nothing else than to keep my brain from being used for experimentation. I had no idea what I would do if the need actually arose, but I knew I would either kill someone or myself. I was suicidal, homicidal and ready to become genocidal.

None of this was necessary. I never saw an Oakley dormitory again. I was taken to an annex across the road, which became known as Wolfe Home. There I met Sister Flack. To this day I can recall the image of this woman. She was tall, well built, with blonde hair and large eyes that bored through me as though reaching into the innermost depths of my psyche. Inexplicably, I was drawn to her. For the next few weeks she was truly my saviour.

I was to be a patient for aversion therapy. I was given no facts or information on this therapy. No choice, either — again, if I had not agreed to it voluntarily, I would have been committed. I had no idea of what the procedure, the effects, the short- or long-term consequences, and the desired outcomes were. I have no idea whether Sister Flack knew either, or indeed the male nurse who administered it to me.

It was an afternoon performance, and that, in retrospect, was what it must have appeared to any observer. I was not permitted to eat lunch. Around 2 p.m., with an empty stomach and in a dressing gown and slippers, I trudged with Sister Flack down Wolfe Home's driveway, across the road and into the main block at Oakley. It was humiliating; people in cars stared at us, pointed at us, and made faces as they passed, sometimes slowing down to have a better look at this woman in the 'funny farm'. I was led into a dimly lit room. A man in a white nurse's coat was standing behind a mocked-up bar, his back reflected in a wall of mirrors behind him — on the shelves of which was an array of liquor bottles. He introduced himself, although I have no recall of what was said. My eyes were glued to the commode placed facing the bar: a wooden armchair with a hole in the seat under which, I learnt, was a bowl. Sister Flack, bless her, explained that I was to sit there as she was going to give me an injection. This happened so quickly that I was barely aware the needle had gone in. One lot of serum was followed by the phial being unscrewed, the needle remaining in me while a second phial was attached and its contents disgorged. What was meant to happen? I had no idea — but I found out within the space of a matter of seconds.

The sweat started to pour off me, my vision became blurred, and my heart was racing. The nurse standing behind the bar with a glass in his hand was asking what I would like to drink. Sherry seemed a good idea. I have no idea how long I sat there. I could not control my bowels. I could not control my bladder. Every time I vomited, another glass of alcohol was placed in front of me which I was forced to drink, and that would be ejected as well. My sides ached, my throat was raw, my eyes were streaming, vomit was blocking my nose, and tears were mixing with the contents of the bowl on the bar in front of me. Finally, it was over. They cleaned me up, and Sister and I walked — we *walked* — back across the road, back to Wolfe Home, back to the safety of my room. (How glad I was for that room to myself.) I was confused, alone, humiliated, demeaned, and the sense of abandonment was overwhelming. I was helpless; I had nowhere to go and no one who wanted me, and I was twenty-three years old.

My medical records state that I endured the torture of this experimental therapy for *eight days*. By the time Pat Savage arrived to stand in the corner and watch me, the very smell of alcohol had my stomach heaving and bile being regurgitated. How I hated his presence in the room. I hated being watched as if I was a rat in a laboratory, but I hoped at the same time that he was impressed enough to believe that the experiment was working. He must have been impressed; sometime later I was discharged. I had obviously convinced the decision-makers that the 'cure' had worked, although my eating disorder was still rampant. Nothing had changed regarding my anorexia and bulimia, and I was now smoking close to fifteen cigarettes a day. I had no job, my mother was horrified at the way I looked, and my father found it almost impossible to be around me.

The 'cure' had far from worked. In a matter of weeks I started drinking again, but *this* time I decided to white-knuckle it and control it. I had a plan, a serious plan, and I could not afford for it to fail. My troubles were all because I had been brought back from England. I did not want to be in Auckland, or even New Zealand. If I went back to England, I could start afresh and all would be well. I had to get out of this country — forever. Away from scrutinizing parents, away from a society that wanted to ignore me, away from gossiping tongues and condemning eyes; most of all, I had to escape from being condemned to further medical horrors. The possibility of a lobotomy or the dreaded black-box therapy loomed on the horizon. My case packed, I bought a one-way ticket, and I was leaving on a jet plane.

Chapter 7

The geographical escape

A geographical change is never without consequences, but the reason for moving determines what happens. I failed to even contemplate the fact that wherever I went, and wherever I go today, I take *me* with me, along with whatever emotional baggage I may have. So it was when I boarded the plane with my bottle of Cointreau and my bottle of Johnnie Walker for the great escape back to England.

Somehow I recall shimmering tarmac, and jack-booted figures with — rifles? AK47s? Who would know? An atmosphere of heavy silence permeated the plane. It was 1967, and our route took us over the Middle East. I had no idea where we were; I must have dozed off into an alcohol-induced stupor, as the first thing I remember was being shaken awake. My two bottled friends were nowhere to be found. I have no idea what happened to those bottles: all I remember is the free-falling panic in my stomach when I realized I had no more alcohol available. I defy any but those addicted to a substance to understand the sheer terror that situation provoked in me — again. Fortunately, I must have consumed sufficient alcohol during the flight to sustain me until I found a bottle shop in Earls Court, near where I had arranged accommodation. My sister, although living in London, was not even thinking of offering me a sofa to crash on. She was well aware of my antics over the past few years.

I now felt a freedom that was bordering on euphoria. No parents, no bottle-shop owners, nobody around to look at me strangely or try to avoid me. I failed to understand how normal such reactions were for anyone who had seen my behaviour maybe twice, let alone with monotonous regularity. But now I was free to do what I liked, when I liked. *What* meant to drink. *When* meant any time, day or night.

I had been in London before, in the early 'sixties. I knew the pubs, I knew the bottle shops. I knew Earls Court and South Kensington, I knew King's Road and Fulham Road, I knew Knightsbridge and I knew Chelsea. It was fortunate that I did. On the nights when I somehow found my way home to my flat in an alcoholic blackout, it must have been with a pre-programmed homing instinct.

At weekends I would stay with relations or old friends who lived out of London. I kept my drinking under what I considered to be a certain amount of control. Many of my old friends were heavy drinkers, so they may have failed to notice the changes in me when I drank. As an active, drinking alcoholic, every time I drank I did not necessarily pass out, but by this time I was unable to do two things simultaneously: I could not control and enjoy my drinking at the same time. If I was to control it, I could not enjoy it; if I was to enjoy it, I could not control it. Once I had crossed that line of control, I could never go back. But I tried, I tried very hard.

Then came the weekend that was to have an earth-shattering effect on my life.

As I grow older, I look back and see how one thing precedes another, and another, in life. Some are really minor incidents at the time, yet can remain lodged in the memory for some inexplicable reason until the significance later becomes clear. One such incident involved my father's secondary-school tie. He had been educated at Clifton College, in Bristol, England. After World War II, the family's New Zealand-based import/export business, H.T. Merritt Ltd, had required him to make regular trips to Japan. His young daughters always met his return with breathtaking excitement

— not only were his gifts of transistor radios a novelty, but there were also battery-operated, head-nodding and tail-wagging dogs, ballerinas on little stands that pirouetted to music when we wound them up, and kimonos, fans and parasols.

For some extraordinary reason I remember a conversation between my parents after Father's arrival home one evening. He had invited an Englishman for a drink the following night, the result of a chance meeting in the hotel at which they had both been staying in Tokyo. My father had been wearing his Old Cliftonian tie, and a man had approached him saying, 'It is so nice to meet another Englishman here.' My father replied that he was not English, but a New Zealander. The Englishman asked how he came to be wearing an Old Cliftonian tie; Father explained; and in the resulting conversation learnt that the Englishman, John, was an insurance agent with South British Insurance.

John and his wife, Sally, visited us in New Zealand on several occasions. Subsequently, I came to know them in England, and that fateful Friday night in October 1967 I caught the train from London to stay with them for the weekend at their home in Ascot. The top to my hot-water bottle was of utmost importance for the weekend ahead. If it did not fit snugly, then the gin I was smuggling inside would leak out. That would be a disaster: John and Sally would then know that I was definitely a secret drinker. Who in their right mind would put gin into a hot-water bottle? I carefully screwed the lid onto the bulging container. Turning it upside-down, I shook it rigorously, examined the whole surface closely, and breathed a sigh of relief. No leakage. Whew! Gingerly I placed it in my suitcase, ensuring that a cheap old plastic raincoat was wrapped around it — just in case.

As I skimmed my eyes over the other items to pack, my thoughts remained with the rubber container and its contents. What a comfort to know I did not have to be alone for the weekend. I had my friend, my lover. Whenever I felt that gnawing discomfort, all I needed was the warmth from the bottle's liquid, kept safe by that little plastic cap.

I finished my packing, but anxiety had started to worm its way into my mind. What if I was to lose that cap? How would I cope with my fears and insecurities, my loneliness, if I misplaced this small item and my liquid solution to life escaped? Fear gripped me now. What if the little rubber washer, an integral part of this incongruous piece of plastic, should be lost? What if the bottle *did* leak? In the suitcase? On the floor? In the dresser drawer? How would I erase the easily recognizable, acrid smell that would emerge from the seepage? Mustn't think like that. Just be extra careful, I cautioned myself as I headed on my way.

John and Sally took me to their local pub before we went back to their house. That was the last memory I had when I awoke on Saturday morning. What I *did* remember was the copious quantity of gin I had consumed before boarding the train. The heart palpitations, cold sweat and stomach-churning which announced the panic rising in me began. I told myself that there was probably nothing to worry about. After all, we had all been drinking and I could just pretend, if anything was said, that I had been tired and the alcohol had hit me rather hard.

I had reckoned without Sally.

John had left for golf. I sat at the kitchen table in my dressing gown while Sally poured me a cup of coffee. She placed the cup in front of me and drew out the chair opposite. I felt her direct gaze as she sat down. I remember how excruciatingly painful it was when I met her eyes. She knew. Without any preliminaries, her words were direct and to the point: 'Liz, you have a drinking problem. I know, because my mother-in-law died of alcoholism. I have called a friend of mine who is a recovered alcoholic and she will be here in about ten minutes. I want you to listen to her.' Not 'I want her to talk to you' or 'I want you to talk to her'. No. 'I want you to listen to her.' There was nothing I could say. I just nodded.

The sitting-room window overlooked the driveway, so I saw the Daimler arrive. British racing green. It could not be her. An alcoholic with a *Daimler*? But I heard Sally greeting her, thanking her for coming so promptly, and I can still hear Jean's reply: 'We so often change our minds within an hour. It's important to catch us while we are vulnerable.' I felt my hackles rising. What was this 'we'? I was not an alcoholic; my father had told me so.

The diamond clasp of the double string of pearls blinked on the baby-blue twinset (it had to be Pringle!) as a shaft of sunlight enveloped her. She entered the room ahead of Sally. A faint whiff of *Femme*, my favourite perfume, caressed my nostrils as she took my outstretched hand in hers and enveloped it like a cocoon with her other one. Grey-blue eyes filled with caring and compassion held me in a steady gaze. 'The mornings are the worst, aren't they?' 'Yup' was out of my mouth before I even realized I had opened it. Squeezing my hand, she turned to the armchair under the window, plumped up the cushion and sat down.

It is extraordinary how some events in life can be photographed by the mind. I will never forget this particular image. The pale green and blue chintz of the chair, the primrose-yellow cushion, the golden October sun streaming through the window behind Jean's silver-grey hair. The trees outside weeping their fiery leaves, almost empathetically acknowledging the emotions I was experiencing. Tears at Jean's understanding, anger that I had not had my guard up to protect my feelings, and fear as to what else she was going to tell me about me.

How arrogantly wrong I was about what was to happen next. Sally brought more coffee; I needed it even if Jean did not. Her hands cradled the mug (how did she *know* I needed a mug, not a dainty cup?), and the rainbow of light from her diamond-and-sapphire ring — which I sarcastically assumed had to have been on loan from the Tower of London — danced around the room. For a while she and Sally exchanged news of their latest golf scores, news of their children, news of their dogs, women's news; then Sally remembered 'needing to meet John', and Jean and I were alone.

I had made up my mind that I was not going to have any more discussions, or answer any more questions. I had had enough. Parents, friends, doctors, nurses, psychiatrists, psychologists.

Jean placed her mug on the small glass table beside her chair, and I waited for the first question. It was not a question; it was a statement: 'Liz — I'm Jean and I'm an alcoholic. I'd like you to listen to my story.'

I was thrown completely off-balance. No one had ever requested me to do *that* in my entire life. Why would she want *me* to listen to *her?* Wasn't she going to ask me to tell her about me? Self-centred as I was, I was completely oblivious that, in the space of a bare sixty seconds, I had gone from silently deciding I was not going to answer questions to being infuriated because I wasn't being asked any. Little did I realize that Jean had a PhD in out-manipulating the controlling manipulator that I had become. I was thrown so off-balance that I paid attention. This elegant, wealthy, expensively dressed, serene, relaxed, lie-detecting (I was to experience that later!) woman began her story. It was a story that was to change my life (and, since that day, countless other lives as well), for she started to do something nobody else had ever done with me before. She started to tell me what it had been like for her. In telling me her story, she was telling me mine.

She told me how lonely she had always felt, even as a child, as though she were an alien not only in her own family but in the world. How she had always striven to be better than anyone else at whatever she did — just to feel equal, just to belong, but not knowing *who* she wanted to belong with. As a child, she remembered fear. Fear of people, places, things. Fear of being left out. Fear of not being good enough. Constant fear that became more desperate as she grew older.

She remembered her first taste of alcohol; her parents had decided she should grow up with an appreciation of wine. She recalled how she had coughed up the first mouthful, unused to the strange abrasive sensation down her throat. How eventually she had kept that one glass down, and the hole with the wind whistling through it inside her had started to fill up as the warmth of the wine spread through her. The lightheadedness, the sense — at last — of her inside matching the outside of those around her.

For the first time in her life, she felt she belonged in the world; she had found the answer to all her problems. Jean talked and I listened, absolutely spellbound by this elegant and compassionate woman in front of me.

It was around 2.30 p.m. when Sally and John returned. Jean said she wouldn't stay for lunch, but would be back again the following day (Sunday), around 10 a.m., for coffee. Perhaps we could talk some more. Perhaps a walk now would be a good idea — for my head to clear. But on my own, I said. In reply to Sally's obviously concerned frown, Jean replied, 'Let her go, Sally. It's better that way.'

Again, I was taken totally off-guard. Here was this woman whom I had known for not even twenty-four hours assuring someone who had had I knew not what kind of experience with me the night before that I could be trusted to walk wherever I chose — alone. I was beginning to feel a trifle paranoid. I simply could not understand how she could infiltrate my head in such a short space of time. Numerous psychiatrists and two trips to a mental institution, along with all the head games that had been attempted on me there, had been to no avail, including use of a truth drug. Yet here was a sophisticated woman who without any apparent shame labelled herself 'alcoholic', and who predicted that I could be trusted out alone after Heaven knows what sort of performance the night before. It was obscene! I was terrified and fascinated at the same time. Terrified of what else she knew or could predict about me; fascinated as to how she was able to do so.

Sunday came. We sat in the same chairs. The diamond clasp blinked — this time on pink. I mean *pink!* Who wore *pink* in the 'sixties? Jean did, and looked almost ethereal. This time I also noticed her signet ring, heavy compared with the dancing diamonds. Without thinking I started twisting my own, the one my grandmother had given me for my twenty-first birthday. My grandmother who had spoiled me, as the eldest granddaughter. Who had taught me to burn the stems of poppies to make them last longer in water. Who, religiously, at 10 a.m. every day she was home, sat on the veranda while the housekeeper brought her coffee, her gold case with the Senior Service cigarettes beside the coffee pot from which she would carefully extract one of the two she rationed herself to each day. The grandmother I always ran to find every Sunday when we went for lunch after Sunday School. Strange what the memory chooses *not* to forget.

I started my story for Jean.

It was a story of whining and blaming, a story of disaster after disaster. A story of fear and panic, loneliness and isolation. A story of lies and deceit, of reasons, excuses and rationalizations. There were exaggerations and minimizations and real stories and fabricated stories. It was *pathetic*. I was so sick that I didn't know *how* sick I was. Jean listened, never taking her eyes off me. Finally, she said, 'Liz, I would really like you to go somewhere for a while. Sally and I have been talking. John called your parents in Auckland last night and spoke with them.'

The panic started to grip my stomach. It crept down to my toenails and to the ends of every hair on my head. In those few seconds, memories started to shoot through the neurons in my brain like a forest fire. I started to recall the hospitals, psychiatrists, prescriptions, the abuse both physical and mental that somehow I had survived, and an icy shudder shook my entire system. Through intuition, experience or just sheer observation, Jean took my hand and, looking directly and calmly into my obviously fear-distorted eyes, announced: 'They will be tough, but kind.' Somehow I relaxed, somehow I trusted her, somehow I felt confident that she would make sure I stayed safe.

Several days later, Jean packed my bag with me, after arranging with my sister in London to collect the remainder of my possessions from the flat and pay the other girls my rent owing. I knew little about the 'somewhere' to which I was being taken. For an inexplicable reason, at the time I was willing to do whatever Jean said I should. I really did not have much choice: I had nowhere to live, only my clothes for the weekend; I was nearly out of money; and I had run out of energy to fight both Sally and Jean.

Also, something had stirred inside me. Some flicker of conscience, some flash of recognition, and a blink of curiosity. On Sunday night, Jean had taken me to a small church hall in Staines to meet friends of hers; she told me this was a regular occurrence for her every Sunday night. When we pushed open the door, through a haze of cigarette smoke I encountered what I thought was a room full of *Dad's Army* men in mufti, along with some of their wives! There were not many — certainly nowhere near a platoon's worth — but all of them had to be over forty years old. Jean knew all of them; as I stood there staring at this motley lot, I thought 'My God, what is this?'

The majority of them looked like they had come from the local council estate. There was the woman in her pink slippers with red pompoms on the toes, the man in the blue suit and green tie, the Ena Sharples look-alike pouring tea from a large metal teapot beside a plate of gingernut biscuits, and a couple of men who looked like they could compete with the Kray twins, standing with their backs to the wall smoking roll-your-owns. The man in the tie and tweed jacket looked incongruously out of place, as did Jean in her Pringle and pearls, but they seemed blissfully unaware of their differences.

I did the circuit feeling like some freak who had been brought in from a circus, except that there appeared to be no curiosity on anyone's part as to where I came from or what I did. By the last handshake I realized that my paranoia had got the better of me at first, and these people were really welcoming me.

The meeting lasted an hour; it seemed an eternity. All I can remember is that each person, when asked to speak by the chairman (one of the 'Kray twins'), started off with 'My name's ___ and I'm an alcoholic.' Like dawn breaking, I came to realize I was in a room full of alcoholics. They didn't smell like drunks or alcoholics, they didn't talk like them, and certainly they didn't act like them. I was intrigued, bewildered and curious all at once. Why did they call themselves alcoholics? How come some of them said they had not drunk for five or for fifteen years? What did they mean by 'working the programme'? They mentioned God a lot, but quotes never came from a Bible. They had a large blue book that sat on the chairman's table, to which they kept pointing. As we left, they said 'See you next week' to Jean and 'Keep coming back — it works if you work at it' to me.

'Those people and others like them helped save my life,' Jean told me. 'How?' I asked. 'Because, when I had had enough of the life I was leading, I went back and asked them to' was Jean's answer. 'Only *you* can decide when you have had enough. I went to a meeting like that years ago, looked for all the differences, ignored the similarities, picked holes in everything they said, came up with numerous excuses and rationalizations as to why I couldn't be like them, and drank for another two years. I went back because, deep down in my soul, I knew they had the answer I needed to do something about the life ruled by alcohol that I was leading.' For the final minutes back to Sally's house, I mulled over what she had just said. In retrospect, a crack had appeared in the walled fortress that I lived in.

Jean and Sally drove me to the 'somewhere'. Down country lanes, past the old houses with their magnificent oak trees that were English history-books if only they could speak, to a funny little village. We turned down the lane opposite the pub and stopped in front of a pair of wrought-iron gates. The house name was discreetly embedded into the brick wall. I had to be hallucinating: my life could not have come to *this*. A black-clad figure appeared, and, opening the gates, beckoned us in. And there she was on the front steps. At least six foot tall, the silver cross on her ample bosom gleaming from years of daily polishing, the starched white wimple squeezed around her face, and the black robes billowing around her. The Mother Superior herself. I had been brought to a *nunnery*.

Chapter 8

School for wayward ladies

The nuns tried so hard, they really did, but we were an incongruous lot. After the initial shock of realizing I was back in a boarding-school environment, I started to survey my surroundings and my fellow 'inmates' and 'jailors'.

The nuns were an interesting collection. There was Sister Joan, the doctor, who reminded me of a mouse cartoon. She was small and frail with round wire-rimmed glasses, through which a pair of laser-sharp eyes would watch every movement of everyone in her immediate and peripheral vision. She would have made a great detective. She never missed a move, and silently scuttled when she went anywhere.

Sister Bridget was in charge of the laundry. She always had a wisp of hair projecting out of the left corner of her wimple. She could not have been older than thirty-five at the most, and for a long time we wondered why on earth she had ended up as a nun. We finally discovered the answer: she had had an affair with a 'high-profile' member of the House of Lords, and after the abortion could not face everyday life in the tiny English village in which she lived. Entering a convent had been the option she chose, and The Nunnery had attracted her because she thought that through her own experiences she could help other 'wayward women'. *Wayward* was a complete understatement for the majority of the group. Many of them were bordering on incorrigible, and the fact that The Nunnery was for 'young ladies' simply meant that someone in each person's background was financially liquid enough to keep them out of a mental institution or jail.

Sister Agnes looked like a bear. Her head appeared round because her chin and jowls seemed to flow into a horseshoe shape that bulged over her wimple. She had a large Roman nose, a flat top to her head, and large, thick-lensed horn-rimmed glasses. She spoke with a lisp. We all knew why she had to be in a church order — where else could she go?

Sister Catherine I came to admire, respect, and finally trust, all of which turned into a friendship that lasted until she died, more than thirty years later. I will be eternally grateful to this tough, compassionate, no-nonsense Yorkshire nun who intuitively knew how to handle me. Sometimes the teacher appears in life before the pupil is ready. In the confines of the convent, I *became* teachable as this woman relentlessly chipped away at me. Sister Catherine was in charge of the kitchen and was cooking daily for up to fifty people. I was to spend a great deal of time with her — later.

There were thirty of 'us' and fifteen of 'them'. Some of the women had been there for months, some for weeks, and some were retreads, back for the second or third time. A couple, like myself, had only arrived in the preceding few days. I needed time to take stock of the group and discover where I fitted in.

Pam was interesting. She was tall, with beautifully coiffed dark hair that was pulled back on either side of her face with large tortoiseshell combs. I never saw her without her face impeccably made up. Later I discovered that she never removed any of it; like Elizabeth I, she piled one layer on top of another. She was strange. Apparently, she had not only tripped once too often with LSD, but she also had long-term consequences from ECT treatment. Harmless, but away on some planet in outer space most of the time. I would have died for even one piece of her designer clothing.

Sarah had an eating problem. One only had to look at her to know, poor woman. She was gross. Her medication prevented her from becoming suicidal, although somebody had to be with her every minute of the day as she could not be trusted on her own.

Patty also had an eating problem: she *wouldn't* eat. She was tall, looked like she had been rescued from Belsen, and minced on tiptoe when she went anywhere. Her face was gaunt, with large owl-like eyes, and her fingers continually fidgeted with the buttons on her coat.

Shannon was a nymphomaniac. She wasn't allowed any bananas or sausages, and her permanent mission was for one or other of the girls (preferably the newcomers) to have their visitors bring in some bananas and give her at least half of one. It rarely happened, but when it did she made too much noise at night not to be discovered. I know. I was one of three who shared a bedroom with her.

Then there was Natalie.

Natalie knew she had a problem with alcohol, as it was causing difficulties in her life and had been doing so for some time. But Natalie was only twenty-seven years old. She had long blonde hair, cornflower-blue eyes, and a figure that should have been on a Hollywood film set; and she knew it. She was forbidden to wear stilettos as they 'ruined the floors', but we all knew it was because she used them provocatively. On visiting days, there was not a male eye that didn't ogle her. I learnt later that Natalie was from a well-known aristocratic family whose genealogy could be traced back to Henry VII. She led a double life, of which one part was as a high-class prostitute around the town-houses of Mayfair and Chelsea. It was her way of rebelling against an emotionally abusive family, particularly an autocratic, alcoholic father. Natalie and I teamed up. We were the 'normies'.

There were also a couple of heroin addicts, along with women addicted to diet pills (amphetamines) and to tranquillizers like Valium, Halcion and Librium. There was a cross-section of ages, but the majority of the cars that pulled into the grounds on visiting day were Daimlers, Jaguars, Bentleys and the occasional Rolls Royce.

In our twice-weekly group-therapy sessions, conducted by Sister Joan, I discovered that a number of the women, amongst

Left

My dashing father and vivacious mother on their wedding day, December 1942.

Right

Who could mistake the three sisters? Me (far right) with Jenny, Georgina and friend.

'You must attend as a title of, or character from, a book': I loved my ostrich feather hat. I am fifth from the right, back row.

My first major leadership role: Woodford House school prefects, 1961. I am second from left, front row.

Above

As a debutante, 1962. My official launch into Auckland society.

Left

My one and only attempt at Miss Auckland — 1962.

Right

My anorexia was progressing rapidly. With Anna Caughey in England, 1963.

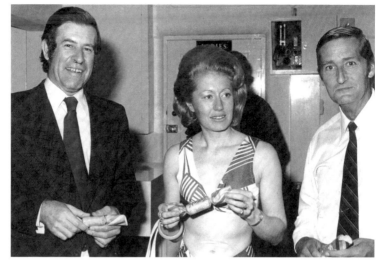

With John (left) and my then Nestlé boss, Frank Edwards, at a Nestlé Christmas function, 1973.

17 May 1973: the day I became Mrs John Jamieson.

Graduation at the Naval Base, San Diego, California, 1983.

The only international, female civilian to graduate from all three of the US Navy's substance abuse training courses in San Diego.

Receiving the Humanitarian Award from Captain Steve Chappell, Commanding Officer, San Diego Naval Training Centre, 1984.

As a presenter at one of the numerous international conferences on Alcohol and Drug Abuse, USA, 1996.

Above

'Let me tell you what drugs do to your brain . . .'

Right

Vanity, thy name is woman! (Facelift, 1988.)

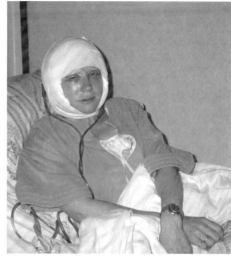

Another school, another group wanting to learn more from me.

With Ian and Pat Booth on Radio Talkback, 1986.

Police and Trust join in sponsorship: Variety Club bash, 1993.

Drug educator and gambling police officer — what a combination! Casino fundraising.

Celebrating Ian's promotion to Detective Superintendant, 1994.

Toastmaster of the Year, Auckland, 1992, with former International President John Fauvel of Auckland on the far right.

With Ian and my mother at Kermadec Restaurant on my fiftieth birthday, March 1994.

Left
. . . and not a stitch
on underneath!

Right
With the love of
my life on our
wedding day,
7 March 1998.

Cops and
gangsters formed
a formidable
presence.

Ian with our
adopted 'children'
on Waiheke
Island.

'I now pronounce you half a Dame'! CNZM investiture, April 1998.

Georgina, Marjorie (Ian's mother), Ian, me, the Barrett-Boyes (the Governor General and his wife), Jenny, and niece Emily at my investiture.

The family that was never going to speak to me again!

their conglomeration of problems, appeared to have significant incidents that arose as a result of their drinking. To me this was blatantly obvious: their lives were a serious mess. It seemed to me, as well, that a lot of the meetings outside The Nunnery to which Jean eventually was allowed to take me had people present who needed to do something about their drinking. They had crashed cars, been asked to leave jobs, had wives, husbands and children walk out on them; some had even been to jail for varying periods of time. Nearly all of them were forty-plus years of age, and nearly all had faces like road maps as a result of their experiences. Natalie and I agreed: *we* were in our mid-twenties — we still had places to go, people to see, things to do. We were far too young to be alcoholics. The fact that I had run out of private hospitals in New Zealand that would look at me and was now in one on the other side of the world did not seem that big a deal. *We* had not crashed cars, lost jobs (no — I had left before they could *ask* me to leave), or been in jail. What had happened to *us* was bad luck and interfering people. How cunning, baffling and powerful is the alcoholic mind.

I started to rationalize my entire past history of the past four years. I disassociated myself from The Nunnery group, saying only what would keep Sister Joan and the group happy. Most of them were not interested in confronting my lies, rationalizations and excuses; they were either too sedated by their medication or too self-absorbed. Sister Joan, like all the other doctors of one sort or another who had paraded through my life, became just another from which I switched off. I was already planning my leaving strategy.

I had now been four months in The Nunnery. About all I had accomplished was to complete a piece of embroidery in our occupational therapy time, a piece I had begun on my last admittance to Oakley Hospital in Auckland. I had agreed to talk with Dr Glatt (a world-renowned psychiatrist and expert on alcoholism, as I later discovered) on several occasions, but I have no memory of the outcome. I had attended meetings that Jean took me to, but normally I didn't listen, and when I did I found so many differences with the people there that they became boring. They said much the same each week about how manageable their lives were now, how grateful they were, how they had finished making amends to people, and how they knew that 'it worked if you work at it'. Whatever the 'it' was, I was not interested in finding out. I had not had a drink for four months and I was ready to leave.

What I now know is that my disease of alcoholism was still thundering on the door. Stopping drinking, I was to discover, was not and is not an alcoholic's problem. Anyone can do that. For the alcoholic in active alcoholism, the problem is the inability to stay stopped and be free of the obsession around alcohol. My days were never a problem when I was drinking; I just drank. My days were a problem when I *wasn't* drinking; when I was recovering from whatever I had consumed the day or night before. My problem was I couldn't live life without alcohol. I was *obsessed* with alcohol: it was continually with me, for I was *always* thinking, planning, recovering, or feeling shame and guilt around what I had done while in its grip. I was restless, irritable and discontented. I was never free from its stranglehold. *That* is alcoholism; and I would not, could not, let it go; even by then, I had not had enough happen to me in life to want to let it go. I had not yet reached my rock-bottom. I was by no means desperate. I still had the insane idea that someday, somehow, I would be able to drink like other people. But only in retrospect is the insanity in the idea clear.

I fully believed that I now had the beginnings of a new life, but in actual fact it proved to be my entrance into Hell. Winston Churchill once said, 'When you're going through hell, keep going.' Thankfully I did, and I came out the other side. Only a small percentage ever do. Most die, go insane or end up imprisoned, either in a government jail or in a jail of pharmaceuticals often prescribed by well-meaning but totally ignorant, sometimes arrogant members of the medical profession. The last category of prison is usually where the more affluent end up, but it is a prison nonetheless. A place where you are helpless, hopeless, surviving in a half-world, not knowing if there is a way out. If you are reading this book and can identify with that form of imprisonment, just keep reading. There *is* a way out.

On a day when I was allowed to visit my sister in London, I had made an appointment to see the Public Relations Manager of a large hotel on Holland Park Road. They had an advertisement for a PR assistant that I had answered. My shorthand and typing were not the best, but I knew I was an excellent organizer, physically presentable, and I was sure my New Zealand accent would be an asset. Ten days later, at the second interview, I was offered the position.

The nuns were far from happy. They did not believe I was ready to leave. I was still underweight (in their estimation, not mine), and according to Dr Glatt I was a high relapse risk. The only one who did not have an opinion was Jean. 'Your choice' was her comment; followed, however, by a memorable statement which went something along this vein: 'I am not going to tell you what you should or shouldn't do, Liz. You can find groups of people and meetings to attend in London, and here is a list for you. You know what you *need* to do; you have heard it often enough. If you do what you have heard so many of us say we do, then you will get what so many of us have got. I cannot lead your life for you or make decisions for you, but remember this. You are responsible for every decision you make, every action you take, and every consequence that arrives as a result. I am on the phone for you, but I have my own life to lead and will not spend time trying to find either your phone number or where you are — you call me. God keep you safe until we see each other again.'

The full extent of the incredible significance of her attitude and words was lost on me at the time, but I could not fail to interpret them as she meant me to. She was releasing me into the world with compassion and love. Without a doubt, she knew that I had more drinking to do. Without a doubt, she knew, as every recovered alcoholic knows, that the drinking and the consequences would only get worse. But her experience had taught her that dictating, threatening, cajoling and morbid anticipatory statements were a waste of time and breath. The greatest experience she could leave me with was the knowledge that the door back was always open. She could see that I was in really bad shape. I was four months 'dry'; arrogant, ignorant, young and well-educated. A lethal combination when coupled with the illusion that I was 'cured'!

I needed to celebrate my 'escape'. But I was *not* going to drink. I would show 'them' that I was right and that they were wrong. I was *not* an alcoholic. I had stopped drinking for close on five months. I might have had a problem with alcohol, but I was not suffering from the disease of alcoholism.

My sister and I had dinner, my uncle and I had dinner, my 'Spanish' godmother and I had dinner. I showed them and others over the ensuing months that I was 'cured'. Meantime I was progressively, on a daily basis, slowly going crazy. I was suffering from untreated alcoholism and didn't know it. I had not rung Jean, I was not attending meetings; I hadn't even bothered to check them out — the last people I wanted to be around were what I saw as self-righteous non-drinkers who called themselves alcoholics. My teeth were gritted, my knuckles were white, my laugh was false, my jaw was set, and the veins in my neck pumped like a kangaroo treading water. Each day I was suffering from an attack of the dry-drunk syndrome, and finally I took the only medicine that worked for me to relieve the pain, the gut-wrenching, head-exploding, relentless emotional pain. I took a drink. I knew, I just *knew*, that it would take away the emptiness, the darkness, the despair, the black hole inside me and the excruciating, heart-breaking loneliness.

That Friday night, my boss offered me a glass of wine to celebrate a successful promotional evening at the hotel. She smiled at me, with the classic statement: 'Just one instead of the ginger ale, Liz. A little wine won't hurt.' And I took the wine. I didn't take it because

I thought that this time might be different. I didn't take it because I thought I could handle it, or it wouldn't hurt me, or to join the other drinkers. I took it because *I didn't think.* I took it because my disease took it for me. I had no defence against that first drink. *If my problem is alcohol, then all I have to do is to stop drinking.* But if there is no such thing as alcoholism, then there would be no need for detox or treatment centres.

For a split second after that first drink my soul went into indescribable panic mode, and all I could hear was a voice in my head saying: 'It was not the third or fourth drink that grabbed me — it was the first. It's not the carriage on the train that hits you, it's the engine.' With that one glass I started a chain reaction where my past was to become my future. That night I only had that one glass of wine, which had hardly any effect on me. I didn't understand that the most likely reason for this was that my poor liver had had time to do a major amount of repair work on itself, and that in conjunction with this my tolerance had increased considerably. That lack of effect from the one glass of wine was the worst possible consequence for me.

Chapter 9

God looks after drunks and fools

Our recollections are fragmentary at the best of times, and this is compounded when the disease of alcoholism is rampant as well. What I recall of the following months is careering from one unmitigated disaster to another, leaving a pile of debris behind me that could only be described as the work of a Sherman tank out of control. Fragments of the journey are remembered; fortuitously, the entire rampage is not. Unbeknown to me, I had passed through the doors into chronic alcoholism.

That one drink activated my disease as if I had turned the ignition key in a car. I quickly moved through the stages of sneaking drinks, having stronger drinks than those around me, manipulating situations and adopting strategies to get more drinks. My blackouts (memory losses) increased in length and frequency. My reasons, excuses and alibis became less and less believable. I was gulping the first few drinks, and for a long time now had been carrying my own supply. I avoided people and situations where they did not drink as I drank, and the capacity to regulate my drinks had passed into mythology. I was beset with guilt, remorse, and a complete lack of self-esteem. I was re-interpreting events in a totally paranoid way, and now I was heading for another job loss. This time a humiliatingly public one, as an entire chain of hotels would be privy to my behaviour.

One night, my evening continued in the bar at the top of the hotel overlooking Hyde Park, where the promotional photographer and I had decided a Friday night 'party' would be in order. Security was called on Monday morning when I attempted to enter the hotel. Two men in suits, carrying walkie-talkies, were summoned when I explained to the concierge that I had lost my ID badge. I was informed that I had not lost it; it had been taken from me. My long-suffering sister Jenny was present as my witness while it was explained to me that what had occurred now saw me blacklisted from this particular chain of hotels, not only nationwide but worldwide.

'There was nothing illegal in ordering room service to your office, Miss Merritt. Nothing illegal about inviting a promotional photographer into your office, either. However, at the room service delivery man's request, Miss Merritt, we entered your office to find you indulging in inappropriate sexual behaviour. It is against hotel regulations to treat any of our offices as establishments in which to conduct sexual intercourse. Should you set foot in any of __ Organisation's hotels in the future, you will be arrested as an undesirable person. Your belongings are in security and your sister may collect them.'

I spent the rest of the day in the King's and Fulham Roads, in and out of bars and off-licences. My final journey had begun, and, without knowing it then, I would be left with only four options: a mental asylum, jail, death, or recovery. The insanity was already there: I *still* refused to give up a life of complete failure without a fight. Jenny took me to her doctor, who suggested I limit my drinks. That didn't work. I ended up drinking my two-year quota in a matter of weeks. It was impossible for me to take a drink and be *comfortable* not to take the next, and the next. I lied that I had kept an appointment at St Thomas's Hospital: I could not leave the bathroom of a hotel as I had decided to drink while taking Antabuse (disulfiram), a chemical that interferes with the body's processing of alcohol. I was sweating, my heart was racing, I was scarlet in the face — the doctor would have *known* what I had done. I was lying now even when I had nothing to lie about, and when it didn't matter. I earned my money sorting cheques at the British Caravan Club by day and frequenting the small hotels around Chelsea and Knightsbridge by night. Redheads with foreign accents were few and far between, and I was not a threat to the big-time operators.

Even areas of London can become too small, and other areas were unwise to visit during daytime; certainly not at night and definitely not under the influence of alcohol. I needed a change, I decided. It would be better in the country. A businessman with six children looking for a full-time housekeeper sounded ideal. Dorking would be nice — not too big, not too small. I could have a life being useful with a ready-made family, and live happily ever after.

I found the off-licence liquor store only twenty minutes down the street, so my alcoholic dream had materialized. The four eldest children were at school during the day. Mr Cunningham (within a few days it was Andrew) commuted to London daily, and I could walk the two youngest — one in a pushchair and one on her tricycle — to the shops each morning. I had a roof over my head, far from onerous duties to perform, a busy, lonely man to 'look after', and free time from seven in the evening. I was in alcoholic heaven.

I had reckoned without Mr Cunningham's eldest daughter, who took an immediate and obvious dislike to me. Perhaps she knew intuitively that there was something strange about me. I felt her watching my every move; and, paranoid as I had become, it was unnerving. Unnerving because the physical symptoms of my drinking were becoming more and more obvious to her. My hands were unsteady in the morning; I found it difficult to pour the juice or milk unless I did so at the kitchen sink, my back blocking the amount that was spilled. My thinking was confused, so talking was difficult at the breakfast table, and I had obviously forgotten some conversations of the night before. My memory was failing and my recollections of evening events were gradually becoming non-existent.

I had no idea of the time factor in my steady deterioration while I was in Dorking. What I now know is that it was over weeks rather than months. In the mornings I would, as silently as possible, dry-retch into the bowl I kept under my bed, due to chronic gastritis. On my hands and knees I would pray 'Please, God, let me keep this one down' as I sought to control my shaking with a slug of vodka. I was experiencing stomach cramps, which I now understand were signs from my liver that all was not well.

My consumption of alcohol had reached a point where I could no longer live with it, but I was powerless to live without it; a horrendous dilemma. Liver damage meant that my tolerance levels had plummeted from a bottle of vodka a day to needing to keep just enough in my system to ward off the shaking, the panic attacks, and the voices that had started talking to me in my head. My hands and feet would at times tingle with 'pins and needles' or become numb, and my left ankle would buckle and I would risk falling. Now I *had* to drink, and I knew that I was dying; indeed, on some days I wished I could. If I did not drink, I could barely get out of bed; my head would play games with me, as I would imagine what I had done the night before and could not differentiate fantasy from reality. I operated in a world of total confusion and paranoia.

One day Sister Bridget and Sister Joan were in the hallway, which convinced me I was seeing ghosts — but they were real. Mr Cunningham had contacted my sister, who had contacted The Nunnery, and the two nuns were there to quite literally rescue me. I was completely disorientated, had no idea what I was saying, and learnt later that I was in the midst of delirium tremens (DTs) as I was withdrawing rapidly, dangerously rapidly, from alcohol. In that state, the possibility of convulsions or an epileptic fit was highly probable, and the only remedy in that instance was alcohol. Enough alcohol to stall the withdrawal symptoms and keep me alive until I reached The Nunnery.

The flowers in the entrance hall and the two Dachshunds were a figment of my imagination. My babbling about the vodka bottle in my trunk of clothes must have been irritating, although understandable, as I was guided up the stairs and into the infirmary. The injections were the most excruciatingly painful ones I have ever had. One was paraldehyde (to calm me down); the other was Parentrovite (a massive dose of vitamins B and C). Whatever else I was given, and took without question, knocked me out, for how long I have not the slightest idea. Weeks later, I learnt that if I had stayed in Dorking any longer I could not have survived. I would have been physically unable to gain a continuing supply of liquor, which would have meant risking convulsions that, in conjunction with the DTs, would have meant certain death.

The nuns, bless them, knew not only how to keep me alive, but also how to keep me alive in such a way that I would remember forever the road to recovery, and what a boulder-strewn road it was. My poor stomach would accept only stewed apple (*cold* stewed apple), jelly and ice-cream; the nursing sisters fed me liquid through a straw as I could not sit up. Injections came with monotonous regularity, and at set times Sister Joan would place an apomorphine tablet under my tongue and instruct me to let it dissolve as slowly as possible (apomorphine therapy was used in the 1960s as way to reduce anxiety and cravings).

Children's voices and telephone bells sounded incessantly. There were no children on the premises, and the nearest telephone was completely out of earshot of my room: I was suffering auditory hallucinations. The bugs were worse. Little grey, flat, ridge-backed ones that scuttled constantly over the walls and ceilings. Every now and again, one would fall on the bed and I would watch it scampering over the blanket while I called the duty sister to come and deal with it. I was also suffering visual hallucinations: in the clinically clean infirmary there was never an insect in sight.

The days meant nothing to me as they passed. The apomorphine and other drugs reduced my anxiety, my cravings, the shaking and the nausea. Now that I could sit up in bed, I wanted two things. My embroidery (how that *ever* survived all my travelling I will never know), and something to read. But the all-too-familiar feelings of fear and panic began to envelop me as I found I could neither embroider nor read. First, I could not focus my eyes on the embroidery, as I could not see the stitches without them blurring; then, when I attempted to read I could fathom the first half-dozen words but the rest would melt into a sea of black-and-white fog. I was going blind. I needed glasses. Oh no, not my eyes. Anything but my eyes. I would not be able to read or write, or sew.

Sister Bridget was on duty when my tearful call was heard, and with cups of tea for both of us she sat and told me that I would be all right, and that the 'blurs' would pass. It was an opening for her to describe the frightening, sickening, life-threatening train of events that had ended with my re-admittance to The Nunnery. I had drunk myself into chronic alcoholism. My liver was badly affected, hence my yellow eyeballs, and she showed me the yellowing of the palms of my hands. Alcoholic poisoning had manifested itself in my swollen neck, ankles, feet, wrists and hands. My body was undernourished and the alcohol had depleted it of B vitamins, which was one of the reasons that I had had the DTs, the shakes. Neurologically, mineral and vitamin deficiency in my brain had caused much of my auditory and visual hallucinations. My sister, Dr Harris (yet *another* psychiatrist!) and Sister Joan were going to talk with me that afternoon: I could not stay at The Nunnery forever.

Jenny could not believe it was her sister in the bed, and she told me later that it took an enormous amount of self-control to hold back the tears. Telephone calls had already been exchanged, yet again, not only between her and my parents but also between The Nunnery and New Zealand. Sister Joan — with Dr Harris impassive beside her, and my sister on the end of the bed — informed me that they had exhausted all known methods by which they could help me. I had been treated with aversion therapy (emetine), the truth drug (methedrine, sodium amytral and pentothal), and — as far as they knew — with antidepressants and tranquillizers (although these probably still had Auckland City councillors tearing their hair out, wondering why the harbour tides had stopped operating for a while — drugged up on my prescriptions!). I had drunk on top of Antabuse, at present I was on apomorphine, and Dr Harris was the sixth psychiatrist who had tried to help me. Next time, the only solution would be committal to an institution.

Jenny descended from the bed and left, and I could not blame her. For all our sisterly fights and petty jealousies over the years, I was still her big sister and she was helpless to stop my slow, painful suicide that was taking place before her eyes. The room emptied, and I was alone. Nothing registered from the confrontations. Perhaps I was numb; perhaps there had been so many dramas over the years that I treated this as just one more. I would simply move on; find somewhere else; I was a survivor. Somehow, none of what I had heard appeared real.

But somewhere, someone or something had other plans. I awoke that night lying rigid, enveloped in sweat from seeing images of ECT machines and little old ladies searching for each other's nits. I could not move, and for a few seconds I was totally disorientated. I could not recall where I was. The walls suffocated me; the darkness played tricks, creating swirling wraith-like images throughout the room. My tongue was dry, I could feel my heart thumping, and I realized I was not breathing, I lay in abject terror. I was alone; nobody cared any more. Wherever I went, I left devastation in my wake. I was *not* mad — I *knew* I was not mad — but soon people would put me somewhere because they believed I was.

They had all *told* me I had to stop drinking, how it was killing me; God knows I had enough evidence that it was doing that. But nobody told me *how* to stop. Nobody had given me a solution. Nobody had been able to tell me how to fill the hole in my soul, the emptiness inside that currently only alcohol could fill. They all had degrees in one type of medicine or another, but they did not *understand*. I could not *not* drink, for I could not live in the world out there — I would rather die.

A lump worked its way out of my throat and the tears

started. They were tears of guilt and remorse, of anger and fear, of helplessness, hopelessness and loneliness; tears of frustration, self-pity and confusion; tears of resentment, hurt and, finally, tears of despair. I had no idea what to do. I was broken and desperate. I did not want to live, but I was too scared to die. I called out like an atheist on a sinking ship, for I did not believe I would be heard, but it was all I had left to do — I called out to a God I did not believe existed, and my call was answered. In the depths of the black hole with the hound of death snapping at my heels, I remembered Jean, *Dad's Army* in mufti, and a room full of a motley lot of people who told me to 'keep coming back'.

Jean arrived after lunch the following day, accompanied by the pearls, the signet ring and the pale pink Pringle cardigan. She paused for a moment in the doorway with Sister Joan, murmured to her and then stepped in, closing the door behind her. Making her way to the window beside my bed, she stood staring into the distance for what seemed an eternity. Then she backed away, pulled a chair up to where the sheet turned over the blanket on the bed, and placed a hand over mine where it was fidgeting with the sheet hem. With eyes that saw through to my soul, she asked a simple, uncomplicated question: 'Do you think you are one of us now?'

Instinctively, intuitively, without even contemplating the question, the answer came, just as simple and just as uncomplicated — yes. The floodgates opened, unlocked as much by the chemicals as by the despair. No parent, sister, doctor, aversion or truth-drug treatment, let alone a bunch of psychiatrists, had been able to penetrate that wall. I had been poked, prodded and swamped with questions, interrogations, ultimatums, threats, warnings, orders, admonitions, and even sympathy at times. Nobody had ever given me what Jean had introduced me to and was sharing with me now. She was not sympathizing but *empathizing* with me. She had been where I was, knew the hole in the soul, had looked into my eyes and seen the pain, confusion and incomprehensible demoralization. She saw not only the broken body, but also the broken heart, broken spirit, broken life and broken dreams. She heard me cry not from my mouth but from my heart and from my soul. What comes from the heart touches the heart.

For years, people had looked at me with embarrassment, disgust, contempt and sometimes even compassion, but never with empathy and understanding. I was not consciously aware of the fact, but I had hit the bottom. I had nowhere to turn but to Jean and her friends. Whatever it was that she had and that I saw in her — serenity, strength, freedom, peace of mind, acceptance of life on life's terms — I wanted, and I was prepared to put myself in her hands to get it. For me, pain often happens when I *fight* change, not when change actually occurs. I realize now that change can only happen when holding onto something is more painful than letting it go.

I told her I wanted what she had, and she never asked me to explain what that was. 'If you want what I have, then you need to do what I did. I am not going to make suggestions any more, Elizabeth.' (She said that was the name I had been given, and I should use it!) 'I'm going to *tell* you what you need to do, and if you do not like it then find someone else to help you. While you are here, you need to do everything the nuns ask you to do. I will talk with the Sister Superior, for I will need to take you out on a regular basis in the near future. Meanwhile, there is a book here I want you to read, particularly the stories in the back.' She bent and kissed me, and her face softened. 'Remember, from now on you do not *need* to drink again. There is no cure for us, but there is a solution.' And leaving me with that riddle to contemplate, she left.

Chapter 10

The road less travelled

For all of us, pain and suffering in life come accompanied by self-pity and, so often, the 'why me?'s. My life has been lived forwards and learnt backwards, so that all I know today has been gained through a voyage of self-discovery, much of it as a result of pain and suffering.

Without a shred of realization at the time, I had finally cracked the wall that was surrounding me by surrendering to the knowledge that *I had had enough* and was willing to do anything to escape the Hell in which I found myself. The wall had protected me, but it had also isolated me. As I built it thicker and thicker, I became more and more lonely. Jean had penetrated that wall; something which no doctor, psychiatrist, family member or prescribed chemical had been able to do. She had cracked it with hope and with her inner strength. It was not the outstretched hand, or the smile, or the kiss on the cheek that did it — it was the loving kindness, the spark of humanity that she touched in me with her compassion; one human being who knew my pain because of her own scars, reaching out to another, someone inextricably bound by her past suffering to my present experience. My courage had gone, and the world was threatening and unsafe. I had no home, nowhere to go. I was deaf and blind to anything except my own agony and despair. She, by her very presence, showed me that there was a way out. I intuitively knew that she could show me that way. I had no idea how or by what means, but I knew she knew the path. What she instilled in me was *hope*.

Sister Catherine was still the kitchen Sister, and that was where

I was put to work. Not very willingly, and my face indicated my lack of enthusiasm. I would have preferred the garden, as it was spring and the sun was soft and gentle as English springs are. (I had actually started to *notice* that this was so!) But other plans were afoot for me. Looking back, I believe the nuns wanted to observe my eating habits to see if my patterns had changed. They had definitely improved, but my food consumption was still far from normal. Although I was no longer starving myself, no longer placing stones, soap or other weights in my pockets or underclothes to disguise my real weight at the weekly weigh-ins, the bulimia was still occurring three to four times a week. It was still a huge 'secret'. I believe they hoped that working in the kitchen would alter my eating habits. However, for me the frustration at not being able to compulsively eat was not conducive to any recovery.

Sister Catherine had her own way of handling me.

'You have a choice, Elizabeth. You can continue to resent working here, for this is where you are going to be, *or*, if you choose to co-operate, I will teach you how to cater for the fifty people you are aware we feed on a daily basis.' This was one of my early lessons on choice. We win or lose by the way we choose. I was not able to change the circumstances, but I *could* choose my attitude in that (or any other) situation. Jean's words rang in my ears: 'You must do everything the nuns ask you to do.' As I was talking to Jean every day, I knew I had to co-operate. I would need to tell her what Sister Catherine had offered. Jean's reply to much of what I was expected to do if I still wanted her help was 'Do it and you will come to understand.' She would follow up a few days later with 'Well, what did you discover in *that* instance?' I began to discover that we learn best what we learn for ourselves.

Sister Catherine started me at the beginning: on the scullery floor with a bucket and scrubbing brush — her lesson in humility! She condescended to a pair of rubber gloves after a while, only because of a graze on my hand that threatened to become infected. Quite rapidly I graduated up the scale from the floor to the vegetables, to cakes, biscuits, scones, then meat, and finally puddings. I was really good at pudding making, eventually introducing the entire establishment to Baked Alaska, achieving the ability to serve ten of these items all at once!

'She was the chief assistant of a staff of five and proved to be very efficient and capable and able to take responsibility . . . I would have no hesitation in recommending her for a post in a kitchen or catering department.' Such was the letter of reference from the Sister Superior on my departure.

Sister Catherine and I maintained a correspondence for thirty years, until her death. Some people come into our lives for a moment, some for a season, and some for a lifetime. As with anybody through the years, she was an unexpected teacher in an unexpected environment in an unexpected way.

Now ready to take the next step, the advertisement I saw in *The Lady* magazine seemed ideal. Lady Katherine was a divorcée with three children. Again a woman to whom I owe a debt of gratitude, because although she was aware of my entire history she was still prepared to entrust her three children to me in the capacity of a live-in nanny.

Without the protection (or perhaps confines) of The Nunnery, many of my fears and anxieties started to return. However, the enormous relief of acquiring a job *despite* my handicaps gave me a small amount of hope, which was a new experience for me. Jean was adamant that I stay in contact with her on a daily basis, that I continue to read the 'textbook' (as she called it) that she had given me, and that I continue to attend and participate in the various meetings from the substantial list with which she had provided me. Lady Katherine was agreeable to my having most evenings free, so long as it was not inconvenient to her.

Although I was still shaky and with some degree of the visual and other problems from my alcohol poisoning, Jean had been taking me regularly to rooms where groups of recovered alcoholics met. Her requirements were simple, clear and non-negotiable. So far as she was concerned, she was too busy to give me 'private tuition', as she described it. I would learn about myself and my disease of alcoholism in two ways: from hearing the experiences of others, and by doing what I would discover I needed to do. I alone had to make the changes, but I did not have to make them alone. There were people who would support me. I would discover that the meetings had not changed, but if I stayed around them they could change me.

Jean set requirements that I needed to bring to these rooms each night: to look for the similarities and not the differences when people shared their stories, to keep an open mind, and to be willing to change. She had already drummed into me that dishonesty was no longer an excuse or an option. Honesty meant I was not to cheat, steal or tell lies of either omission or commission; it meant acknowledging my conscience (once it had woken up, for I'd anaesthetized it for years), and learning to listen and listening to learn. I was to sit at the front of the room and, when asked to speak, to state my first name, why I was there, and that I really wanted to stay stopped drinking for I believed I was an alcoholic. No more, no less, for I had nothing to contribute yet. Everyone there knew how to drink; I was there to learn how to stay stopped, and to acquire the peace of mind and serenity to lead a life where I would no longer need or want to drink.

The urge to drink had not left me. I could not understand how so many of the people could talk about the desire having left them. I knew I could not live with alcohol any more, but failed to comprehend how I could live without it. 'Sure you can,' Jean would say. 'Today you can, just for today you can, and if you feel the urge — call me. I may be able to talk you out of the drink, but I cannot talk the drink out of you.'

Slowly, very slowly, over the weeks and months I came to understand the simple philosophy for living that these people shared and the principles they attempted to apply in their lives day to day. However, I had a plethora of questions. I wanted to know what membership list I needed to sign; there was none. They told me I was a member if I had a desire to stop drinking. There were no dues or fees to pay, but if I could afford to put something in the bag at the end of the meeting then that helped to pay for the rent and tea and coffee. The whole organization supported itself from members' contributions. As the weeks progressed, my curiosity grew increasingly stronger. What other organizations did the money go to, and with whom were we affiliated? Did we endorse any causes? Which ones? Who was the head of the organization; where were the managers; what were they paid? What was everyone supposed to do apart from meeting in various halls at various times and talking about themselves?

I became more and more confused, until a blonde who reminded me of Diana Dors sat me down in a Lyons tea shop one afternoon after a meeting with the words, 'Let me explain what we are, luv, and what we do and do not do. We're a bunch of ex-drunks, alcoholics, lushes, whatever you want to call us. It does not matter what our names are, where we live, what jobs we have or how big our house is — even whether we *have* a house. We are all people with a past who do not wish to repeat it. Our main purpose in life is to find peace of mind so we do not need alcohol or any other mind-altering substance any more. We don't attach ourselves to any other organization, as we have only one other purpose apart from staying sober ourselves, and that is to help others like yourself to achieve this peace of mind in life. Getting involved in other organizations would take our focus off this. Nobody is paid for helping another, although the office in Chelsea has someone who is paid because they do office work, such as distributing our literature, answering phone calls, and keeping the financial records when we send money in there so we *can* keep the phones going and the office open for anyone wanting to find out about us.

'What else do we do? Well — not much. We just help each other help each other. Just cleaning the ashtrays, and washing the dishes, and talking to someone who looks a bit lost at the meeting is what *you* can do. Very importantly, we do not tell other people who comes to these meetings. So if we see someone who we may recognize — whether from the world of media, business or politics — it is essential that we do not divulge their presence. It's important, first, because it may be a risk to them in their work, but, secondly, if they go back drinking again and cause havoc, then people may believe that all that we do is a waste of time and doesn't work. Of course we can tell each other amongst ourselves who we are and our last names — otherwise how would we know which ward Bill is in if he is in hospital? — but a person discloses that from *choice*, not because they have to. I do not want to know your last name unless you choose to tell me.'

I had one final lesson to learn about alcohol and me. Lady Katherine, the children and I went to stay with her parents in their baronial castle in Scotland for the school holidays. Her parents had no idea of my background, other than that I was a New Zealander who was on a working holiday.

I was so preoccupied with the castle, the sight-seeing, the trips to Edinburgh, that I never did what Jean had told me I must do when she heard I would be there for a few weeks. 'You need to find the meetings there and go to at least four a week. Lady Katherine, I know, will be agreeable.' I could not be bothered. It was too much of an effort, too long a drive; I was fine now, and really did not need those people in those meetings any more. I was 'cured'.

Half a bottle of vodka and an evening I could not recall was a final convincer. It was 14 September 1971, and it was to be the last drink I ever took. I had proved finally that I was totally powerless over alcohol.

Jean had me writing and ringing her, and attending meetings, and writing and ringing . . . making a list (again) of all the areas in my life that were unmanageable: my job losses, my relationships, my handling of finances, my eating disorder. How was I going to gain peace of mind unless I started to clean up my life? But how could I do that if I did not *list* the areas that needed cleaning up?

'Don't just *think* about it — being alone with your head is not a good idea. Write!' So I wrote, and from this I started the in-depth work on myself with Jean's guidance. I needed to face the hurt I had caused and the wrongs I had committed, both to myself and to others. What were my objectionable character traits? What were the assets in my character? Did I use them or did I squander them? What were my attributes, my talents, my shortcomings? I was being guided on a journey that I had not known to exist. I was on a voyage of self-discovery. I was dismantling my wall, one stone at a time, not only to discover who I was, but also to do something about the hideous mess my behaviour had created, not only in my own life but in others' lives as well. I was willing to get out of my prison.

I learnt that nobody could ever *get* me well. No doctor, no psychiatrist, no counsellor, no friend. The doctor could write a prescription; the psychiatrist, psychologist, therapist, could make suggestions — but *I* had to take the prescription, *I* had to do whatever was suggested, *I* had to do the work. I learnt that it was a type of insanity to be doing the same thing over and over again, yet expecting different results. Only I could change my behaviour, and I had to take responsibility for my life.

It was made very clear to me that I was not a failure and never could be. I had had plans in life that had failed; it was the *plans* that had failed, not me. I needed to find different ways of handling situations, and if I did what these people at the meetings did, then (given time) I would have what they had.

I, and only I, could do the work — but I did not have to do it alone. Jean and others would help me, but I needed to ask them. This was another lesson in humility: learning to swallow my pride, and realize that I was powerless over alcohol, my life was a mess, and I needed to find some other Power that could help me get well. *I* heard 'religion' here, and with that came memories of chapel twice a day at boarding school, the long trek to church from the school grounds each Sunday, the lectures from pulpits, and what I saw as the hypocritical lives some adults led while professing to be Christians.

A woman who reminded me of Princess Margaret opened the door to my understanding of what a Power could be. 'I don't believe *in* a Power,' she said when she was talking at a meeting one night. 'I believe *that* a Power can help me, and for me I hear messages in all sorts of ways. Originally, the person who first helped me was more powerful than me; she had a strength that I could feel and I wanted.' (I immediately thought of Jean.) 'I find that there is some atmosphere when I am with all you people that is very powerful and allows me to feel safe, although it hurts at times! I hurt because here I hear truth, and yet there is a freedom in that. The truth sets me free. Why does it hurt? Because it is my *conscience*, and with no alcohol in there to shut it up I have to listen to it. I *know* the truth when I *hear* the truth, and this is what got me well and keeps me well. It's that little voice inside which I can no longer ignore, nor can I anaesthetize; you people have guided me to the understanding that it is the spiritual essence in me. Religion is a dogma and that's not what we have here; spirituality is the essence of every religion, and spirituality is about principles. *That's* what we talk about: attempting to live our lives by spiritual principles which are universal. Humility — the courage to admit when we are wrong. Courage — to change what we can. Compassion — empathizing with others. Acceptance — discovering the peace of mind to accept what I can't change. I can't change the fact I'm an alcoholic, but I *can* choose what sort of alcoholic I am. I can be drunk; I can be dry, which means I'm not drinking but still causing chaos in my life and other people's; or I can be sober and out there helping others to tread the path to find that peace of mind that I have. At long last I have a purpose to my life.'

I spent a whole day with Jean after I had listened to that woman (whom I never saw again), because I finally wanted to know more. Fear and despair had crept back in at the same time as my new-found senses of excitement and anticipation. I did not want to be a person with a past so much as be a *new person*. My fear was that I would never have the capacity to feel compassion or empathy; my despair came when my head started to tell me that I could never be like the people I heard and saw. 'Right *now*, Elizabeth, are you better than you were?' I knew that I was. 'Well then, you have made progress' was Jean's wise observation. I also had to acknowledge that I had only been a matter of a few months off alcohol, whereas some I had heard had not had a drink for several years. Jean suggested that I take a look at where I had come from, particularly in terms of my thinking and the life I was not leading any more, and compare myself only with myself, not with others. I would have ten years of not drinking and the equivalent peace of mind *after* I had lived those ten years and done what I needed to do, not before. But *I had started*. I did not want my old lifestyle, I knew alcohol was no longer an option for me, but in addition to that I knew I had to start cleaning up myself and the wreckage of my past. All this could not be done in a day.

One morning, unexpectedly, a letter arrived with familiar handwriting that I could not place until I turned the envelope over and read the back: *P.B. Shield*. I found it almost impossible to believe. It was from the boy with whom I used to exchange letters, secretly, on a Sunday morning after our expeditions to church from school, and he wanted me to return to New Zealand. A very grown-up 'boy' now. He had finished his stint with the New Zealand SAS in Vietnam, and wanted me back in the country to see if there was anything still between us.

As was my wont, I turned to my mentor Jean, who immediately suggested that I write out the pros and cons on a sheet of paper. What was to keep me in England? What could I return to in New Zealand? Marriage was no longer a priority on my list (who would want to marry a twenty-seven-year-old alcoholic, bulimic woman?). I had accepted that I might never marry, but I still had to move on with living. Nonetheless, the thought and hopes were still there, of a husband, children, house, car, boat, and perhaps never needing to work again. How totally erroneous that image was to be! I decided to return home, and in doing so I never saw Jean again. Unbeknown to me, she had developed cancer of the throat and her days were numbered.

Chapter 11

The courage to change

I am not the person today that I was yesterday. Today, I am the person I was yesterday plus the experiences of yesterday and its lessons, and so I was when I returned to New Zealand.

My parents were dubious about my returning, particularly when a letter to Dr Richwhite from yet another psychiatrist in England arrived, stating that 'returning to New Zealand is obviously going to be a very great strain on her. She will be trying very hard to retain her poise and self-assurance.' Mother informed me categorically that I could remain in their house only until I found a job and a place to live. If there were any 'incidents', then I would have to go immediately. I found this hurtful and harsh at the time, but in retrospect I can hardly blame her. She did not want a repeat of my past behaviour. Trust can never be demanded; it has to be earned.

The whirlwind trip to visit Paul in the South Island lasted forty-eight hours. Although we had spent time together during our teenage years — for his sister Janey was my best friend and I had had summer holidays in the Marlborough Sounds with her family — we had travelled totally different paths since then. SAS training and his Vietnam experiences had covered Paul with a veneer that confused me, and my years of torment had obviously changed *me*. We both accepted this, and I returned home. I would never have made a farmer's wife anyway — too much mud, sheep dags and early-morning shearers' breakfasts for a city girl to adapt to!

When one door closes another opens, and I had learnt enough from my motley lot of mentors in England not to stand too long in the hallway getting chilled by the wind. Within a day of returning to Auckland, I knew what I was going to do. I would apply to Air New Zealand for hostess training: I already had concrete evidence that they would accept me. Two letters I had retained from the early 'sixties — one from BOAC (now British Airways) and one from TWA (Trans World Airlines, an American company) — had offered me training plus an annual salary from BOAC of £530.00. I had never taken either company up on their employment offers because I had returned to New Zealand, and then on my return to England I was far too involved in my life of inebriation.

'You are a little underweight, Miss Merritt, but apart from that everything else is satisfactory and there is no reason why I cannot recommend to the employment board that they offer you training as a hostess. We have a high regard for BOAC's selection process, and these letters will suffice.' The Air New Zealand Medical Officer shuffled the papers together on his desk and reached for the stapler as he nonchalantly queried, 'Is there anything else I need to know?' My mouth went dry. I felt the palms of my hands start to sweat and my heart thump against my chest. I knew I had to say it: I did not *want* to say it, but I knew I had to. 'Well actually, there is. I am a recovering alcoholic and have not drunk for nearly three months.'

The stapler and sheaf of papers hung in mid-air. Slowly he brought them together with a click that sounded to me like a pistol shot ricocheting around the room. 'Thank you for your honesty, Miss Merritt. We will obviously have to review your application and let you know.'

The letter arrived three days later: 'We regret to advise . . .' I was furious. I stood in the hallway at home stamping my foot and banging my high-chair. Why me? Why do *I* have to be an alcoholic? Why? Why? Why?

I knew what I needed to do, what I should do, what I ought to do (but didn't want to). I needed to find a group like those I had felt comfortable with in England. It was no good talking to my parents. I would just be told to get over it, that I should not have told him 'that'. It was not the 'done thing' to tell everyone I was alcoholic; it would affect our standing in the Remuera social scene. But I refused to co-operate with this approach. Not because I wished to cause my parents or family any angst, but because I had the courage to tell the truth. I would rather that people put an 'alcoholic' label on me than believe I was nuts.

I did what I needed to do. In the pouring rain, on the other side of Auckland, and after trying to open three locked doors, I finally entered a room to find about twelve people sitting around a table with cups of tea and a plate of the ubiquitous gingernut biscuits. A man was talking; he paused while I sat down, and then continued without missing a beat. I knew I was in the right place. There was the familiar blue 'textbook' on the table, cards pinned to the walls with such sayings as 'First Things First', and other items with which I was familiar. 'Yes' was my reply when I was asked if I would like to contribute, and I launched into something — I have no idea what else I mentioned apart from my hostess predicament.

Nobody offered advice or opinions; they just nodded their heads periodically until I had finished. Then the only woman there spoke. She talked about how she had learnt to keep away from people, places and things that would tempt her to drink or interfere with her peace of mind. She had not returned to her work in catering because there was too much alcohol involved, and now worked as a receptionist. Initially, she had been angry because she thought it would be such a boring job, but now realized how much better it was: she had regular hours, she met and talked with a variety of people, and all her evenings were free. She had learnt to accept the seemingly bad along with the apparently good; she didn't know which was which until she looked back at her life. I was amazed — yet again — for I was hearing what I needed to hear and knew that I would scrutinize the daily paper the next day. Flying the friendly skies would certainly have been high-risk for me at that point in my life.

The people I met that night were far removed from *Dad's Army*. They appeared as if they belonged to the local Rotary Club, and two of them were to play a significant part in my life. One was a dentist, Bert; the other a lawyer, John.

The advertisement had jumped out from the page: the Head of Marketing of The Nestlé Company was seeking a private secretary. I had not touched a typewriter in at least two years, and my shorthand was as rusty as a neglected piece of farm machinery. But nothing ventured, nothing gained; dressed in my smart green-and-brown suit, my nails painted, and my hair back-combed in that bouffant style of the 'seventies, I presented myself for an interview at the company's New Zealand headquarters in Parnell. This time I would *not* mention my struggle with alcohol. I felt it unnecessary. This position did not require a medical certificate.

Peter Bowes was a cigar-smoking, golf-playing, extremely intelligent and astute South African, with an engaging smile and a pair of piercing blue eyes. I liked him immediately. The deal was that I would be on probation for two weeks, and then a final decision on employment would be made. That day eventually arrived, and sitting in the chair across the desk from him I held my breath, hopefully and optimistically awaiting his decision. I was not disappointed. 'I would like to employ you as my secretary, Liz. How do you feel about the position?' I told him I would be delighted to accept the job; and then, without thinking, my mouth opened and I dumped the statement on his pad of blotting paper like an ink blot: 'Mr Bowes, there is something you need to know about me. I'm an alcoholic in recovery and I'm trying to change my life.'

I waited for the embarrassed apology, the averted gaze, the self-conscious clearing of the throat — none of which materialized. He held my anxious, awkward, agonized gaze with blue eyes that never flickered. 'What you do in your private life, Liz, is no business of mine, but if it ever interferes with your working life then we need to address the circumstances. Do not be concerned,

I appreciate your honesty.' Several weeks later, as I was taking dictation, he off-handedly remarked, 'Oh, by the way Liz, thank you for disclosing your involvement with alcohol. Mr McClelland asked me this morning if I knew that you had had a problem. Apparently there are a number of people in Auckland who are aware of parts of your past.' I was so relieved that I had disclosed my secret.

I went on to hold that position for eleven and a half years. Most bosses change their secretaries — I changed five bosses in those years! One of the great benefits I enjoyed during those years was the overwhelming pleasure I gained from being able to help others in the company who came to me for assistance with relations, friends and loved ones with a similar problem. I broke an image for many of what they perceived an alcoholic to be.

The time had now arrived to commence repair work after my anorexia and bulimia, for both had dissipated over time. Changes in my behaviour around food had been tied into my drinking circumstances, so that as I progressively changed my lifestyle and thinking for the better, the compulsion to binge-eat and vomit became less acceptable to me.

I had also become worried about some physical changes caused by my behaviour. These were changes that I was too frightened to discuss with anyone, which made things difficult for me, as keeping secrets was becoming harder in my new way of life. I had started bringing up small clots of blood during my purging and also had a constant sense of indigestion, which I now know were signs that I was in danger of rupturing my oesophagus. Although my period had returned, I suffered from chronic constipation and my teeth were tender when eating. There was no question in my mind that I needed a thorough medical and dental check-up.

I started with Bert. He did not need to spend long exploring my mouth to discover that he had seen skulls with healthier teeth! My incessant vomiting had constantly bathed my mouth with hydrochloric acid from my stomach, and this had worn off much of the enamel on my front teeth; my gums were red and receding, swollen from neglect. Capping and gum repair were not Bert's forte, but a referral and several thousand dollars and several months later saw me with nearly half my teeth capped and my gums in repair from what had looked like a great white shark's attack. The orthodontist/periodontist had Christmas and Easter arrive in his bank account all at once!

I had lost the hair down my spine, but Peter Restall (a general physician and Nuffield scholar) explained that my eyebrows would never grow back as a result of damage to my thyroid. It was essential that I eat as little meat as possible, making sure that fruit and vegetables formed the major part of my food consumption. I needed to be aware that I might have complications later in life from my extensive use of laxatives. After comprehensive blood tests and all manner of other explorations of my system, Dr Richwhite could barely believe that I was as healthy as I was.

I believe there were many factors playing a part in enabling me to regain my health and emerge, physically and psychologically, from the bulimarexia. Physically, because I had often eaten and then drank until I lost consciousness, much of the food had been absorbed and I actually gained weight. My body must have been ecstatic — food at last! Physically, it could have been so much worse.

Psychologically, my whole outlook on life had changed. I was developing a consciousness of now having a group of friends who accepted me for who I was — not for what I did for a job, what school I had been to, where I lived, or who my parents were. With their help I was able to start discovering my talents and attributes, the obnoxious defects in my character, and shortcomings that had become habits but were not serving me well. It was a revelation to me when I discovered that I had lived so much of my life in fear, and that the fear was obscuring my strengths. Fear of what people thought of me, fear of criticism, fear of not being liked, fear of saying the wrong thing; constant fears, some of which had no name. As I began to peel the layers off myself, I found that I started to become much more free as a person. Nobody *told* me to take a look at myself; they just explained that when they did it they felt this incredibly heavy rock being lifted off their shoulders. A rock that they never knew they had been carrying for so long — the weight of guilt, remorse, shame, despair, fear, resentment, hostility. The list was like worthless tools in a workman's box.

I discovered that when I talked about my worries, my feelings, situations I was having difficulty handling, I felt better and would be open to suggestions (not put-downs) as to how I might cope with them. I learnt to disagree without being disagreeable. I no longer had to deal with anger by shocking people with my emaciated appearance, stuffing it down with mountains of food, or anaesthetizing it with alcohol. In learning to trust another person (first Jean and now Bert, for he had become a mentor to me), I was learning to trust myself. More than anything, I was learning that achievements that were not perfect did not constitute a disaster!

I came to understand that asking for and accepting help in my life was not only a lesson in humility, but also showed strength of character. I had been brought up to believe that asking for help was a sign of weakness. So many of my old ideas and belief systems had to be changed; only I could do that. Asking for and accepting help was going to enable me to grow and change, as I would benefit from the knowledge and experience of others, and so not be limited in my growth. Such a simple lesson, but hard to start practising as my pride got in the way.

My recovery from anorexia and bulimia was of course not simply a matter of an increase in weight. Over the ensuing years, my confidence and self-esteem grew, I developed a more flexible (and less ritualistic, less obsessive/compulsive) attitude to life, and I became more interdependent. As I did so, my need to escape into my previous behaviour around food receded.

My relationships with people were also maturing — I was learning to trust on a certain level, and also I was discovering the meaning of intimacy.

My father was not at all happy with me. Delighted that I had such a high-profile job, that I had repaid the $300 he had loaned me (a large sum in those days), and that I was supporting myself and had even moved into a flat on my own — but not at *all* happy that I was announcing the fact I was an alcoholic to all who wanted to know what had been wrong with me.

I refused to tell people anything else; I was tired of secrets. I was discovering more and more who I was and what I could become. I had lived for so long with a conglomeration of personalities that if you had placed me in a room I could have conducted a group-therapy session on my own! I had a long list of people to whom I needed to make amends for my past behaviour, and I had no intention of being anything but up-front with them. I refused to live any longer according to principles that were detrimental to my integrity. I certainly had no intention of standing on a street corner with a tambourine, but I was perfectly well aware that I *could* help to dispel the myths and perceptions that society had of what an alcoholic looked like. I was cleaning up my past as best I could. I was demonstrating that it was possible to lead a productive life despite having the disease of alcoholism, and I was certainly not ashamed any more of who I was. Ashamed of what I had done and the hurt and embarrassment I had caused, yes; but I was attempting to repair this, too, as best I could. I no longer wanted to live with lies, fakes, deceit and dishonesty. An inner strength was growing where one harsh word no longer made me bleed for days. I was beginning to acknowledge when I was wrong, admitting to it and moving on. The approval or disapproval of my parents no longer controlled me. I was starting to gain an emotional maturity that was surprising to me; but I was not achieving this on my own.

I was well aware that without Jean as a mentor any longer I needed to find someone to whom I could turn for guidance as I had turned to her. I also knew that for me it was necessary that this be an individual who understood me as an alcoholic, and whom I could trust. I could not find another woman to whom I felt connected, but did discover that I could talk to Bert, the dentist from the meetings.

He and John Jamieson were the best of friends. There were few professionals in Auckland who were recovering alcoholics in the early 1970s — a large number who probably *needed* to change their drinking behaviour, but few who had actually done so. I was flatting in Remuera, Bert was in Greenlane, and John lived on his own in Mt Eden. John had been separated but not divorced from his wife for two years; he used to say, jokingly, 'I'm too busy getting other people their divorces to do anything about my own!' He would often call in while Bert and I were meeting, and soon I was visiting his office in High Street for a cup of coffee if I went into the city after work. We began to eat dinner and mix with other alcoholics, and eventually it seemed ridiculous that we were maintaining two residences when one would suffice. I surrendered my living quarters and moved in with John.

Several months later, I discovered that Bert had cornered John into making a decision. John already had a woman in his life apart from me, his ex-wife and his secretary: she was a professional, and still married. 'You had better make up your mind,' Bert had told him. 'You know it's unfair on Liz. Do you want to make a decision or do you want her to find out?' The mistress was asked to return the key to the front door.

Of course I had to tell my parents, or it would only be a matter of time before they discovered that I was no longer living where they thought I was. Father came home from his office for lunch, at my request, and Mother had made coffee and sandwiches for all of us as we sat in the drawing room and they waited with bated breath for what I had to say. I am not always good at pausing before I say something, to explore 'Is it kind? Is it necessary?', but

I had thought through this whole change in my life and decided that it *was* necessary that they know from me, rather than discover the circumstances from elsewhere. I also wanted to do it as kindly as possible.

I have no idea what they were thinking. I had brought us together to talk, and they could never have predicted what was about to be blurted out. I commenced with a number of prefaces and preliminaries, and then out it flew: 'I've moved out of my flat and am living with someone. He's fifteen years older than me, a recovering alcoholic, still married, with six children. He's a lawyer called John Jamieson.'

I thought my father was going to have an apoplexy. The profession was obviously acceptable, but under no circumstances was the pedigree! About the only part of his face which retained colour were his blue eyes. The rest went the colour of chalk on a blackboard. Without touching his coffee or glancing at the sandwiches, he strode from the room with the words 'You'll pay for this, my girl.' Mother froze as if she was posing for a portrait painting. I returned to work. The letter came two days later, right out of a Victorian melodrama: 'having brought *further* disgrace on the family I disown and disinherit you as my daughter'.

He was *furious*. Whenever I went back to the house, he would disappear out the back door as I arrived in the front. What made the whole situation even more unbearable for him was that all he heard around the professional and social scenes of Auckland was 'John Jamieson? A fine lawyer — enormous admiration for the man — commands respect throughout the profession — how wonderful for Liz'. Mother, having survived the shock and done her own detective work, thought she had better explore my living conditions.

Armed with one of her ubiquitous tins of homemade shortbread that served the purpose of either peace offerings or Christmas presents, she satisfied herself that the west-facing, sunny, two-bedroom flat in Mt Eden was a far cosier place for me than the east-facing basement one I had left. Over the ensuing years she became incredibly attached to John, and liked nothing better than to be stimulated by his, as he called it, 'rubbish-bin mind of life's flotsam and jetsam' and his puckish sense of humour.

Jenny arrived from England for a few weeks' holiday and promptly performed like an enraged fishwife. She shredded Father. How dare he? After all I had been through, who was he to tell me who I could or could not live with? Look at what I was doing with my life! She refused to attend the cocktail party Father had arranged specifically for her unless John and I were present. Needless to say, she won. Whatever the outcome was between them after this avalanche I have no idea, but at least Father no longer exited through the back door on my arrival. One interesting result was that, after John and I had married, Father made John one of the directors of his company and behaved as if nothing detrimental had ever been a part of their relationship.

The Anglican Church's policy in those days was that no divorced person could marry, but they had reckoned without Jim Thomas, the vicar of St Mark's in Remuera, and Ron Banbury, vicar in Mt Albert. Whether Bishop Gowing gave a special dispensation or not, I have no idea. All I know is that Jim Thomas vowed he would perform the ceremony anyway, and that we had better include John's vicar Ron Banbury, because the last time one vicar had not worked for John so maybe if we had two this time it would!

Bert gave me away, John's eldest daughter was my bridesmaid, my wedding dress was bought off a shop rack, and our plumber friend, Jimmy, was John's best man. With tears in his eyes, he confessed that he had never been asked to be best man before — he had always been too drunk. His blue suit was probably from the City Mission, and the white socks and brown shoes made me wince, but Jimmy had one of the proudest moments in his life — he was a lawyer's best man for the day. As he sliced the wedding cake into pieces, I could have sworn he used an axe.

Two days later, John was in California honeymooning on his own — I had no holidays owing, so could not take time off from work. He had met Chuck and Elsa Chamberlain (actor Richard Chamberlain's parents) while they were holidaying in New Zealand, and from then on we were both to have a close and wonderful relationship with this truly inspiring couple.

John's eldest daughter asked if she could come and live with us; then the second daughter wanted to bail out from her home, with the third threatening to follow suit in a few years. We had to move, and move we did: back to Remuera. Living with a stepdaughter who was closer to me in age than her father was not an easy situation. She was strong-willed, extremely bright, pragmatic and surprisingly emotionally mature for her age. Her whole attitude, at age nineteen, to her parents' situation was 'Don't involve me. It's not my fight.' This unfortunately used to antagonize her mother, with the result that she ended up 'living with your father and that skinny bitch!' Mary Elizabeth and I still keep in touch, spasmodically, and she has followed in her father's footsteps, being now a successful lawyer herself.

With one stepdaughter at university and one at teacher's training college, the house was a hive of activity. This, coupled with the fact that most weekends John and I would have people to lunch (usually ending up with more mouths to feed than anticipated), our lives were full and fulfilling. We enjoyed a stimulating, happy, laughter-filled trip around the world, staying with friends in the States, my relatives in England, and an extremely memorable few days with Peter Bowes, my original boss, in South Africa. We discovered more recovering alcoholic friends amongst the Americans; I was able to make many amends for past behaviour to people in England; and Peter Bowes was genuinely pleased to be able to show us Kruger National Park and some of the Zulu dancing ceremonies.

My parents were not only delighted at how their eldest daughter had 'turned out', but also glad she was now in such a socially acceptable position: married to a lawyer, living in Remuera, and secretary to the chief executive of an international food company.

They had accepted that there would be no children from me (John said it had to be my decision, but with six already he really did not want any more) and tried to ignore my mentoring of alcoholics. Life could not have been better.

Chapter 12

Love never dies

The girls were away during teacher's training college and university holidays when John laboured up the back steps about a week prior to Christmas 1977. Intuitively, I knew something was not right. Was it the stoop in his shoulders, the lack of energy and enthusiasm in his walk, his bowed head? Maybe all of these. As he rounded the corner of the sink bench, I stood glued rigid to the floor, my head racing in a thousand different directions. Had he drunk again? Had there been bad news for his legal practice that he was so bravely piecing together? Maybe it was one of the girls?

He placed his bag on the floor, and the inevitable stack of files that came home on a chair, and reaching into his trouser pocket, he pulled out his white handkerchief and slowly peeled it open. I looked with shock and mounting horror at the large patches of scarlet phlegm that were revealed sticking to the white linen. 'Oh my God,' went my mind, 'oh my God.'

He just stood, holding the handkerchief with both hands as his mouth quivered, his lower teeth sunk into his upper lip to control its shaking. His eyes filled with tears, and his shoulders drooped and sagged as if all energy had suddenly been sucked out of him. This six-foot-two, solid Scotsman, who made people laugh with his incredible verbal agility, who always had an open door to his office for an alcoholic in trouble, who found humour in the trivialities of life, and who would have given me the world if I had asked for it, was helpless in the face of something he had no idea how to handle. I learnt that for weeks he had been washing the handkerchiefs before placing them in the washing machine.

Somehow we managed to live through the visits to doctors, the medical tests, the X-rays and the consultations that could be squeezed into the days before Christmas. The biopsies showed a malignant tumour, and because it was small-cell carcinoma there was the possibility that there might be secondaries. Radiation treatment was advised for as soon as possible, but everything was closing for the Christmas break. We could only take life one day at a time.

John was a heavy smoker, to the extent that one of his clients had jokingly observed that he was not sure whether the stop smoking sign on the office door was to keep the smoke in or out! His smoking may have caused the cancer; I believe it aggravated the remains of a melanoma that had not been completely removed from the middle of his chest several months before. Whatever the cause, we were faced with the challenge of doing all we could to arrest and hopefully cure the condition. But there was an enormous problem: try as he might, John simply could not stop smoking. I had attended the Seventh Day Adventists' five-day course the previous year, and had at least been able to reduce my consumption. I was willing to stop again, but John, for all his intelligence, could not do the same. I was powerless to do anything. What could I have done? He was going to continue smoking anyway. When people kept telling me to make him stop, my answer was a simple one-word question: 'How?'

I remember nothing of that Christmas and little of the ensuing holiday period, except for one incident that is indelibly printed in the photograph album of my mind. New Year's Eve. It must have been one of those chilly New Years that descend now and again, because I remember our gas fire was burning. John and I were sitting alone as we were not feeling sociable enough to celebrate, when around eleven o'clock we both winced at the unexpected *bang, bang* of the front door knocker. In the misty light of the front porch stood three figures: two adults, and a child of around eleven years old. 'We thought you might be a little lonely, so we've come to have New Year with you.' Dr Fraser McDonald, his wife Jackie

Fahey and their youngest daughter, Emily, stepped into the hallway. I was one drop of water away from tears falling on my cheeks. Apart from Bert, there was perhaps only one other in our vast, intriguing accumulation of friends and acquaintances who could have lifted John's spirits to any height; and here he was, quizzically, scrutinizing John with a twinkle in his eye as John helped them all remove their coats.

Fraser was one of the psychiatric profession's mavericks, possessing an empathy with and understanding of alcoholics that was both baffling and intriguing. He and John had become the greatest of friends over the years, sharing not only that puckish sense of humour, but also intelligence, an ability to connect with anybody, irrespective of race or creed — and an eleventh finger that they found impossible to amputate: the cigarette. There were many who loved Fraser in a very special way until the day he died.

Both Fraser and Jackie brought a light-heartedness to the evening that allowed us all to laugh for a while. How grateful I am, again and again, for the people who entered my life when I was not aware that I needed them. As I heard a man say once: 'I'd rather pray and find there isn't a God than not pray and find there is!' I had said enough prayers, consciously and unconsciously, over the years to believe that *something* was taking care of me, often by sending people my way when I was ready and willing to accept them. My new-found recovering alcoholic friends had certainly helped me to discover my own understanding of a God that I chose to address with that title. Name it what you will, when the chips are down and your back is up against the wall, there are few people who do not cry out to *something*; there are few atheists on a sinking ship.

Finding the serenity to accept what I cannot change is never easy, and now I was facing, yet again, another situation that I had no idea how to handle. What could I change, what couldn't I change, how could *I* change, to cope? I started to talk to people, lots of people, to discover what I could do.

Dr Richwhite told me that I must stay in my job, as this would provide a semblance of normality in my life. Elsie Rainer, John's secretary, was devoted to John. She had left the firm John had been with, and, when he arrived back in Auckland after a time at Queen Mary's Hospital in Hanmer Springs, she had presented herself for her old job back. During his radiation and chemotherapy treatment, Elsie held his practice together. Bluey, an old, weather-beaten seaman and longtime friend of John's, arrived on the doorstep announcing that he would cut the hedge and mow the lawns for us. On the days when it was difficult for John to be in the office because of the effects of the chemotherapy, other ex-drunks, as some of them called themselves, would line up to drink the eternal cups of coffee and keep him company.

During the following soul-wrenching eighteen months, I tried to never let John see my tears. Radiation treatment had effectively erased the growth in his chest, but as the carcinoma was the small-cell type there was a risk that it would spread to other areas of his body. Chemotherapy was recommended; we entered this whole torturous process completely oblivious to the toll it would take on both of us. John's Shetland Island constitution allowed him to endure each chemical blast with the most mind-boggling fortitude. For my part, with the support of Fraser McDonald and my amazing group of friends in a fellowship I had resisted for so long, I challenged treatments, medications and medical jargon incessantly. Three days in hospital for each chemotherapy session was unnecessary. There was no reason for him to lie there for a day before the treatment, and little reason to remain for a day afterwards. I delivered him in the morning and collected him in the evening, as he was nauseous and vomiting and far preferred to do that at home in his own bed. Every form that was placed in front of me to acknowledge that I was taking responsibility for him was signed with a flourish, and staff were questioned only for information on what to expect as an aftermath from the treatment.

With the help of the loyal Elsie, John's legal files and clients were well cared for, and his new partner Eion Castles was able to take much of the responsibility when John was unable to go to work. I knew John's law was his lifeline; it gave him his identity. His staff gave him their support, his clients (for many months) wanted to go nowhere else and gave him their loyalty, but most of all his work gave him a purpose in life. Intuitively, I knew that John's ultimate destruction would not lie in the cancer he was fighting; he would be destroyed by a sense of uselessness. I needed to protect him from despair over this worthlessness: for as long as he had meaning to his life, he would go on. He knew what he had to do, he knew what he ought to do, and he knew what he wanted to do. No matter what, I was determined to defend his right to do this.

By the time September arrived, we had decided we needed some Californian sunshine — but the thought of three weeks away from the chemotherapy perturbed the doctor who was treating John. I was adamant we were going, and so reluctantly it was agreed that we could depart on the condition that we carried a referral letter with us. If, for any reason, there was a need for medical assistance, then the letter from the doctor at Greenlane Hospital could be handed to the appropriate person; it would contain a list of the chemicals and the forms of treatment that John had been prescribed. The following day, an extremely concerned Elsie was on the telephone to me at work. Did I know where John was? He had not arrived at the office, and there were two clients waiting. I had no idea where he had gone. I'd understood that he was collecting a letter from the hospital and then driving to work. I had barely put the telephone down when Bert was on the line: please could they excuse me from work, as John was with him having opened the doctor's letter. Although the envelope had stated 'To Whom It May Concern', John had opened it and read the contents. Halfway down the page, following the list of chemicals to be administered, was the fateful line: 'This man of course is living on a very short amount of borrowed time.' We had been led to believe that John stood a chance — this told us that the cancer had in fact run rampant.

On our return from the sunshine — flowing from our friends as much as the environment — we lived each day as it came. I took up ballroom and Latin American dancing to retain my sanity, gaining bronze and silver medals in both. John began to turn more files over to Eion, yet each evening arrived with an armload to pore over on the floor for a couple of hours, along with the ever-accompanying cigarette. As the cancer spread and grew, we were faced with even greater challenges. John's short-term memory started to be affected, until I no longer felt it was safe to leave him alone — and he was now spending days away from the office. Eventually I discovered he had started drinking again, possibly kick-started by all the chemicals in his system. After two weeks in Kingseat Hospital to dry him out, I had to fight to take him back; their recommendation was that he remain there for three months.

By the middle of 1979, even though I was with John every day, it was noticeable that his deterioration was accelerating. A spell in Auckland Hospital had me refusing to leave the ward until they had increased his pain medication, for now the pancreas was under attack from the cancer and the pain was excruciating. I stood my ground, giving the best medical lecture I have ever given on what it means to be an alcoholic and how that person's tolerance for painkillers is dramatically higher than that of a non-alcoholic. Yes — for Heaven's sake, I'll take responsibility. Where do I sign?

By this stage, John's two daughters who had been living with us had moved on. Mary Elizabeth had married, with John still able to 'give her away' at her wedding, and Cathy demonstrated her compassion by finding friends with whom to live, allowing me to spend the last few months alone with her father. We began the long way home for John; back to where life's pains and sufferings are no more, and peace and the companionship of those who have gone before are waiting, across the great divide over which we all must pass.

Every morning at seven, one crazy Irishman who John had helped to stop drinking would arrive in his three-piece suit, don a pair of overalls, and shave, bath and dress John, and place him in his chair by the fire, all accompanied by a never-ending string of Irish banter. By eight o'clock the first of the rostered group of friends would arrive, the last one leaving at five when I returned home from work; every one of them either recovered alcoholics or their wives.

Later in the evening, and always on a Saturday and Sunday morning, Rosie would walk her five-minute journey from her parents' home up the road. Rosie was God's gift to me at this time. She was probably the sickest alcoholic I have ever known! We had been at primary school together, and our mothers both played bridge. Rosie had just returned from her second spell at Queen Mary Hospital; this time for four months, an unheard-of period to stay. She came because she never wanted to drink again and she wanted me to help her. She explains to this day that watching me cope with a dying husband and yet not drinking was the inspiration which kept her going. For my part, her arrival meant that I was taken out of myself, busy helping her to gain a different perspective on life. She was my angel in disguise.

My parents were on tenterhooks — they were sure I was going to start drinking again. Lloyd Richwhite, meaning well, offered me sleeping pills, tranquillizers and antidepressants. 'Lloyd, I can't take these: I'm alcoholic. It's like eating my booze rather than drinking it.' 'But Liz, this is different' came his reply. 'No, Lloyd, nothing is different' was my retort. 'I have a philosophy of life, something I don't fully understand but I believe in, that will keep me safe and it is the greatest support system I could ever hope for.' And so it was.

As John grew thinner, weaker and more forgetful, so I appeared to become stronger, more competent, more capable: the balance that was necessary to keep our lives functioning. He spent his days and now his nights either in his chair or kneeling in front of the gas fire in the sitting room next to the kitchen, the warmth from the fire helping ease the crippling pain in his back. I took to sleeping either on the sheepskin on the floor next to him or on the couch within arm's reach. Thankfully, with the kitchen next door and the bathroom only two open doors away, he could always hear me; he would call out if there was a moment's silence, terrified of being alone. Pathetically, he would shovel food into his mouth, trying to keep it down, knowing it would keep him alive; then would sob like a child as I held a bowl for him to vomit it up again. His urinal was always handy, too, as it was becoming an enormous effort for him to walk to the bathroom.

I was now administering 'Dr Nolan's mixture' on demand. This consisted of liquid Largactil, Librium and morphine — nausea and pain medication along with a sedative — which I had to top up with brandy. How could I possibly dispense this concoction every four hours, as prescribed, to an *alcoholic*? That would have been torture. I gave it to him on demand. What was amazing was that at no stage did I even contemplate touching this mixture myself. It simply never occurred to me. I had totally lost the desire to drink or change reality in any way. Old hedge-cutting Bluey had said something very profound to me: 'You can either see that John is dying of cancer, or you can learn to live with it. One day you may be able to share this experience in your life to help another.' This weather-beaten old seaman had showed me I had a choice, I always have a choice: it is not what happens in my life that matters as much as what I *do* with what happens.

The day came when I knew, reluctantly, that I could no longer cope with John at home; he had to be taken to hospital. How kind and gentle those ambulance personnel were as they placed him on the stretcher and into the vehicle. Now I could no longer hold back my tears as I looked into John's eyes, for he knew — without a shadow of a doubt he *knew* — what this journey meant. My hands were not free to wipe my nose and my eyes on that journey; they were clasping John's. The ambulance lady held a handkerchief to my nose periodically as the stream threatened to become a river. I knew I just had to cope with that day; do whatever had to be done; not think about tomorrow, but just take everything a step at a time, a decision at a time . . .

I shall be eternally grateful to The Nestlé Company, for through all the emotional turmoil of the following ten days my boss was more than generous and understanding in terms of time away from the office and hours at my desk spent on the telephone. I pleaded with friends and family not to visit John, at his request. Weeks earlier, he had asked that only certain people come back to see him. He found visits exhausting, and I wanted people to remember him as they had known him: the honest, generous, funny, articulate, caring man that he was, not the crumbling, worn-out shell he had become.

The children, Bert and a few others were there along with me to help him blow out his fifty birthday candles. John's father had died young, of a heart attack, never living to see fifty. John had always been determined to make that number, and he did; how incredibly powerful the mind can be. The next day it was my sister Georgina's birthday, and as usual I was at John's bedside at ten o'clock that night after the family dinner. 'I think you should stay,' suggested Pauline, the nurse, as midnight came and I rose from the chair in which I had been dozing. I never even asked why as she left the room after squeezing my shoulder: I simply pulled the chair closer to the bed and took one of his thin, cold hands in mine.

Many thoughts meander through the mind outside death's door; some spoken, some unspoken. Periodically, as I reminisced and shared my memories aloud, there would be a weak squeezing of my hand — they say that hearing is one of the last senses to leave. There was the funny time when John had wondered whose shirts I was ironing apart from his; they belonged to my new boss from England whose wife and family had not yet arrived in the country. There was that embarrassing time when I could not remember the drunken performance I had given at one of his legal colleagues' dinner parties before I had sobered up; and the poignant times of our long walks on the beaches surrounding Auckland.

Without a shadow of doubt — and no one will ever convince me otherwise — there is a time when the spirit leaves the body which cannot contain it any more, to travel elsewhere. Experiences are memories that are never erased, and if ever I am forced to choose between those and academic information I will choose experiences every time.

The last whisper I heard was not from John's mouth, but from his heart and his soul: 'Let me go, Liz, please let me go'; and I came to understand the true meaning of letting go and letting God take what is His. The suffering and pain that was left was not for John but for myself.

The darkest hour is just before dawn, yet in the silence and the dimness there was a peace and a tranquillity that enveloped me as I prayed. My prayers were ones of gratitude — gratitude that John was now free of his pain and torment; that *I* was now free of the powerlessness, hopelessness and helplessness I had lived with for so long. They were prayers of thankfulness for the years that we had had, few though they had been, and for the wonderful times and memories we had shared and with which I had been left. But perhaps, over and above everything, I felt grateful for the knowledge that never, at any stage, had I found it necessary to extract myself for one single moment from any experience of those heart-wrenching months. No pill, no potion, no panacea had anaesthetized me against reality. It was through my own suffering that I came to greater knowledge of myself and made discoveries of strengths within me that I did not know existed. The strength to walk away from the self-pity which was in danger of consuming and destroying me, just like a cancer — but one that attacked not the body but the emotions, threatening to erode my strength, my courage, my humanity, but most of all my ability to love and be loved.

John's funeral was one of the largest Auckland had seen for a while, and the 'recovered drunks' came from as far away as Dunedin and Queensland. Perhaps the greatest and most humbling eulogy of them all was the simple statement from a legal colleague: 'I believe John to have been one of the greatest pleaders in mitigation this country has known.'

In the solitude and quietness of that night, I found that silence has its own eloquence that can be more comforting than words. I had come this far in life, and through all the pain had discovered strengths in me that I never dreamed existed. I would grieve, but I knew there must come a time when a fresh meaning to life would be needed, rather than a preoccupation with death — or the latter would destroy me.

I was thirty-five years old.

Chapter 13

Suffering is optional

Pain is necessary; suffering is optional. I am not responsible for what happens to me much of the time, but I *am* responsible for what I do with it and for my subsequent attitude.

Grief is painful. It enters all our lives in various disguises along with its companions, sadness and suffering. These in themselves are not a tragedy: the tragedy is that too many of us waste the experiences they present and the discoveries they offer. I was not grieving for John; he was free of his pain and suffering. I was grieving for myself, which was unavoidable and probably natural. The last thing I wanted from well-meaning people was platitudes: I needed empathy, not sympathy, for the feelings that were competing for recognition every day.

My instinct was to wallow in self-pity over the terrible deal life had given me. I was angry and hostile, bitter, resentful and questioning — *why me?* But I never stopped meeting with my recovered-alcoholic friends, I never stopped showing up at work each day, and I never stopped seeing or talking to Rosie on a daily basis. As a result, drinking never entered my mind, although my anorexia kicked back in. I found it extremely difficult to eat. It was not that I did not *want* to eat, it was that I had lost my appetite. In hindsight, I realize that this was a stress reaction to the grief I was experiencing.

Boils broke out on my face, under my arms and down the side of my legs, followed by shingles. I had shingles on my scalp, and from my chest to my hips around the entire middle part of my body. I was a mess. Although I was not due any leave from work, it was necessary that I take some and it was Christmas anyway. Dear Rosie, who was like my shadow, insisted that I spend time with her and her family at their beach house at Ti Point. Here, I virtually lived in the sea, the most healing environment for all my agonizing skin ailments.

Some people, like Jean, have played enormously significant roles in my life over the years, and Rosie was and is one of them. She never drank again, and we have been privileged to share more than a third of our lives together. She was such a help to me at this difficult time. Her father, who was a lawyer, had known John well and was full of anecdotes to help me through my grief, while Rosie did not want to drink because she had decided she would take care of me! Meanwhile, I was so busy helping *her* that I was forgetting to pity myself.

In my sorrow, I was discovering the things that really mattered. There was a meaning to all my shameful and horrendous past: I could help others who were wanting to confront theirs, deal with it and move on. There would be meaning in the grief and pain I was undergoing now, but I had to move through the darkness to discover what that meaning was — and I did.

The world appears to be riddled with loveless power, yet if one stands back one can still see the power of love, weaving its strands through the debris to comfort and heal. It is non-judgemental and unconditional; it is the freedom to be oneself while sharing what we are, and what we become, with another. It allows us to grow in our own way, in our own time and on our own course, and to make our own discoveries about ourselves. It was through my pain and through walking the days with Rosie that we each made our discoveries; perhaps we unconsciously realized that remorse and resentment, like self-pity, are cancers as well. Not benign but malignant — for they will erode our dignity, our enthusiasm, our self-respect, our courage, our empathy and our compassion. Most of all, they destroy our capacity to experience love; they cause a slow, painful and self-inflicted death.

Time is a great healer. As the days and weeks progressed, I

learnt to apply the principle of *living* a day at a time and realizing that love never dies. Sometimes one of the containers in which we may experience it does, but love itself comes in a variety of forms. There is sexual and erotic love, the love in friendship, and the love of compassion, one human being reaching out to another human being in pain. One can give without loving, but one cannot love without giving, and this is not displayed in words but in actions. In the atmosphere of love and companionship provided by my recovered-alcoholic friends, I started to heal, and in this healing I discovered hidden strengths that had been locked deep inside me. In these depths, I discovered myself. I had my own life to live, my own purpose to discover, my own destiny to fulfil — with or without another person.

The myth that happiness, usefulness and contentment can be found only within an intimate relationship with another person was exploded for me over the ensuing years. This is not to say that relationships are not important, but to believe that fulfilment in life is purely dependent upon an intimate association with another is totally erroneous. Often, being free of such ties allows us the time and energy to explore and practise our creativity. This was one of the myriad lessons I was to learn over the coming years.

Chapter 14

What shall we do with the drunken sailor?

Fraser McDonald rang me one Wednesday morning. 'I have a Navy psychiatrist visiting from the United States, Liz. He is speaking at the Auckland Medical School tomorrow night and needs ten people for a panel. Can you come with nine others?'

I was fascinated with psychiatrist Dr Joe Pursch's story of how the US Navy's alcohol and drug treatment programmes originated. Fascinated because of my parents' naval background and because of my involvement in the Auckland Navy League, into which I had been reinstated. I learnt how a retired US Navy captain had spoken with a doctor at the Naval Hospital at Long Beach, California, about his own alcoholism, and how that conversation had started a chain of events which had led to the Navy having several treatment and rehabilitation centres throughout the States. That evening was to be yet another turning point in my journey in life, one which was eventually to take me in a direction that I could never have envisaged in my wildest dreams and imaginings.

Around the same time, I got to know Gordon Nicholson. He was a quiet, kind, warm and unassuming gastroenterologist, who was sympathetic to alcoholics but had the humility to admit he had little understanding of them. Like many in the medical profession, he avoided them if he could. But over the years he had come to recognize that some of his patients had managed to recover with help from other, sober, alcoholics. Ward 5D at Auckland Hospital, where Gordon worked, was an area that had several beds allocated to people withdrawing from alcohol, and Gordon was keen to have individuals such as myself up there on a regular basis to talk with some of his patients. Rosie was with me the night I met Bill there. Bill was due to return to the Devonport Naval Base, and was concerned as there was virtually no support for non-drinkers in that environment. Could a group of us perhaps talk to the doctor there, to see if there was a chance we could find a room to go to once a week, just to share experiences to give people strength and hope? I remembered Joe Pursch's story about the Long Beach Naval Hospital, and thought to myself 'Well, the worst thing the Navy doctor can do is say no.'

I had no conception of the magnitude of the task on which I was about to embark; all I wanted to do was help some unfortunate naval rating to remain sober. By the end of the exercise, spanning all of the ensuing years, I came to realize that I had opened up a hornets' nest and started a 'war' that would shake the very foundations of a long-established and male-dominated institutional rite: a sailor's drinking. The ripples would spread wide. I had not only antagonized certain naval personnel, but in doing so I had also threatened the entire drinking culture of the New Zealand military. If the Navy was forced to confront their drinking behaviour, then so, too, would be the Army and Air Force. Thankfully, it never occurred to me to examine possible consequences of unwittingly challenging New Zealand's entire defence force. At this stage I was only concerned with discovering a way to approach the doctor on the naval base at Devonport.

I rang a couple of recovered-alcoholic friends on the North Shore the next day, one of whom gave me the name and number of a petty officer whom he knew had not had a drink for eighteen months. On my speaking with Petty Officer Buch, he confirmed that he would be only too willing to accompany me as a recovered alcoholic in the Navy — should I be able to persuade anyone to listen to me!

I knew that I would need to find some 'heavies' as back-up: a civilian woman, simply calling the doctor to discuss the topic of alcoholism in the Navy would not get me far. Sir Leonard Thornton was my man. He had had an extremely distinguished career in both the Army and the Diplomatic Services, and was the current chairman of the Alcohol Liquor Advisory Council in Wellington. We had met on several occasions, and when I asked him if I could use his name to 'cut red tape' he was only too willing, if it would help to instigate any awareness on the Auckland naval base. He suggested I call Admiral Neil Anderson, Chief of Naval Staff, who was in Auckland at the time; after a brief conversation, Admiral Anderson assured me I could use his name as well.

Captain Peter Robinson agreed to see Buch and myself for fifteen minutes after work later that week. When we left his rooms — nearly two hours later — we had a brief far exceeding that of merely starting a meeting! I was to be in the front line, spearheading a drive to break the denial within the Navy that there *was* a drinking problem spiralling out of control.

Brian Gubb, an old legal friend of John's, called me when he heard news of my involvement with the medical team at the naval base. Had I seen the paper that day? (*The New Zealand Herald* of Friday, 29 August 1980.) When I replied in the negative, he suggested I read page four, under the headline 'Jailed for Causing Car Death'. Brian had just finished defending a thirty-four-year-old seaman who had 'previously pleaded guilty to three charges of driving with excess blood alcohol, careless use causing death and careless use causing bodily injury'.

Brian was angry; the seaman concerned was on his third DWI (drunk while under the influence) charge and his second excess alcohol charge; he had had a noted alcohol problem since 1975, and now he had been convicted of causing death while drunk. Brian had been acting for both commissioned and non-commissioned naval personnel for the past fifteen years, and he was prepared to state in court that all his criminal work with Navy people was liquor-related; this was substantiated by a retired Wren officer. It was the fact that the naval base commodore had told Brian that there was no problem with liquor in the New Zealand Navy that had made Brian furious. They were still issuing the daily tot of 120 per cent proof rum, reportedly a strength sufficient to dissolve a pickaxe, which immediately placed the consumer over the limit for driving (and at a time when the legal limit was 100 mg per 100 ml of blood, not today's lower limit of 80). Yet no one in authority had the moral courage to go down in the annals as the individual responsible for removing the rum ration; New Zealand being the last country in the world to keep this tradition alive.

Alcohol-related incidents were now starting to become less of a secret, at the same time as some of the hierarchy's resistance to change was becoming louder. The Navy refused to divulge the amount of liquor consumed in the messes, yet they knew that some sailors were driving off the base with excess alcohol in their blood. A high-ranking officer admitted to Brian that he knew that the bars should be closed at a certain hour, but 'did not want to upset the Navy way of life'. The lieutenants and lieutenant commanders were strongly opposed to any Navy alcoholism programme because of accelerated promotion — others being promoted over the top of anyone with a drinking problem. All hell was starting to break loose, as the alcohol-related incidents were becoming more frequently acknowledged, and four-stripers (captains) and above were starting to confront drunken behaviours in their commands and amongst their peers.

Although few knew me by name, as Peter Robinson remarked during my first meal with him in the Officers' Mess: 'They all know what you look like now, Liz. Those personnel at the other tables are all officers. I would not be too worried — most of them are frightened of you!' I was five foot two and 50 kg, a redheaded, widowed member of the Navy League who lived in Remuera and had a top secretarial job. There was no way they could touch me! What's more, I had agreed to work one night a week, unpaid, with Navy psychologist Peter Sutherland. It was an unofficial appointment, and yet I would be there, so far as the clients were concerned, as an officer of the Royal New Zealand Navy.

❧

Meanwhile, although I was grateful to have a job which gave me a reason for starting the day, and Nestlé was a stable company to work for, it was somewhat stuffy. I yearned for another employee to arrive who contained a little *oomph!* She appeared unexpectedly one Monday morning. Toni arrived like a bird of paradise amongst a flock of sparrows. She was a voluptuous bottle-streaked blonde, in her early thirties, and wore mini-skirts with stiletto-heeled shoes. In addition to all her physical assets, she was an extremely competent secretary, and within a week she and I had decided we were going to clear the cobwebs and put some colour into our Dickensian environment.

We must have made a formidable pair: one blonde, one redhead; one divorcée, one widow; and both in the prime of our lives — our early/mid-thirties. The die-hards who were determined to end their days glued to their desks ducked for cover, while those grovelling for excitement in their lives shared our table at morning and afternoon tea (yes, we still had tea breaks *and* a tea lady); the other secretaries would huddle in a cluster, drinking their sugary beverages and watching us with their peripheral vision.

The marketing group were the most fun. They had some spark to them, and the rumours were flying for a while when one of their fraternity, Rick Stevens, arrived at work on a Monday morning with his leg in plaster and hobbling on crutches. Unbeknown to Toni and myself, money had been changing hands as people laid bets on whether I would accept Rick's proposal for a night out. I did; we had a great platonic evening, but Rick had an accident on the basketball court the following day. Nobody believed him! I was never again invited out on a date by a member of The Nestlé Company.

Rick was barely off his crutches when our next piece of excitement came along. The Round The World yachts had arrived in town, among them the Swiss entry *Disque D'Or*, for whom naturally the contact base was Nestlé. The company provided their dried food, Nescafé, Milo, chocolates, and an office from which they could send telexes and make telephone calls.

For the three weeks that the yacht was in port, neither Toni nor I slept more than four hours each night. We partied on the boat, we partied in our homes, we partied in other people's homes. Francis (the co-skipper) barely drank, in deference to me but also because he said he didn't like to. John Potter, my new boss, was incredibly patient with me, as I arrived each morning having obviously had an exhausting night in more ways than one. I never asked him, as I never felt it appropriate to, but I wondered whether he was sympathetic to all I had lived through during John's illness, and maybe was pleased that I was finding that living and life could have meaning again. Whatever the reason, I was extremely grateful for his tolerance and for his understanding of the aftermath — when the yachts departed on their next leg, I was shattered.

All I could think and talk about was Francis. He had become an obsession with me that was all-consuming. Again I could not eat as my appetite had genuinely disappeared, and I started to lose weight which I could ill afford to do. I wrote to him, and the letters were returned unopened; I tried to find his telephone number, but to no avail. He monopolized every conversation in which I attempted to engage, and nothing and nobody could rid me of this obsession that I had developed. Luckily, what I did have were my friends, and what friends they were.

With extraordinary regularity throughout my life, as I have kept participating in those meetings with my alcoholic friends, sooner or later I have heard what I needed to hear someone say when I am in a particular situation and don't know what to do. It is in the *doing* that I have found I can change, so long as I hold on to three values: the honesty to acknowledge that I need to change; an open mind to hear what I must do; and a willingness to do whatever needs to be done. Simple — but often far from easy. 'Pain comes from hanging on, not from letting go,' I heard. It was what

I needed to hear. That door was closed in my life; I had to stop beating my fists against it, live with the pain until it subsided, and use my energy elsewhere.

It was only a matter of weeks before a dramatic change in my focus occurred. Captain Robinson, Peter Sutherland and I spent many hours over the subsequent months and years attempting to discover a way in which to deal with the Navy attitudes and the alcohol-related problems, which they recognized were far greater than were being acknowledged by the majority of those at the top of the chain of command.

I discovered not only an interest but an enthusiasm in my life that I had not felt for a long time. My vacation time from Nestlé was now spent in the United States around the naval alcohol and drug rehabilitation centres, talking with the personnel involved in the area of addiction. Joe Pursch let me spend time at the Long Beach Naval Hospital to experience how the treatment centre operated. Some of my alcoholic friends introduced me to Hal Marley of the State Department in Washington, who arranged for me to meet with personnel at the Pentagon. A year later, Commander Jere Bunn was conducting me on a tour of the San Diego Naval Alcohol and Drug Training and Rehabilitation Centre, describing a programme that had been operating for nearly fifteen years.

I was hooked. I *knew* this was what I wanted to do, and where I needed to do it. I was tired of sitting behind a typewriter, tired of trying to discover places in New Zealand that offered quality training for addiction counselling, tired of talking to social and welfare workers who could not envisage as I could that we in New Zealand were heading for addiction problems to a range of chemicals apart from alcohol, and totally frustrated at the condescending and patronizing attitude of some of the academics who were operating from the neck up and would not have recognized an alcoholic unless they had fallen over one — and that one would be in their image of the man with the brown paper bag in the gutter. There were a few, a handful, who were supportive and encouraging: among them Kim Conway and Gordon Nicholson in Auckland, Tom Maling and Robert Crawford from Hanmer Springs in the South Island, and unreservedly my long-term friend Frazer McDonald.

I had no idea how I, as a New Zealand civilian, was going to be permitted to enter a United States Naval facility for training, but what I had learnt over the years since I had stopped drinking was that asking for help usually turned up people who would be willing to do so. I was not to be disappointed. Captain Peter Robinson wrote to Brigadier Brian McMachon, Director General of Defence Medical Services in Wellington, who wrote the following:

> This letter is to introduce Mrs Jamieson, who has for the last four years been of great assistance to the New Zealand Armed Forces and the Royal New Zealand Navy in particular in drawing attention to, and assisting in the setting up of, programmes relating to our endeavours to control alcohol abuse and addiction. She has monitored the literature, provided us with reports of the seminars she has attended and generally stimulated us in the preparation of our policies relating to alcohol.

This was followed by a set of travel orders explaining that I was 'a consultant in alcohol education and rehabilitation for the New Zealand Ministry of Defence . . . She is responsible for her own expenses on a per diem basis.'

I panicked. What was I doing? Here I was in a secure job, with a top secretarial salary from an international company, a member of their pension scheme, with a mortgage-free home, a car and loving friends — and I was contemplating entering a military training programme on the other side of the world! I started asking people around me what I should do. My father almost had another fit of apoplexy. My mother suggested it was 'my decision'. Most of my friends told me that I had not dealt with John's death and I was doing a 'geographical', in other words running away; and Frazer McDonald said, 'I think you should go.'

Rosie was not sure she would survive without me, but I told her that I thought the postal and telephone services were operating quite well across the Pacific. Father told me not to call him when I ran out of money. A married couple I knew were looking for a new place to rent (that took care of the house), a girl at Nestlé bought my car, and John Potter, my boss, wrote a note on my resignation present which concluded with the words 'with thanks to an excellent secretary but a lousy typist!'

Excited, optimistic and terrified, I felt the surge of the aircraft as it left the tarmac and I began to wing my way towards an unknown but unparalleled great adventure.

Chapter 15

Every girl loves a sailor

I am convinced that the mass sigh of relief exhaled as I left New Zealand was enough to blow at least one naval frigate across the Waitemata Harbour. However, little did the élite realize that, like McArthur, I had vowed to return.

There is no way you can live in California without a car and, of course, a driving licence, but to acquire the latter requires venturing onto the freeways. I could not recall being more terrified as I set forth on what seemed to me to be a public raceway. Six lanes one way, six lanes the other, with spaghetti loops every few miles. I was sitting in the driver's seat on the wrong side of the car, on the wrong side of the road. Everything was back-to-front — the gear lever, the rear-vision mirror, the seat, the road lanes, the roundabouts. Pedestrians had right of way. I could turn right at a red light if nothing was bearing down on me from the left, and the slow lane was my fast lane — or perhaps it was my fast lane that was the slow lane! I passed the test in my orange Pinto, but this did not alleviate the terror that stalked me for weeks every time I ventured onto that race track. However, there was (and still is) a mitigating factor: the average American driver would allow me to make any move providing I indicated with my lights what I was doing. Within a month, I put rubber to the road on the Los Angeles freeway — *that* was a real adrenalin rush!

My room in the Bachelor Officers' Quarters (BOQ) was sparse but comfortable, and I came to make great friends with Dan, a gay, African-American ex-cocaine addict who had the day shift at reception. A very courageous man, he had dealt with all three prejudices against him from many in society, and was now finding an amazing fulfilment in his life by helping others who faced similar rejections. I came to believe that he was probably employed where he was to see how many people still had any issues around those factors themselves.

The Administration, Training and Advisors Course was not difficult for me, apart from the fact that I had to translate all the American 'enlisted' ranks into our 'rating' ranks, and learn their rules and regulations around alcohol consumption and other disciplinary measures. The US Navy had dry ships (no alcohol on board or to be consumed on board), unlike the British and New Zealand Navies which not only permitted alcohol on board, but — in the case of the latter — had the traditional tot of rum. The majority of people on the course with me were non-commissioned officers, i.e. petty officers or middle management, and higher-ranking enlisted men and women. They were first of all fascinated with my accent, and secondly amazed at the information about the rum tot. Did I think that when a New Zealand ship hit port, the crew did not get into trouble in bars? I disagreed: of course they did. Then they found it unbelievable that there was no programme such as the one the US Navy had for people with drinking and drug problems. (In the US Navy at this time, the early 1980s, a commissioned officer with an alcohol-related infringement was given one chance; but caught under the influence of drugs, including marijuana, was immediately court-marshalled out. An enlisted man was given one chance with alcohol and one with drugs, and then court-marshalled out.)

We had a variety of personalities in the large group, around thirty of us, and of course there was one pain-in-the-neck. Chuck was a know-it-all petty officer who continually challenged the two instructors. None of his interjections was constructive. He thought the curriculum needed changes, he was opposed to any self-disclosure as he considered his and his family's life to be no one else's business, and was there because his commander had ordered him to go. By the last day, I had had enough. I was a foreign civilian with no US military rank, so I told hi to 'put a sock in it!' A leaf could have been heard falling in the room, and I believe this was the final qualification I needed to enter the Institute of Alcohol Studies (IAS), undergoing gruelling counsellor training that was to leave me a stripped, exhausted survivor. Washington later compelled changes to be made to this programme, as there were too many casualties who were either 'deselected' or opted out of their own accord, unable to cope with the psychological pressure.

I entered the IAS training half a day late. I had been given the wrong time on my 'Navy Order' sheet, and proved it by waving the piece of paper at an obstreperous marine; this did not endear me to him at all. The other trainees were already seated in the room as I made my flounced entrance. There were four naval personnel (including a four-striper who I was to discover was a Navy pilot), two from the Army, two from the Marines, and me! I had a strange sensation that the following weeks were not going to be easy! Nor were they; and I have been fortunate never to have needed to repeat that harrowing, grinding experience again.

As with anything in life, no one can have any idea of what an experience entails unless one has been through it. This US Navy counsellor training programme had to be the toughest available anywhere in the world at this time. Anyone can acquire information — for example, history can be a self-taught subject from sufficient books — but to be able to confront any military officer and break down his or her denial system around drinking takes skill and tenacity in addition to knowledge. All addictions are diseases of denial, and the disease will get worse, never better, if left untreated. My own past had taught me that, so I needed no convincing on that score. However, the first requirement for a successful counsellor is that they have dealt with their own prejudices, grief, anger, and any other garbage from the past. How can I possibly help you if you are gay and I am homophobic?

Our trainers had been handpicked by the programme's manager, a small, wiry, charismatic man whose eyes bored through into the depths of my psyche. Instinctively, I liked and trusted him. Among his staff were a Navy psychologist, a Marine psychodramatist and a Navy clergyman (I always suspected this last was there to pick up the pieces). Somehow, I and four others (including the captain, but not the two Marines) survived the emotional and psychological hammering that was necessary to ensure we had the strength to deal with the people who would be placed in our path. We practised C.C. GRIPES until we could almost demonstrate it under hypnosis! Concreteness, Confrontation, Genuineness, Respect, Immediacy, Empathy and Self-disclosure; and if we had to choose between Genuineness and Respect, Genuineness won every time.

We did have our break times, some structured, some not, where I learnt that even military personnel are human! There were dances and social evenings at Camp Pendleton, the Marine base between San Diego and Los Angeles, barbecues with the other trainees' families, trips across the border to Mexico, and every morning during the week an hour of physical fitness before breakfast — another requirement for staying the distance of the course. If a trainee did not pass the physical fitness test, then they were 'deselected'. Running within a time limit was not a problem, press-ups were not a problem — but pulling myself up on a bar so that my chin was over the top not once but *six* times (twelve for the men) was! At exam time I nearly throttled myself on the last heave; there was no second chance.

In the final weeks of training, my presence started to cause problems for the training establishment. Although I had all the official letters, travel orders and other documents required to participate in the course, I was nevertheless a civilian from a country which was part of the ANZUS agreement — and politically this agreement was on ground that was starting to become shaky due to New Zealand's growing resistance to nuclear ships and the nuclear armaments which the US Navy never confirmed or denied they were carrying. Placing me in any position dealing with personnel who were privy to confidential information was high-risk, for under pressure, or in a fit of anger, it was possible that disclosures could be made which could have repercussions. The question arose as to what to do with me. I could be an embarrassment to the Navy's training programme if I did not complete the course, so I needed to do my practical — but how? I had not only stirred up a hornets' nest in the New Zealand Navy, but now I was in danger of repeating the process with the US Navy.

There was no way they wanted a political incident on their hands. The solution was found: I would complete the NADSAP (Navy Alcohol and Drug Safety Action Program) course, as there was a low security risk in the facilitation of this programme, but my counselling skills would still be monitored. NADSAP had a thirty-six-hour curriculum developed by the Human Sciences Department of the University of Arizona. The programme had originated in the early 1970s as an alcohol safety programme under the auspices of Commander Jere Bunn, but had grown, developed and been refined over the years, as it was found necessary to include drugs other than alcohol in the curriculum. (It has since undergone further revision and name changes, and is now known as the United States Navy's Substance Abuse Education and Prevention Program.)

The trainers for this course were not Naval personnel, but (mainly) civilians from the University of Arizona. I formed a lasting friendship over the following months with Sara, one of the facilitators, and after my graduation from the IAS course she had a great idea. The mother of one of her room-mates was attempting to find a lodger, and Sara believed she could match us up. Having finished the course and working part-time as a facilitator, it was no longer permissible for me to be living at the BOQ, yet I still needed to increase my practical experience by attending classes at the base, particularly in group work.

I was drawn to Anita within five minutes of our 'interview'. A fifty-year-old New Yorker, originally from Brooklyn, she was in the middle of divorce proceedings against a highly intelligent San Diego State University faculty member whose alcoholism she was no longer able to tolerate. Her smile was as broad as the Mississippi River at its widest point. She was articulate and funny, with an energy and a turn of phrase that at once endeared her to me. Even after her suggestion that I might like to consider one of her friends' places for rent nearer the beach, I was convinced that I wanted to know her better. I moved in, and we have remained the closest of friends ever since, sharing travelling experiences together, and the funny and sad moments in both our lives.

My voluminous correspondence with New Zealand agencies, including the Defence Department and the Alcohol Liquor Advisory Council (ALAC), had not ceased while I was in the States, although it had reduced during my training. So the wedding of my youngest sister, Georgina, in November 1984 was a good excuse to return to New Zealand to investigate areas and organizations that might be interested in employing me. Many people replied to the letters that preceded my departure from the States; all of them interested in my achievements and grateful for the work I was doing and the information I was feeding them, but none of them able or prepared to find any finances to help me offset the 20,000-odd dollars it had cost me thus far.

Some people were helpful. Kim Conway in particular, at Eden Clinic at the time, was extremely supportive, finding moments in her busy schedule to keep me up to date with all that was happening. John Robertson, chairman of ALAC, and Dr Robert Crawford, Superintendent of Queen Mary Hospital in Hanmer Springs, also took time to relay relevant information to me.

I was excited and optimistic as I headed back home, anticipating a wealth of opportunities opening up for me so that, on my return to the States, I could tie up any loose ends and then leave to contribute the results of all my hard work to various areas in New

Zealand. After all, I had completed training in administration and advisory roles, I was a trained counsellor and facilitator, and the US Navy's NADSAP was not only an employee assistance programme (EAP), but it was also accepted by the City of San Diego (with its large military population) as a first-conviction drinking-driving programme. I had also completed the San Diego State University's twelve-hour Drinking Driving Facilitator Training Programme, including a session of 'practical work' — riding with the San Diego Police Department for a night as they apprehended and arrested drinking drivers, most of whom vomited in the car before we got them back to the cells. (Regurgitated Mexican burritos are *disgusting*, and the ride was even worse with the windows open: I nearly froze to death!)

Kim had advised me that the 'impaired driving' area was 'a real mess'. The Ministry of Transport and the Health Department were trying to do it 'on the cheap', but treatment services around the country were saying that they were 'not going to comply with legislation because a doctor has to sign the assessment form, which they regard as unethical and impractical, and because there is no requirement for treatment or extra money available for treatment services'. Kim went on to say: 'we've been suggesting they set up special programmes for drivers convicted of drinking offences, but there seems to be no way they'll entertain the idea . . . ALAC has given up trying to influence the MOT and Health Department which is where the problem lies.'

Peter Robinson, the Navy doctor, was cautious but optimistic: 'Defence Council Order 76 has not been updated, so initially there has been no change in the Armed Forces attack upon the problem,' he wrote. 'It would appear that there is certainly no intention at this stage to set up any form of Tri-Service alcohol/ drug Rehabilitation Centre. Your expertise would be of great value to us . . . I would certainly look forward to seeing you on your return.' A letter from Surgeon Commodore Tony Slark at Defence Headquarters in Wellington, in which he stated 'I shall look forward to your visit back to New Zealand when we can discuss the possible work that would be helpful to the Defence Department', also encouraged me as I winged my way home full of enthusiasm.

Frazer MacDonald had asked that I send a short press release to him, which I compiled as follows:

Mrs Elizabeth Jamieson, who has just returned from 10 months in the United States, is a woman totally dedicated to her work in the field of Alcohol and Drug Abuse. At her own personal expense she became the first New Zealander to attend and complete all the United States Navy's alcoholism and drug addiction training/administration/counselling and education programmes. Mrs Jamieson has also accomplished several other firsts in this area — the first New Zealander to be employed in the United States Navy's Substance Abuse Prevention and Education Program, dealing mainly with those convicted of drinking driving offences, and the first New Zealander and first international member of the United States National Council on Alcoholism.

In addition to her United States Navy involvement she also attended many civilian workshops and seminars. Mrs Jamieson met with a wide variety of personnel who specialise in such areas as Women and Addiction, Drinking Driving Education Programmes, Adolescent Education in Alcohol and Drug Abuse as well as occupational programmes for substance abuse in general.

Her purpose in attending the various United States Navy's alcohol and drug abuse schools, which are recognised to be the best in the world, was to gain first-hand knowledge and experience from these schools. The principles taught are adaptable world-wide to suit particular national requirements. With the basic training and principles Mrs Jamieson is hopeful of finding how the two countries could continue to co-operate and work together in the sharing of experience and information to the mutual benefit of all concerned.

Currently she is working as a group counsellor in the United States Navy's Substance Abuse Education and Prevention Program at the San Diego site in California and will return to that job following her home visit. [This programme] is taught on a worldwide basis at 160 locations from Holy Loch, Scotland to Subic Bay, Philippines; from Jacksonville, Florida to Okinawa, Japan. The University of Arizona, under contract to the United States Navy, is the current [programme] provider with over 1400 persons on the payroll. She has proved as a New Zealander and a civilian that this programme is capable of teaching and reaching all nationalities. She is convinced that people from all nations can meet in this area without political differences which normally separate us. That there is a common purpose which allows co-operation and communication internationally in combating drug abuse of all kinds which threatens the people and the future of the free world. The Navy funds these sites on an international basis using, in addition to Naval personnel, local personnel trained to teach the programme.

At present Mrs Jamieson is in New Zealand to meet with officials at both Government and Military of Defence level. In addition, she will confer with those New Zealanders in the Alcoholism/Drug Addiction field so she can make the most of her time when she returns to the United States for a period to continue her practical experience. It is her ultimate goal to return home and become a part of the team of already dedicated professionals here in New Zealand.

He believed it would help to open a few doors during the time I was back.

I travelled the country for six weeks at my own expense. I wrote proposals for the Ministry of Transport and the Ministry of Defence for an education programme for first-conviction drinking drivers and for alcohol misuse and abuse in the armed forces. There were goals and objectives, specific aims, suggestions as to participants and to how the programme could be partly funded by the participants themselves. I noted that when the US Navy had surveyed their programme (NADSAP), they found a recidivism rate of 10 per cent, the San Diego County Programme having a rate of 33 per cent. The Navy also noted that 52 per cent of those convicted on first-offence drinking-driving charges would re-offend within a year if they did not complete the Education Prevention Programme.

I met with representatives from the Ministry of Transport, ALAC, and the defence forces; I spoke with Community Alcoholism Services in Auckland, the Salvation Army, Presbyterian Support Services, and numerous other agencies and services. They were all delighted with my accomplishments, appreciated the avalanche of material I had provided for them, agreed to consider where I would fit in or how they could use me, but could offer nothing concrete. By the end of the fifth week, I was tired, frustrated, irritable and wanting to hear someone say 'Great, Liz, come back tomorrow and we will see how we can start something rolling.' Instead, I got a call from Murray Deaker — a call that would change both our lives. 'Liz, I need your help.'

Murray had had a public career in drinking similar to mine, although in a different arena, and like me he had stopped and pulled his life together. We had met over the years at varying times through mutual friends, and he and my late husband John had shared a similar verbal agility and sense of humour. Murray had a woman friend who he believed should meet me, as he was suspicious that she had a drinking problem. The three of us sat outside at a wooden table with our coffee, and must have talked for at least an hour. Whether I made any impression on her or not I will never know, but I certainly did on Murray.

I told him I was leaving to return to the States the following week, as I could find no employment in New Zealand, and so I would apply for an extension on my visa to continue gaining experience under the auspices of the University of Arizona. I was not prepared to beat my head against brick walls in New Zealand, when I could enjoy my work and gain a wealth of experience in California. I was also convinced that what was happening in the alcohol and drug scene in California would be happening in many other places in the world sooner rather than later. Not only had AIDS just arrived, but San Diego was dealing with a new substance, and a rather frightening one at that. Known by several names, the labs in which it was manufactured — mostly trailer (caravan) parks and motels — often exploded when some of the highly flammable chemicals used to produce it caught fire. The substance was methamphetamine — crystal, crank and the smokeable form 'ice'. I was about to return to New Zealand's future.

I also had another reason to return to the States — it was a place where my work was appreciated. A few months before my departure, I had received the following:

> It is a great pleasure to inform you that you are the recipient of the 'Naval Alcoholism Rehabilitation Center Humanitarian Award'.
>
> This award is given in recognition of your unselfish and untiring efforts in the field of alcoholism prevention education. At your expense you sought out and obtained extensive education in the field of alcoholism counselling and prevention education. You

are the only non-USA citizen to have ever attended and graduated from all three of the U.S. Navy's substance abuse/alcoholism orientated schools, to wit:

Institute for Substance Abuse (ISAS) — 10 weeks
Alcoholism Administration, Training and Advisor School (ATA) — 2 weeks
Navy Substance Abuse Prevention Program (NASAPP) — 36 hours

In addition you were selected to participate in facilitator training for NASAPP and after a period of arduous training/supervision, you were designated as a 'NASAPP Group Facilitator'.

Thus in recognition of your most outstanding efforts you will be presented with the NARC Humanitarian Award, 8 June 1984, at the NARC San Diego, California. The award will be presented by the Honorable Duncan L. Hunter, Congressman of the United States for the Forty-Fifth District of California. He is a member of the House of Representatives 'Select Committee on Narcotics Abuse and Control'. I am looking forward to seeing you.
Sincerely
Stephen F Chappell
Captain, U.S. Navy
Commanding Officer

This letter stunned and excited me. It stunned me because I had no idea the Navy thought so highly of my 'adventure', for that is how I saw the whole experience; and it excited me because I thought 'Now people in New Zealand will want me, I can be useful.'

The eighth of June was a glorious summer day. The Naval personnel were in their dress 'whites', the Marines more sombre in their khaki, and, as I sat on the dais in my pale-pink silk dress and blue hat with blue and pink roses, there was an enormous lump in my throat, and tears in my eyes that blurred the scene before me. The medals and the gold braid along the front two rows danced in the sunlight, the commanding officer and the congressman sat either side of me, and overhead the American and New Zealand flags fluttered in the sea breeze. From the many messages of congratulation received by the commanding officer, only three telegrams were read out: one from Peter Robinson, the New Zealand Navy Surgeon General; one from Prime Minister Robert Muldoon; and one from Sir David Beattie, New Zealand Governor General. The award read:

> To Elizabeth A.S. Jamieson:
>
> For exceptional commitment to the field of substance abuse, and for extreme personal sacrifice in the interest of gaining knowledge and experience for the betterment of the lives of her countrymen. At her own expense she sought out and obtained extensive education in the field of alcoholism counselling and prevention education. Her unselfish and untiring efforts in the field of alcoholism prevention education have been truly remarkable.

I heard the acknowledgements, although my own thoughts were louder. Past memories flooded in: of the people who had helped me through life, the places I had been to and escaped from, and the things that I thought had been so important and now were no longer so. From a psychiatric ward to where I sat seemed a lifetime away — and it was. A lifetime of joy, pain, acceptance, and an unshakeable belief that there was a purpose to my life and that this day was only a part of it. God had plans for me that I did not know about. What I *did* know was that I was doing the work I loved, and loving the work I was doing.

Hopefully *someone* would want me back home, but in the meantime I would keep building my credentials, my friendships and my experiences in the Californian sunshine.

Chapter 16

California girl

When Winston Churchill gave a prize-giving speech at his old school, Harrow, his words were ones no boy could ever forget. He spoke for all of sixty seconds: 'Never give up,' he boomed. 'Never, ever give up; never, ever, ever, ever give up.' Then he sat down. Churchill is one of my heroes, and his words have remained with me during all my years of growth and learning.

I continued my work with the US Navy's NASAPP programme that had evolved from NADSAP, honing my skills. I was supervised on a regular basis by University of Arizona staff to ensure that my facilitating was up to standard. If it hadn't been, I would have been stood down and put through a process to discover what in my own life was interfering with those skills. Programme classes took me to El Centro, where the crack pilots in the Blue Angels are based, to the Submarine Base on Point Loma (Navy Seals), and onto the ships and aircraft carriers of the Pacific Fleet based in San Diego. I learnt to facilitate classes of enlisted men, Marines, and one never-to-be-forgotten class of male petty officers.

These petty officers were *not* a happy bunch. They were not happy to be spending a week participating in a thirty-six-hour-long primary prevention course on substance abuse; they were not happy that it was a foreign civilian who was conducting the course; and they were *certainly* not happy that this was a woman! They *had* to attend; they had been commanded to do so. How did they object? With the silent treatment.

I called the roll. No one answered, so I stated that, since I had ten persons present and there were ten on the roll, I presumed they were all there. I did all the talking that day, which was not how the course was meant to be conducted — I was supposed to facilitate *their* communication. At 1600 hours (4 p.m.), I told them I would be back the next day (I learnt later that not one of them believed I would be).

At 0800 hours the following day, I took the roll. All present. (At least they answered the roll this time!) Then I said: 'OK guys, let me tell you the drill. I'm on board for the rest of the day. I will be back again tomorrow, and the day after, and the day after that, because I'm being paid and I need to eat and pay rent. On Friday, I will be submitting a form as to your behaviour — not what you have said, but your behaviour — to my site co-ordinator. This will be passed in turn to your command. You either co-operate and have the consequences, or don't and have the consequences. Your choice. Now, we'll have a five-minute coffee refill break while you decide.' I was *not* having them run me off that ship.

Every one of those men graduated with a certificate of completion, but what was of real interest to me were the various anonymous remarks that they wrote on their evaluation forms. Two of them had Post-It notes attached with requests for a date!

Each class of enlisted men was a challenge; often humorous, ribald and poignant, but never boring. Many were off the streets of places like Los Angeles and had run away to sea from unhappy lives. Others were following a family tradition because earlier family members had been to sea; yet others had entered the Navy to learn skills; and some, often the children of immigrants, to better themselves. Most wanted to see the world and have fun. Some brought me bunches of flowers at the end of the class, others wanted to write to me, and nearly all would be out in the parking lot to mend my car if there was anything that needed fixing. Not only did they come from all walks of life, but from an amazing mix of cultures: Puerto Ricans, African-Americans, Philippinos, American Indians, Mexicans, red-neck Americans from the South, and wise-cracking New Yorkers from the North. They came with their own attitudes, beliefs, prejudices and experiences, a real liquorice allsorts of life. Brazen, curious, sceptical and fearful, by the end of the week they had made discoveries about themselves that they found challenging and exciting. My job was to guide them through this process so that hopefully they could discover whether alcohol or other substances were interfering in their lives. I was also responsible for recommending that they either return to command, or be referred to an outpatient programme or a more intensive residential treatment.

I have no idea how many lives this programme has saved, as NASAPP has been operating on numerous US Navy bases world-wide. I do know of at least one. He was obstreperous from the beginning, and only my instinct allowed me to permit him to stay for the full length of the course; but at completion I recommended inpatient treatment for him. He was furious, and vowed that once he got out he was going to find me — I was 'in for it'. Not a pleasant thought, but over the following weeks, with more classes, more people, more recommendations, I forgot about him. Until one night.

Sara and Di, two of my facilitator friends, had invited me for dinner at a Mexican restaurant, where one of them suggested we call in at the local NA (Narcotics Anonymous) dance being held that night. I had never had that experience before, so I agreed, slightly apprehensively, to accompany them, not having the vaguest idea of what I was in for. The place looked like a 'sixties dance hall, once we got past the bouncers on the door: strobe lights, dark corners, an enormous wooden floor, gyrating bodies, ear-splitting music, and Coke and 7Up cans littering the long trestle tables. 'No one here is either stoned or out of it,' Sara yelled in my ear. 'The only way they can get in is the way we did. Those guys on the door have done time — they can smell a user a mile away!' I just stood as though my feet were stuck in concrete; I found it hard to believe that they were all clean and sober, but realized cynicism was not going to endear me to any of them.

I drank more 7Up than I intended, and on my way back across the empty dance floor to join the others to leave, my heart suddenly missed a beat, my mouth went dry and I could feel my skin start to crawl. There, walking towards me, was the 'in for it' guy. I stopped, rooted to the floor. My eyes darted around looking for an escape route, but it was useless: he was already close enough for me to feel his breath on my face, and his arms had mine pinned to my sides. As the pressure intensified, I heard the crack in his voice as he whispered, 'Thank you for saving my life.' For probably another three seconds he held me in the hug, and then turned and disappeared into the crowd on the other side of the room. Perhaps I could have found out what had happened to him over the months, but somehow I just wanted to let it be.

It was yet another lesson in the joy to be experienced from having the ability to play a part in another's life of change. There truly is a beauty and a miracle in being alive, made even more so for me when again and again I see evidence, in my own life and in others', of the results of practising empathy, compassion and, sometimes, tough love. I was slowly discovering how I could contribute to, rather than subtract from, others' lives. Life had meaning.

Meanwhile, Anita had not been entertained on such a scale in years, and her three sons became extremely protective of me, as my life started to stretch to unmanageable proportions — and all to do with men!

There was Juan, the Mexican Marine who took me to open-air concerts; and John, an Employee Assistant Co-ordinator (he was dumped because the boys thought he could be 'an abuser waiting to happen'). Then there was Keith, my 'sugar daddy', who took me to lunch at his golf club in La Jolla; Larry, who lived in Waxahachie, Texas, and was a divorced officer on one of the ships; and Paddy (Irish, of course). Like me, Paddy did not drink and he had a history as chequered as mine. He was separated from his wife, had three sons and owned a BMW motorbike. I had never ridden a motorbike in my life. That was all about to change! I bought leather pants and black boots, a white jacket with reflector stripes, and leather gloves; Paddy provided the passenger helmet. To gain my learner's licence as a pillion rider, we took to the side streets around Point Loma near the submarine base, graduated to the city streets, and finally hit the freeway. It was months before I could send my mother a photograph — not because I needed her approval (that had been long gone as an issue), but because I did not want her having sleepless nights over imagined escapades. It never occurred to me until later that nothing could have surpassed her insomnia during my drinking days.

Paddy and I saw Bisbee in Arizona and San Antonio in Texas; we drove up the coast to Monterey and Carmel, as far north as Mendocino, and south to Rosarito in Mexico. Paddy taught me fun, freedom and a certain high-risk craziness that liberated me in a way I had never experienced before. This life was a far cry from the rigidity of boarding-school days and the eternal need to keep up appearances in the social scene of Remuera. There was no way it could last, but the shock was still unexpected when it came.

Paddy and his wife decided to give their marriage one more chance, and so I went over one Saturday morning to pack up my few clothes from the cupboard and drawers in his room. I arrived back at Anita's that afternoon in a state of shock. I had become totally addicted to the excitement, the adventure and the craziness of Paddy's lifestyle, and I started to have withdrawal symptoms. I cried, I could not sleep, I was angry; I could not erase Paddy from my mind. When the postman left a packet at the front door with Paddy's handwriting on the label, I had to have Anita open it. Inside was a note saying: 'You left this.' It was my vibrator!

Anita swore she would nail him to the door if she ever found him. One son, Terry, quipped that at least now they would not have to climb through the window to enter the house (the bike used to be parked in the front porch); another son, Michael, was wonderfully empathetic; and Lee was my shadow as much as he could be.

Lee had been a regular marijuana user for some years, and soon after I started living at the house he had arrived back from an extensive trip through Europe. When he discovered why I was in the States and the nature of my work, initially he avoided me; then he became curious, and finally started questioning me. Were there any effects from using; any withdrawal symptoms? He had difficulty sleeping, had bad nightmares and vivid dreams, could not remember words that he knew were familiar, and found that he would seesaw from anger to depression and back again without knowing what he was angry about. Gradually over the weeks, as he came to trust me, there were other symptoms he talked about. Night sweats and clammy hands, sometimes stomach cramps after eating, diarrhoea, restlessness, lack of concentration, irritability when more than one person was talking, coughing up phlegm; and finally, although his sex drive had increased when he'd initially started smoking, he was now concerned that he was having difficulty 'getting it up'. 'How about paranoia?' I asked. 'Oh, most of the time' came his reply.

Lee was courageous enough to decide that he would like to set himself a goal of six months without using cannabis. I warned him that although it could be simple it was not easy, and that he needed to live each day of the six months on a daily basis. I could help him. I could not do it *for* him, but I would do it *with* him. Over the next weeks I shared some of my story around my struggles with alcohol, how I had stopped and stayed stopped, the wonderful philosophy for life I had discovered by mixing with other ex-drinkers, and that his life would change dramatically but that it would take time.

I helped him through the night sweats, and for a while the daytime sweats, as his body detoxed. I suggested he had baths rather than showers, as they would help the emotions to relax as well as the body; that he drink plenty of water and cranberry juice, and, because the sweating would deplete his body of potassium, that he eat melons, tomatoes, bananas and green vegetables, all of which are high in that mineral. He returned to his basketball and his tennis; his whole life started to change. Today, Lee is a highly successful attorney, married with two children.

At the time of the Paddy furore, however, what concerned Lee was that I might drink again. But I had made many recovering alcoholic friends in San Diego during my sojourn, and because I saw several of them on a regular basis, I had no desire to drown my emotions. I had learnt that there was always a way to deal with an emotion — I just had to find it. Once again, I heard the solution one night: 'The person I was angry at owned me. *I* was the container that was being eroded, not her.' I came to understand that, yet again, I was being forced to accept a situation that I could not change — but I could change my attitude.

When Paddy decided that he wanted to renew our relationship, it was too late: Shane was on the scene. Shane was a tall, lanky Texan with a drawl to match. Terry was beside himself. He now envisaged a *horse* at the front door instead of a motorbike, but he was to be spared — saved by a letter. The letter was from Murray Deaker.

There must have been some extremely angry and resentful members of both the Education Department and various colleges of education when, in 1984, Murray was awarded the Woolf Fisher Fellowship. This was to enable him to visit the United States, Canada and Britain, accompanied by his wife, to examine what was happening around drug and alcohol education in schools. Many in the Department and the colleges would have felt that it was *their* prerogative to go.

Initially, Murray treated it as a holiday; but he rapidly discovered that, although as a deputy principal he had helped clean up Takapuna Grammar from early substance abuse, he and certainly New Zealand were still in kindergarten with regard to what was looming on the horizon for New Zealand schools. He could see that liberalism, political correctness and individuals' rights — with no mention of individuals' responsibilities — had joined with a breakdown in discipline to open the way for massive drug and alcohol problems in overseas schools. And these same clouds were gathering above New Zealand. On his return, a fifty-eight-page report was sent by him to all of the appropriate agencies and departments. Not only did *not one of them* reply, but they also ignored his follow-up letter. Murray was determined to do something. He gathered his support.

In 1985, he set up New Zealand's Foundation for Alcohol and Drug Education (FADE), with a board that certainly impressed me: among them was the Superintendent of Northern Region Education, the principal of Auckland Grammar School, a Rhodes Scholar, the advertising manager of *The New Zealand Herald*, a psychologist, a lawyer, the detective in charge of Auckland Drug Squad, and my old friend Chris Innes. And I received this:

> The reason I am writing is to offer you a job, to start a New Zealand Adolescent Substance Abuse and Education Centre. You would head the Foundation . . . you would be stationed in Auckland and select your own staff. Be assured I have the finance organised . . .

It was another year before I returned home. A year of conferences and speaking engagements, accumulating of curriculum content and policies, listening to teachers and counsellors (what worked and had not worked in their experience), and saying my farewells to people from New York to San Francisco. Finally, with Anita assuring me that I could return to stay at any time, I was on my way to begin another set of life-changing experiences that could never have been imagined. No one, least of all me, could have envisaged that within four years I would be in a maximum security prison.

∾

Chapter 17

A new job and a new face

I had anticipated the spotlight being focused on me, but not the whole *bank* of floodlights that switched on within weeks of my arrival in Auckland. Murray Deaker had used his charismatic public relations flair to ensure that not only Auckland but the entire country knew of my arrival and of FADE's school project. I was the person who was to place FADE on the map, show up the incompetence of the education establishment in continuing to procrastinate instead of addressing the drug and alcohol problems — slowly growing now, not only in the schools but in communities as well — and produce a curriculum that could be used for education in the schools.

The New Zealand Herald had a half-page announcing my arrival, the *New Zealand Women's Weekly* managed two pages on my achievements and plans for schools, and Sue Kellaway interviewed me on television. Jolted out of their apathy, the educational powers-that-be started to become extremely uneasy, but I had no time to concern myself with them. Within three days of my setting foot in the country, Murray had arranged for me to speak at the Annual Secondary School Principals' Conference in Wellington. I have no memory of what I said, but it must have impressed many of the participants, for invitations to speak at schools grew from a trickle to a flood. From Pompallier College in Northland to Scots College in Wellington; from Otaki in the west to Mt Maunganui in the east. The uneasiness of the Education Department and some colleges of education personnel grew as more and more speaking engagements brought a greater awareness to schools and communities that at long last some organization was doing something about the problem *they* knew was growing.

Possibly one of the greatest acknowledgements that FADE received was during an evening at Pakuranga College. The assembly hall had standing room only, with people crammed into the doorways, students sitting cross-legged on the floor in front of the stage, and some people squeezing two to a seat. Murray spoke, I spoke, Detective Inspector Ian Hastings (Officer in Charge of the Drug Squad) spoke; and finally Barbara Divehall, with her knees visibly shaking — she was the only one of the four of us unaccustomed to public speaking — gave the parents a workable answer: *parent support groups*. Barbara had experienced these while in Chicago: parents meeting the parents of their children's friends, and supporting each other in making and holding their children to guidelines and responsibilities while they helped them through the teenage years. We could not have had a greater impact if we had offered everyone a car in imitation of *The Oprah Winfrey Show*. Before Barbara had finished her cup of tea that night her telephone was in dire need of another two lines. PRYDE — Parents Reaching Youth through Drug Education — was born.

FADE now had a formidable team of speakers. I was working with the students during the day and speaking to parent groups at night, often with Barbara and/or Ian Hastings. Wherever we went the media followed, whether it was the small community papers or the local press. The inevitable happened: two officials who were part of the education establishment requested a meeting with some of the FADE personnel. Attempting to attack Murray Deaker, either physically or verbally, has never been a good idea, so their vitriol was aimed at me. This was a huge mistake. Murray is a wordsmith at the best of times, but that afternoon he excelled himself. He defended me down to my last toenail. He vilified the colleges for their apathetic, arrogant ignorance; their failure to even examine what was occurring in schools around the use of (primarily) tobacco, alcohol and marijuana; their refusal to pay attention to the growing problem of marijuana usage and the subsequent damage to young people's still-developing brains; and when they insinuated that they would prevent me from continuing to work in schools, Murray sneeringly suggested that they try.

That meeting was a disaster for the bureaucracy — for all of the twenty years since it took place I have been, and still am, with students in schools. Yet when several years later I gave a five-minute presentation to a conference at the Auckland College of Education, not a single hand was raised when I asked if anyone had ever been to one of my presentations. In the words of British social philosopher Herbert Spencer: 'There is a principle which is a bar against all information, which is proof against all arguments and which cannot fail to keep a man in everlasting ignorance — that principle is contempt prior to investigation' (*Principles of Biology,* London, 1864).

FADE, the Substance Abuse Education Trust (SAET), the Life Education Trust and others have gained credibility from the work they do and the schools in which they work — yet, amazingly, it can still be a struggle to get their voices heard. These groups are prepared to give time and energy; and in the Trust for which I work, this comes at no cost to the schools.

At the end of 1987, I hit the wall. I was travelling the country speaking in schools, *not* (as some Education Department personnel were accusing) as a 'one-off' speaker, but as a back-up to their pitiful health programme at the time. Often students would come and talk with me after school, or there would be an interview with the local media. Sometimes I would barely have a two-hour break before the evening presentation to parents, and being billeted with teachers often meant that they wanted to continue the conversation before bed. I was also attempting to run the FADE office, and the trustees were wanting a curriculum written. I was living on my own, my father was dying of a blood disorder (my parents had moved from the family home to a small unit), and to cap it off Murray and Sharon Hoggard (she a retired primary school teacher and FADE trustee) returned from Australia with the great idea that FADE (read *plus me*) would become involved in setting up Life Education in New Zealand. Aaaaargh! This was a programme for primary schoolchildren, and was way beyond my training and experience.

Two years after I returned to spearhead FADE into the schools, I resigned. There were disappointments, hurts, frustrations, and a fair share of acrimony between me and some of the trustees, but it was impossible for me to fulfil the brief they had set in place. My love and passion, which has lasted twenty-two years, was and still is to work with teenagers at the coalface — in the schools.

My father had died. I was exhausted and disillusioned; frustrated that so many people in government departments and working in the drug and alcohol field were *still* not prepared to listen to those of us — Murray, myself, Ian Hastings, Barbara Divehall and others — who were giving warning of what Murray termed 'the gathering storm'. There was no question in my mind that during my years in the States I had been where we were going; how sadly true this has proven to be. When I first started to explain foetal alcohol syndrome, the only people who would listen were Plunket nurses, who presumably saw it regularly in the course of their work. I was accused by many in the field of coming back with 'all these American ideas'. What complete cultural prejudice. Many of the ideas and solutions I had had been *proved* to be workable in the States. Would they have discounted me in the same fashion if I had come back with possible working solutions for cancer?

I was frustrated, angry and fed up with the continual attacks on my credibility and integrity, the misreporting — and in some cases outright lies of omission from my talks — that appeared in the media, many of them blatantly defending the harmlessness of marijuana. I wonder why? (Some have now, courageously, admitted how wrong they were.) So I made plans to return to the United States. However, I had reckoned without some very decisive people: several school principals and three individuals who were determined to keep me here — Barbara Divehall, Christine Fletcher (future mayor of Auckland and Member of Parliament), and Detective Inspector Ian Hastings. They started making their own plans to ensure that I stayed; but I was too tired to be interested.

Christmas was approaching, and who should reappear in my life but sexy Toni from Nestlé? She now worked for Garuda Airlines, and dropped into the house one evening to see how I was coping with my sudden change in circumstances. Three months previously, she had barely left my side except to go to work after her boyfriend had shot half his face away in a botched suicide attempt. Sitting in Auckland Hospital A&E at 2 a.m. with her holding his hand was only one of many incidents I have sat through during the years. He was a regular user of marijuana who had not been able to cope with the idea of her leaving him — due to his increase in mood swings, his paranoia and his aimless lifestyle.

Toni could no longer live in the apartment in which the incident had occurred, and wanted to know whether I had a spare bed. The following weeks proved to me, once again, how people can unexpectedly enter our lives when we need them.

We shared a number of conversations that led her to the ultimate question: 'Well, why don't you have a face lift?'

'Whaaaat?' was my immediate reaction.

'Well, why not?'

She certainly had a point. Constant purging and vomiting during the bulimarexia years had swollen my face and contributed to an unseemly puffiness, particularly around the eyes. I had time on my hands while I decided what I wanted to do with my life. Georgina, my youngest sister, was in Samoa for two years on a work-related project of her husband's, so I could recuperate with her, and I knew that the only plastic surgeon I would allow to touch me was still practising — just.

Sir William Manchester's name in the plastic surgery world

was legendary, as was his work during World War II in England with burnt bomber pilots. Our family had already experienced his renowned skills when he reconstructed my mother's face after an appalling accident. Trying to save an opened car door from being blown off its hinges, she had fallen, caught her heel in the door frame and been dragged along the road, resulting in massive damage to one side of her head and face. His repairs on her face were a work of art.

Bill, as we knew him (for he was part of my parents' Remuera social group), was about five foot six and probably one of the only men I would truly call 'dapper'. He wore his trademark red rosebud in the top buttonhole of his jacket no matter what hour of the day or night. I sat opposite him, and his eyes bored into me as he asked me what I understood was his standard question: 'Why do you want this done, Elizabeth?'

I gave him my honest, blunt, no-frills answer: 'Because I'm vain, Bill.'

He never blinked an eyelid. 'Good' was his reply. 'I don't know why more women can't be truthful. See my secretary and make an appointment.'

I later learnt several facts about Bill's attitude towards, and actions in, his work. Many of his patients who had been accident-ally scarred, particularly burn patients and those who struggled to find the payment, were charged a bare minimum for his work; he made up the amounts from those he felt could weather the maximum. He worked on some children for no payment at all. Few people knew the compassionate, unassuming and truly humble man he was, a man who worked to his own ethics and who for me is one of the 'great' people I have known. His charges to me were $5000. Mother mentioned later that he believed being able to erase some of the physical consequences of my past would help me in my work.

Arriving at my hospital bed, Toni burst into peals of laughter. All that was visible of me were two slits of eyes; the rest was a swathe of muslin bandaging. Mother refused to look at me for a week, and Ian Hastings was sworn to secrecy (he was still trying to persuade me not to return to the States). Two weeks in Samoa, scaring poor Georgina, who on meeting me off the plane thought I had been drinking again, and another six weeks hiding out in Auckland over the Christmas holidays, and I was recovered, revived and ready for my next foray into 'the system'.

Chapter 18

Never give up

I was persuaded to stay in New Zealand, although Ian, Christine and Barbara probably had more confidence in my ability to make an impact in the substance abuse field than I did.

PRYDE was growing, and now had an office in Christchurch; Barbara needed non-bureaucratic support for the parents with whom she was working. Government agencies had counteracted FADE's and my approach to informing people of the harmful effects of substances by adopting a policy of 'harm reduction, harm minimization and responsible use'. Not only was this confusing for our young people, it was outright dangerous. How can young people be taught to inhale *responsibly?* And as for drinking, not much needs to be said when we have the consequences undeniably in front of us today.

I have enormous respect for some academics, but in the sub-stance abuse field there are some ignorant, dangerous idiots. I remember hearing one prominent Sydney psychiatrist, who was an advocate of harm reduction, speaking at a conference about heroin addicts being 'drug free' when on the methadone programme — methadone is a *drug!* In the 1980s, many of these people never took the development of the human brain into consideration. Our brain cells do not fully mature, physically, until we are in our early twenties; nor are all the various tree-like connections finalized until then. Teenagers and young people do not have brains that function in the same way as *adult* brains. Their perspective on life is different, and among other beliefs is the one 'It will never happen to me.' Among a raft of other facts some of these academics simply failed to understand are the physiological effects of many abused substances, and what the long-term consequences of an individual's usage could be.

I took stock again of what was facing us, not only in schools but throughout the country as a whole, relating it to the future as demonstrated by the United States. San Diego in the early 1980s was the methamphetamine capital of the world, marijuana was increasing in potency and usage and was rife in schools, and schools there were attempting to repair the incredible damage that had been done by the liberalism that had swamped them in the 1970s. This was where we were heading.

Ian, Christine and retired bank manager David Morgan decided to form a charitable trust which came to be known as the Substance Abuse Education Trust (SAET). Its aims were to continue working not only in schools, but also in the wider community (complementing FADE and the other organizations starting to emerge that had the same philosophy as we did), to help people understand, through a combination of facts and common sense, the detrimental effects of the various drugs that were becoming more prolific. I was asked to be Executive Director. Toni and I set up the electronic typewriter, and started on our mission of sending letters to schools, businesses and other organizations to inform them of the Trust's aims.

The frenetic schedule that had ceased when FADE and I parted company was fortunately not resumed for some months. Murray was now speaking in schools, accompanied by prominent sporting personalities; the police had instigated the DARE programme (no one seemed perturbed that *this* had an American base to it!); Rotary had established their education programme Reaching Out; and DrugARM (a Christian organization) was also adding to the increasing number of non-government agencies in the field.

Because of the decrease in my own school work, I wondered whether I had made the right decision to remain in New Zealand — but within a matter of months I was left in no doubt. With each passing week, the number of requests for speaking engagements increased. Church groups, Girl Guides, women's lunch meetings, Rotary, Lions, schools — and finally the Navy called me. A regulating staff officer with HMNZS *Philomel* and a master at arms from HMNZS *Tamaki* were requesting a meeting.

I could feel the excitement. My heart started racing, my skin tingled, and saliva coated my tongue in ever-increasing quantities. Were they *really* going to ask me? If they did, was I capable of it? Would the US Navy and the University of Arizona allow me to use their material? If not, how could I adapt material without risking plagiarism?

When the Navy officers and I shook hands, I instinctively knew that my excitement was well founded. At long last, the request and the accompanying challenge were being presented to me. The New Zealand Navy wanted me to write an Alcohol and Drug Education Programme, and then train the officers, both commissioned and non-commissioned, who would ultimately take over the teaching of that programme.

My head was spinning. I had faith in my capability to produce a programme, but training New Zealand personnel? Could I do that? I was not so sure. Would they be capable of having the courage and willingness to not just learn the academic part — that would be easy — but to participate in the *process* of the programme, which necessitated a good deal of self-examination and self-disclosure? The training would not be an uncomplicated process. There was no guarantee that every training participant would be capable of then becoming a trainer themselves. So my reply was simple: I would be delighted to sign a contract to write a programme; however, initially I would need to submit a proposal outlying the goals, aims, and where the participants would come from (among other items for consideration), to ensure that I could meet the Navy's requirements. We shook hands again.

I was so excited, yet I realized that I needed to curb my tongue and be circumspect as to whom I shared my enthusiasm with. Unfortunately, certain organizations and individuals would have been delighted to see me return to the States. I had become an annoying, impossible-to-swipe mosquito that the media did not ignore even if the bureaucracy wished they would.

The United States Navy and the Health Sciences Department at the University of Arizona gave me full permission to use the NASAPP curriculum that I had been facilitating, and training others to facilitate, during my time with them, but by this time I had started to panic. My self-confidence had turned to doubt and my enthusiasm had waned as I contemplated the massive project ahead of me. I could see no way that I could maintain my speaking engagements *and*, within a six-month period, produce a three-tiered education programme, albeit starting with established material.

So I turned, as I always have done since my drinking stopped, to examine what principles I needed to implement the request, and to find those people around me who believed in me even though I doubted myself. They were there. Most, of course, were the other recovered alcoholics, who brought humour and sense into my predicament. 'Be an optimist,' said one, '— at least until you hear they are moving the animals in pairs to the top of Rangitoto!' Has anyone told you you *can't* do it?' asked another. 'No' was my reply. 'Well, go ahead and do it.' Then, finally, there was the seventy-year-old man who had not had a drink for over thirty years. Humble, wise and patient, he heard me out with all my doubts and rationalizations. 'Liz, isn't this what you have always hoped for?' His words were so carefully chosen. Not 'wanted', but 'hoped for'. Of course it was and I knew it, but I was full of doubt as to whether I would be able to produce what I had been asked for.

'If you say you can, and you say you can't, you will be right on both accounts. Look back on your journey so far in life and see from whence you have come. You are capable of doing what you have been asked to do; that is why you have been asked.'

I discovered from this man something that I desperately wanted and knew that I could only develop as he had: through listening to another person, mind, emotion and soul. That something is scarcer, finer and rarer than ability. It is the ability to recognize ability. I started to write.

By the end of 1990, I had submitted a three-tiered programme consisting of a basic introductory course, an updated programme to be delivered two years later, and a programme for supervisors and officers. The Trust retained the right to own the programme, and I was to be responsible for all initial training.

There is no experience in life that is devoid of a lesson, and I learnt many lessons from this experience. Satisfaction in life cannot be built out of being faint-hearted. Sir Walter Raleigh scratched on a window pane: 'Fain would I climb, yet fear I to fall'. Quick-witted Queen Elizabeth I scratched underneath: 'If thy heart fails thee, climb not at all.' If every decision I made and every action I took was dependent on what other people might think, then I would never be who I am today or where I am today. Yet I have needed people — to encourage me, believe in me, support me, and perhaps most of all, consciously or unconsciously, to have faith in my abilities. So often, because I am too close to my own mirror, I cannot see these for myself.

'And who the fuck are you?'

Two coal-black, defiant, fearful eyes challenged mine as, seated on the swivel chair at the front of the room, I scanned the faces in front of me.

He must have been thirty-something. The coffee-coloured hands were pock-marked with old-fashioned tattoos — chains, 'love' and 'hate', a bird between the thumb and forefinger. Slouched in the chair, legs splayed, what caught my eye was the nerve twitching on his face below the left eye, and his right leg which appeared to suffer from St Vitus's dance. The body never lies unless the

owner has a PhD in the art of super-intelligence espionage,
and this one had no chance of that. The brown face, the
tattoos, the fiery eyes had far from the desired effect on
me. Kindly, sympathetically and compassionately, I held
the gaze as I replied calmly: 'Well, if you stay here for the
time they suggest, I will help you to discover who the fuck
I am.'

Treatment centres — such as the Salvation Army Bridge programme
in which I was now working part-time — seldom allow such
language, and certainly will not tolerate attitudes such as this
beyond the assessment area, but this man had not been present in
the group the previous week, so was obviously a new admission.
He slouched further down in the chair, reached for his shades on
the top of his head, realized they were not there (as sunglasses
were not allowed in a group setting), so folded his arms and closed
his eyes. I commenced my forty-five-minute presentation.

I spoke of how we all come into the world the same way, breathe
and then start communicating, a lifelong occurrence in one way or
another. First by sound, then by actions, and finally words; and
in all our cultures we learn different words for different feelings.
However, within a matter of a few years we are taught a moral
aspect to our emotions — right and wrong; good and bad — when
in actual fact morals have nothing to do with feelings. Feelings are
simply comfortable or uncomfortable. It is what we *do* with them
that is important. If we bury them, we never bury them dead;
we bury them alive. At some stage they will rise to the surface,
sometimes again and again and again, and often with disastrous
results as we act them out rather than talk them out.

Sooner or later in today's chemical world, we find a way to
anaesthetize the feelings: smoking, drinking, swallowing, snorting
or shooting chemicals into our systems as an answer to the painful
emotions. And the answer works for a while; until when, as if a
spider has enticed us into its web, we are caught and our 'answer'

then backlashes into becoming a problem. And we, the ones who have ended up in treatment centres, we have already tried to *control* the drinking, the substance abuse. If we had been able to do so, then we would not have needed to be admitted to a place like this.

I purposefully used the first-person plural. First, because using second-person would have sounded like an accusation; and secondly, because in sharing the information I was including myself. I watched him with my peripheral vision (a skill most alcoholics and drug addicts develop as part of their survival mechanism). His arms were still folded, but he had sat up a bit in the chair and his eyes were following my scribbles on the whiteboard.

I talked about trust, integrity, honesty and unconditional love, and about how chemicals deprived us of these. I spoke about the need to *demonstrate* that we could be trusted again; that we had to earn it by being honest. I explained that honesty was not just a matter of not stealing, not lying; it was incorporated into integrity — our inside and our outside matching each other. I used the example of sadness: if I was asked why I looked sad, then if I *was* sad I needed to admit to it; but I did not need to say what was causing it unless I wanted to. In being honest, I demonstrated integrity; with integrity came trust; and if I changed my behaviour, then learning about unconditional love would be a series of lessons leading into recovery. I now had his full attention. His arms had moved from being folded across his chest to being crossed in his lap, the tick in his cheek had gone to sleep, and his leg had finished its solitary marathon.

I completed the forty-five minutes with Abram Maslow's hierarchy of human needs in the form of a pyramid. The base shows what we all require in life to survive: air, water and food. The second level shows our next requirement, shelter; and the third, our need for a sense of belonging, to a group or community — few of us are solitary animals. Then I drew, halfway up the pyramid, a thick line in red pen and, above that, the next three tiers: to *know* ourselves, *be* ourselves and *give of* ourselves. I explained to them that in a treatment centre the three primary needs are met, so that while they were there they had the opportunity to discover the next three levels. I explained that, while only *they* could do this, they did not have to do it alone, and that the people who made that journey discovered strengths and answers within themselves that they never knew existed. I was one of the guides; if they stayed for the eight weeks in the centre, this would help them with these discoveries. I was there every Friday to conduct part of the programme.

He was waiting by the door as I cleared the board and gathered my pens and paper together.

'Mohi,' he grunted as I paused to walk through, 'I'm Ngapuhi.'

'Glad to meet you, Mohi,' I replied. 'I hope you stay the eight weeks. You know, it takes more courage to stay than it does to go.' Mohi completed the eight weeks, and left that treatment centre a totally different man to the one who had challenged me that first day.

I forgot about him for the moment, as there were so many others who came and went over the following weeks and months.

Mike looked as though he had shares in a metal factory, and could almost be heard before he was seen. He looked lost when I saw him minus all the steel. Interestingly enough, none of it ever appeared again after *his* eight weeks. Robyn had the most amazing head of auburn hair once the peroxide had grown out; Betty could finally be unaware of everyone's shoes, instead noticing the colour of their eyes; and I barely recognized Barbara with make-up.

Then there was Tim. No one thought he would stay the course. Tim had decided he needed to do something about his drinking and drug-taking when he had woken one night to see his wife standing over him with a butcher's knife. Faye had a broken nose and a black eye, and was about to kill him — she'd had enough. Tim had had his own gang in Glen Innes at sixteen, once been given twenty-four hours to vacate Kings Cross in Sydney, and ran his own successful business — drug dealing. In a moment of clarity, however, he had realized that it was only a matter of time before he was looking at a serious jail sentence. He was — reluctantly — socializing with recovered alcoholics, who suggested that a few weeks in a treatment centre would be a good idea. Like Mohi, Tim took an instant dislike to me. In the months ahead this was to change dramatically, and with unforeseen results.

Jill, the programme manager at the treatment centre, resigned to take up a position at the Drug and Alcohol Unit at Auckland Hospital, and although we were sad to no longer have our weekly contact she promised to stay in touch. True to her word, a few months later I received a telephone call. 'Liz, I'm looking to instigate a training programme here for people involved in the health and social work field. Would you be interested in running it?'

Of course I was. The treatment-centre clients had benefited from what I had been doing with them, and I could easily adapt the model I used in that environment for a variety of other groups. Over five days I thoroughly enjoyed the mixture of participants who chose to attend: marriage guidance counsellors, social workers, nurses, wives and husbands of alcoholics whose partners were in treatment, and a couple of naval personnel, along with several probation officers. At the conclusion of the course, one of the probation officers remained behind, and asked if I had time to join her for a coffee. She had been a strong, open and honest participant over the days, and had helped cement the others into the cohesive group that it had become. She had obviously enjoyed the course, and verified this over coffee. She had a proposition for me: Paremoremo Prison was needing another substance abuse education programme (in true professional fashion, she gave no cause as to why the previous one had folded), and she was convinced that the one in which she had just participated would be ideal. Would I consider conducting this one for the inmates?

There are three items in life that can never be retrieved: a bullet shot, a spoken word, and a lost opportunity. I said I would need twenty-four hours to consider her request. No matter how much I enjoyed the programme and curriculum with which I was currently working, and no matter how impressed and fulfilled she felt after participating in it, I could not envisage any way in which a gang (for that's what I knew I would be dealing with) of men in Paremoremo Prison was going to relate to me and what I was offering. Why would I choose to place myself in a position to be hacked to pieces, mentally, emotionally and possibly physically? Yet, a small voice inside me murmured, 'When anyone, anywhere, reaches out for help, Liz, your hand can be there.'

Chapter 19

Mobsters, gangsters and bad boys

Evil is sinister and silent as it slips through life's highways and byways, seeking the soul. Its fingers creep slowly; feeling, touching, until the soul shivers as it senses the encroaching danger. I came to experience its presence, but first there were corridors for me to walk which prepared me for its fingers.

'Who the fuck are you?'

My God, I thought, *this is like some sort of mantra!* But there was no way I was going to inform *this* group that profanities are for conversational cripples!

The Annex (Unit 6) was the lowest-security unit at Auckland (Paremoremo) Medium Security Prison; I was being eased into the system gradually, as these men were due for release or parole and spent a large portion of their time outside on the farm, growing vegetables, driving tractors or tending the nursery garden. Every one of them had a condition for their release: they must attend a drug and alcohol programme.

The curriculum and contract that I was bound to was five weeks, six hours per week (this was later to change to eight weeks, and subsequently four weeks at twelve hours a week). I explained that he would come to know who 'the fuck I am' (he blinked) in time. The ten brown and two white faces slammed their doors on me. I truly believe (and this was later confirmed by several of the men) that I had taken them rather by surprise. I was dressed as they were — blue jeans, blue shirt — deliberately, in order to blend with the group (clothes are powerful communicators). As I surveyed the assembled participants, I had a flash of *déjà vu*. *Good heavens — I have a bunch of enlisted naval personnel in front of me.* I felt better. 'Trust what you know, Liz,' said the voice in my head. 'You *know* there is so much these men are going to take from these five weeks. You know what you need to do.'

The year was 1990. All of the participants had alcohol and/or drug issues as an underlying factor in their prison terms. Many were there because of an accumulation of drinking-driving charges (there but for the grace of God went I), others had marijuana as the reason for doing time, a few had been involved in heroin, LSD, prescription pills, and there was the isolated cocaine user. From the start, I refused to have a guard in the room with me; there was no way I would be able to work with these men and encourage them to open up with an authority figure present. By the end of the first hour, I knew that safety was not an issue. Seven years of experience with both groups and individuals at the coalface of addiction had trained me to understand, and had helped me to develop skills for handling, the denial mechanism of the disease — but the most valuable factor of all was that I had been where some of them were, not physically, but mentally and emotionally.

I had had an identical set of experiences hundreds of times with the groups of naval personnel I had worked with in the States. The only difference in this situation was the environment. I had learnt navy language, I could learn prison language; I had worked with diverse cultures, I could work with them again. Age, sex, social background, education — all of these differences eventually became unimportant, no longer stumbling blocks for the many who could be brave enough to let them go; and by the end of the course, most of them had.

The prison grapevine carried all the communication that was needed. Some of the men returned for another course. ('Didn't think it would be like that, Miss. Could listen better next time.') Every one who completed received a certificate, for some the first they had received in their entire life. There were requests for photocopies of the certificate to send to families and whanau; we celebrated graduation with tea, chocolate biscuits and bags of potato chips. There were group photos taken (*unheard* of today!), with the promise that there would be a copy for each of them when I was back to start the next group.

Again, the inevitable happened. I was called to meet with the Programme Manager, two Unit Managers from Medium Division, and the Chief Social Worker. Would I consider trialling the programme in two of their higher-security units? I explained that I needed to talk with the trustees of the SAET, that our primary area of work was with schools, hoping that we could at least have a modicum of influence there to ensure *some* did not end up under their 'care' at Paremoremo.

By this stage, we had six trustees on the board: Ian Hastings, Jill Palmer (a psychotherapist), Dave Morgan, Christine Fletcher, Murray Cruickshank (a company director), and myself. There were three issues: my safety, my time and the charges per class.

I stated that I could deal with the safety issue, and believed it was essential that we continue to conduct classes in the prison. Most of the inmates had sons, daughters, nieces, nephews, and each week had started to ask what schools I had been into, understanding that if *they* did not know the facts around some of these substances, how could their young people know. So far as they were concerned, the fact of my working in schools was a credential. It was also becoming a credential with the schoolchildren that I worked in the prison! I agreed to negotiate with the prison so that my time in schools would not suffer.

Financially, the Trust was now self-supporting through corporate donations, funding from other trusts, and fundraising casino nights that Ian Hastings was conducting. (When the critics asked how we could justify raising money for substance abuse education through gambling evenings, our reply was that we were simply cutting out the middle man. Even the Salvation Army was receiving funding from the Lottery Commission.) Our charges to the Justice Department (as it was then) had to be such that we did not exceed the taxable limit for a non-profit organization. Finally the contract was signed, and I entered West Division of Auckland Prison for my initial class.

I never realized how subtly memories are stored. The large key clonked as the lock was turned, the metal gate slammed behind me, and the key clonked again. I started to feel sweat under my arms and on the top of my lip, and my hands started to stick to the handles of my bag as the guard and I made our way down the mirror-clean, vomit-coloured linoleum, gate after gate, to the unit's guardroom. The keys brought back memories of Oakley, the linoleum memories of numerous hospitals, and the key-turning of nurses and orderlies in an atmosphere where I had had no rights. *Dear God,* I thought, *how close I came to the women's equivalent of where I am now.* Instinctively, I knew that in many ways I would be able to identify with a portion of those with whom I would be working.

There were three of them in the guardroom, and as I was introduced I could feel their suspicion. I could not have appeared very professional in their eyes. I was dressed, as usual, in my blue jeans, blue blouse and navy blue jumper. I did not carry a professional briefcase, and when I spoke my social background and education were obvious. Out of the corner of my eye I saw several faces pressed against the large circular window in the door that obviously led into where the inmates were housed. Curiosity was getting the better of them!

I explained to the guards that the men did not need to bring anything with them. That the course would take two hours, but they would need a toilet break halfway through. Not possible, I was told. There were not enough staff available at that time (10 a.m.!) and I needed to finish at 11 a.m. sharp because that was lunchtime. Many people are actually open to negotiations, but not this lot. Fortunately, I had already stipulated that there were to be no guards in the room with me, as I had been assured that all those participating were a low security risk. I could see the guards were not happy as I clarified that situation, so I explained as politely as I could that the whole group process could not take place unless an element of trust was first built in the group and that, with no offence to them, this would be difficult if they were present. One face looked at me as though I was some sort of idiot; the others looked bewildered. Not my problem.

Thank heavens for the prison grapevine! Many on my courses had heard about me, about how the class was non-threatening, and how I worked with schoolchildren. There were still some sceptics, some cynics, some who wished to retain their cultural, sexual and social prejudices — and some who chose to sleep through the entire length of the classes — but at least most of them completed.

And so began my life sentence — fourteen years — at Paremoremo.

You can't teach what you don't know. You can't guide if you do not know the road, or if your head is in it but not your heart. If this is so, forget it — in the field of substance abuse education, addicts and users will switch off from you within ten minutes flat.

I was lacking an ingredient in the prison course which had been concerning me for a while, although I was not fully aware of this until one evening when I was drinking coffee with a number of my recovering alcoholic friends. Colin was on the opposite side of the room; what caught my attention was his laugh. His face looked as though a bus had run over it a couple of times (the result of bar-room brawls), he was over six foot tall, his laugh rose from his stomach and the hand encircling his coffee cup carried trademark prison tattoos. This was the man I needed. He was Maori (and many of the class participants were Maori), an ex-prison inmate, and he had been clean and sober for three years. He had the important experience that I lacked, because he had done time for his drinking behaviour. The men inside needed to hear his story; what it was like, what had happened, and what it was like now. After lots of form-filling, meetings, clearance and assurances from me, Colin came in at the end of the programme and shared his experiences; and I knew we had done the right thing when I saw hope in some of the participants' eyes. Here was living proof that they *could* make changes if they could muster the courage to do so.

Colin and I then began a search: we needed a Samoan and a European. When we found James, Colin already knew him — they had drunk together several years previously. James had not only had a drinking problem but he had become addicted to prescription pills as well. Both he and Colin had suffered the consequences of marijuana use. Clem, who completed the trio, was an ex-biker who still looked like a druggie from the 'sixties and 'seventies.

I have lost count of the number of men who passed through those classes over the years. Some groups were so unwilling to work that I came close to not completing the course with them; and then I would look at the two or three whose whole body language was telling me that there was *so* much they were learning, and I could not bring myself to deprive them of the full experience. There were boring groups and uplifting groups; humorous, challenging and poignant groups; and incidents that will remain forever with me.

A life-size plastic brain in two halves has always been one of my teaching aids, and although I kept an eagle eye on my whiteboard markers (sniffing the ink tip can spin the brain), I often turned my back on the brain. One afternoon I only had one half of the brain at the end of the class, and after searching once the men had returned to their unit, I realized that someone had stolen it. How could anyone think that I wouldn't miss it?

In this particular unit, the door separating the staff office and the prisoners' section was in two halves, a little like a stable door. Many of the inmates could hear the discussion as I persuaded the guards to let *me* deal with the situation, promising that if I could not retrieve the brain part I would hand the whole problem over to them. Like a schoolmarm, in through the door I went, down the stairs, and stood at the end of the hallway that led to their 'houses', as they called them. By now they were either in their cells or at the doors — waiting. This was going to be the highlight of the day.

The best way to talk to a German is in German, to a Frenchman in French, to a prison inmate in prison language — and I had not had to learn much there, as it was not very different to naval language! I had learnt to speak about 'talking shit' and 'fucking up the group'. (Not 'talking nonsense' and 'messing up the group'.) 'OK guys, here's the deal. We've been learning about decisions, choices, actions and consequences. I'm in a school tomorrow and need my fucking brain!' (Hoots of laughter.) 'Someone has half of it.' (More laughter — I was obviously the week's free entertainment.) 'I'm going to stand here, turn my back, and count to ten. If that motherfucker isn't on the fucking floor when I turn around, then every one of your fucking houses will be strip-searched.' I knew that an inmate would eat broken glass to avoid *that* taking place.

I doubt that counting to ten was necessary; five would probably have been sufficient. The brain was sitting there. Part of the spinal column had been broken, but in prison there is little point in being pedantic. Hopefully they were learning that my open-mindedness did *not* mean I was gullible, and that there was more than one way to handle a situation. What I hoped for, and what I believe I earned in that particular situation, was trust and respect. I might add that the incident was used and processed as a learning experience the next week. It's not what happens to us in life so much as what we do with it that matters.

The class debate in the seventh session was the highlight for many, and was an eye-opener for all but the most cynical. The topic was always 'All drugs should be made legal'. At this stage in the course, they had already listed the guidelines they wanted in the group — for example, honesty, respect, no interrupting, no put-downs — and they were encouraged to practise them. Modules on alcohol and drugs and their short-term and long-term effects had been covered, and many of the men had come to their own conclusions on both topics.

They took charge of the group. They appointed two judges,

split the participants into negative and affirmative teams, and had fifteen minutes to prepare their arguments before the judges called for the debate to begin. It has never ceased to amaze me how disciplined the majority of these debates were. Now and again the temperature would rise, and personal accusations ('You're a fuckin' dak smoker — what would you fuckin' know?') would be hurled across the room, only to be immediately challenged by one of the judges, threatening to take a point off the accuser's team's score for foul language!

In 100 per cent of the debates conducted in the groups I ran, the negative always won. None of us can change another's belief system, but with enough accurate information coupled with self-honesty on the part of the recipient of that information, we may be able to influence the person to change their own beliefs. Sadly, we live in a world where, as German philosopher Arthur Schopenhauer has said, 'All truth passes through three stages. First, it is ridiculed. Second, it is violently opposed. Third, it is accepted as being self-evident.' In the 1940s, there were magazine advertisements like 'Smoke Craven A [a brand of cigarettes]. Good for your health.' Does this sound similar to where are we now in relation to marijuana? The men on my courses were working with two vital ingredients — their own experience, and information provided by us that made sense to them — and were thus able to change their belief systems.

Every group was a challenge for me, as every single one was different. There was the group of fourteen participants who presented *me* with a signed certificate at its completion, saying they thought I had survived the tough time they had given me extraordinarily well! Then there was the group of eight which included the president of a chapter of the Mongrel Mob. Right from the start he stood out; his charismatic energy was not threatening, just slightly unnerving, as I realized that he was the leader of *this* group and I hoped we would form a relationship of co-operation rather than one of competition.

It took no longer than two sessions for respect to be earned on both sides, although I felt he understood, grudgingly, that we were not on an equal footing. However, the prison grapevine had told him a good deal more about me than I knew about him. At the end of the last session, he helped me gather the assessment forms, pencils and the brain to place in my bags with a conversation that proceeded, roughly, along these lines:

'I'm President of the ___ Chapter of the Mob.' I continued to gather my papers. 'Best class I've been to here.' Pause.

'You work with kids?'

'Yep.'

'They shouldn't smoke that shit.'

'Nope — difficult to remember your whakapapa when your brain's screwed up.' (This man I did not use profanities with — he was educated and smart.)

'How about the rest of the bros do this?'

'Do what?' I enquired.

'The class.'

My eyebrows raised themselves a few centimetres: 'You mean the rest of the Mob?'

'Yep.'

'How many?'

'Sixteen.'

'Six*teeeeeen*?' I was astounded.

'And me.'

'You again?'

'Yep.'

'Weeeeel,' I drew in a deep breath through my nose and exhaled it through my mouth.

'Great stress-release breathing!' he said. Was that a twinkle in his eye?

I snorted. It wasn't quite a laugh, although I had meant it to be so. 'I'll have to ask the Programme Manager. You know this could set a precedent for the BPs and others in here?'

'You know this could set a precedent for the Black Power and others in here?' The Programme Manager looked sceptical. 'And seventeen of them . . .? I'll think about it.'

The group ran like clockwork. Those who had difficulty with some of the written exercises were helped by others. The surly members had a choice as to how they behaved, but knew they were being watched; the clowns had to be prevented from destroying an uncomfortable group process with humour; but by the end of the course one member had asked for a whole set of exercises to send to his kuia in Kawerau.

These men requested a special ceremony for their graduation certificate, and I was asked to bring my whanau. Mother was in England with my sister Jenny, and Georgina did not believe that a flight from Christchurch was justified, so I looked around for those I thought would be interested in the experience and would need minimum security clearance. Christine Fletcher (an MP at the time) came as a representative of the Trust; Rangi Rangihika, Auckland District Commissioner of Police Northern Area, was accompanied by Liaison Officer Detective Sergeant Loza (I never discovered what the inmates thought about *their* presence); Colin and James were present as a Maori and a Pacific Islander; and a recovered alcohol and drug addict completed this incredibly diverse group along with the Programme Manager and the inmates' Unit Manager.

The men filed in, and even I must have shown my surprise. Resplendent in their flax skirts, they were kitted out for a ceremony which included a haka and concluded with a hongi. Christine still speaks about how this ceremony was a turning point for her that enriched her life. Intimidated by the moko and filled with trepidation at the seemingly never-ending line of hongi, the experience nevertheless challenged the narrow view she had previously held on law-breakers — that they should be incarcerated and the key disposed of. It forced her to face prejudices she never realized she had. She was confronting alcoholism in her own family at the time, which enabled her to take a more compassionate and intelligent approach to the men in front of her, and to acknowledge the deep-seated social problems that confront every race, but particularly Maori. From the men she heard about their passionate wish that their children should not follow them to jail, and the hope that some of their families were attending the schools in which I spoke. For Christine, that afternoon led her to help initiate several projects for Maori, many of which she is still involved with today.

Chapter 20

Concrete, steel and a tokotoko

This time, I knew the meeting had to be serious. Not only was the Programme Manager present, along with three other, obviously senior, staff members, but I was introduced to the Superintendent of the prison himself.

While I knew that I should probably not have conducted a class solely for Mob members, I *had* had permission to take photographs in the Annex, and I was sure that my recovered ex-inmates Colin, James and Clem had totally complied with prison regulations — as had I — so what was the problem?

The problem was that they were not sure whether I would accept their proposal: to now take the programme into the East Division of Auckland Prison — commonly known as Maximum Security. I said I would think about it.

It seemed to be an age, although could have been no more than a few minutes, as I waited by the gate for the group approaching to pass through. I was aware of saliva oozing over my tongue and the need to keep swallowing. The rasping smell of chlorine from the recently mopped floor irritated my air passages, and I became conscious that my breathing had quickened.

Their footsteps shuffled in the distance, and the sound of the shuffling echoed down the long stretch of depressing linoleum.

It grew closer as the gate latch clonked and the gate squealed for an eternal ten seconds. Silence except for shuffling feet. Another clonk, another ten seconds of squealing. More silence and shuffling. Nobody ever knew how long they would be made to wait between gates. Finally, two bodies clad in orange overalls stood waiting on the other side of the chipped white, steel-barred, sliding door. There was no eye contact. Was it shame or was it a cultural way of being? For some, maybe both. The khaki-clad figure beside them made no eye contact with me, either; that's how it was most of the time. For one bizarre moment I thought of orange sunflowers brightening a listless, parched field; the mind works strangely sometimes.

The final clonk jolted the image out of my head; the squealing pierced my ears. I moved aside, and felt the clammy wall at my back, the icy steel bar beneath my fingers as I rested my hand on its chipped paintwork. Two heavy, numb souls continued on their way.

There are times in life when many of us feel there is no way out from where we are. For men inside prison, this can take a mental and emotional aspect as well as the physical. But while they do not hold the key for their physical release, we *all* hold the key to our emotional and mental release. The lock is on our side of the door. *I can guide you, show you, tell you how to unlock your door, but I cannot do it for you.* No more in the years that I had in Paremoremo could I do this for any of those men. What I did do was try to create windows for them so that they could see the sunlight of hope beyond the dark rooms of their lives, and to support them in their search for the courage to unlock the door and take a glimpse outside. They lived not only in fear but *with* fear, although they would never tell you so. The world depicted in *Once Were Warriors* was in the nature of a kindergarten for many of them.

I was not there to judge or condemn; that had already been done. I was there in the hope that, somewhere during the class process, a seed would be sown and perhaps watered a little by the ex-inmates who could share what they had done to change *their* lives. I now had two more who had been given clearance to accompany me for the final sessions: Mohi and Tim — my 'who the fuck are yous' from the treatment centre.

Mohi had relinquished his Mongrel Mob affiliation and returned to Whangarei to his wife and children. It would have been unwise to return earlier: Whangarei was Black Power turf, and Mohi had not wanted another stint inside. Tim had made amazing changes. From a wife-beating, 'unemployed' drug dealer, he had progressed to holding the crossing lollipop at his children's school (dressed in leathers, with his former 'clients' yelling and giving him the finger as they drove past), and then to slowly working towards owning his own painting business. The initiation period for the two men had been classes in the medium-security division, which I was still conducting, and now they were ready for maximum security.

Once through the clanging, electrically controlled gates, the first class was memorable. However, after the initial complication I was not sure that the programme would manage to continue. The classroom was as pleasant as a classroom could be in a maximum-security jail (I was to find in the future that this would not always be so): light, airy, equipped with a table, ten plastic chairs (a couple in questionable condition), and even some very worn carpet. Eight men in blue filed in, followed by a ninth in a khaki uniform.

'Can they have a toilet break at 10 a.m.?' I enquired.

'Yep' came the unexpected reply.

'Great, thanks,' I answered, 'I'll see you then.'

His eyes, eyebrows and mouth (lower lip pouted and turned down at the corners) registered surprise. 'What do you mean, you'll see me then? I'm not going anywhere!'

'Excuse me? There is an understanding in my classes that I do not have any guards present.'

His look was not surprised now, it was incredulous. 'But this is a maximum security prison!' he blurted.

'I'm sorry, but that doesn't make any difference. We obviously need to come to some arrangement.'

Eight blue-clad bodies sat rock-still in their chairs, only their eyes moving, darting from the officer to myself. I knew that this issue could not be resolved by the two of us, either in a discussion or an argument, and it would take longer than fifteen minutes. The men returned to their block, obviously intrigued as to what the outcome would be.

The class reconvened a week later. Different guard, different room, same men. There was a difference for me, however: I now carried a prison alarm button on the belt of my jeans. No, there could not be a toilet break. He would return at 11 a.m. to escort them back to the block. During the following years, including classes in D Block (the highest-security block in the maximum security jail), I never needed to use that alarm once.

There were full-face moko, FTWs (Fuck the World), hearts with arrows through them, bulldog faces, and all sorts of other tattoos adorning the arms, hands, cheeks and foreheads of the men who walked into my classes over the years. Teaching in medium-security had helped me see beyond the markings and search the eyes of the group participants, and I soon learnt to apply this same skill to those confronting me in East Division.

In D Block lower landing, I was given my first bone carving. That class had only four participants, and was held in a concrete cell with no windows. We could not hold a debate, only a discussion; one of the inmates took the class for the topic and wrote the pros and cons on my tiny whiteboard. Again, the negative won: drugs should not be legalized. The stress management session brought surprise and delight on their faces when they discovered their lowered pulse rate (heart rate) after a thirty-minute relaxation exercise, and I clearly and sadly recall their disappointment that there was no follow-up group from what we had been doing. Not one of them remembered committing their crime. (Believable or not? You be the judge.) All of them had been drinking and drugging at the time.

There were the young ones that came into the groups: aged twenty, twenty-five? Often it was hard to tell. Some had no front teeth; a few weeks later they might have a new set. Others lost their front teeth between classes — somebody in the block had found a new toy boy. The bruising, the black eyes, the many 'accidents' in the shower; a blind eye can easily be turned to whatever is going on.

I saw how people become desensitized, when their tolerance level for horror, pain and abuse rises to a level where their whole being becomes numb. I came to comprehend institutionalization: the individual becomes bewildered, frightened and lost when removed from a confined environment, and finds it easier to return to the safety of familiar surroundings, confining as they might be. Some of them re-offend in order to do just this. For them, 'escape' into mind-changing and mood-altering chemicals can also be a relief. I even saw how life can become so bad that the person loses their soul. Evil is 'live' spelt backwards; I knew the feel of its presence and I felt its fingers, as did others in the classes. Often it was secluded silently in one corner of the room, as the rest of the group protected me, or it stayed for a few sessions and then refused to return.

In a maximum-security prison, instinct, intuition and energy amongst the inmates would hit the top of the Richter Scale. In some rooms where I conducted classes, the only moveable objects before I arrived were the white plastic chairs and the bodies sitting in them. Their instinct and intuition would have registered my fear if I'd had any; but somehow, although I needed to be cautious, I knew I would be safe. I had learnt not to allow my open-mindedness to become gullibility, or cynicism to replace scepticism. I was perfectly well aware that they could all smell phoniness, deceit, fear, judgement, prejudice, insecurity, gullibility and hostility — none of which I carried. Of course, it also helped that in both maximum- and medium-security areas my recovered ex-inmates found old drinking and drugging cronies (including relatives they had not seen and who had not seen them in years). It is always better to let our friends speak for us: Colin, Mohi, James, Clem and Tim had accepted me, and the word soon went out on the grapevine.

On 4 September 1997, in the dialogue section of *The New Zealand Herald*, Phil Goff, who was Labour spokesman on justice at the time, wrote:

> In June I visited a programme run at the Arthur Kill Correctional Facility in New York. The 'Stay'n Out' programme operates on the basis of drug-free prison units. The counsellors and staff are mainly ex-offenders and former substance abusers, who are role models and proof that overcoming drug addiction is an obtainable goal . . . Stay'n Out works. With a 20-year record it has achieved a 77 per cent success rate in keeping graduates off drugs. These graduates, who often have long criminal records, commit no further crime and do not return to prison . . . It has been the catalyst for change in the lives of over 10,000 men and women in prison . . . The programme pays for itself within two years of the release of a drug-free, crime-free inmate . . . There is a cost in running such programmes. However, that cost is minimal compared with the cost of the wasted lives of unreformed addicts and the huge community costs they impose of welfare dependency, unemployment, criminal offending and dysfunctional families.

From 1989, when I had been invited by the United Nations Drug Abuse Control Committee to present a paper to their conference in Sydney, I had been giving papers at the International PRIDE (Parents Resource Institute for Drug Education) conference in the United States. I might add that none of these conference attendances were at any stage funded with government money. In 1998, the conference was to be held in Florida. Phil Goff provided me with a letter which enabled me to obtain an invitation from the director of the 'Stay'n Out' programme: 'I am enclosing a brochure that describes our current programs and, although it may be a long day, I will attempt to give you exposure to all components of our agency. I have had the honour of hosting visitors from New Zealand . . .' Apart from Phil Goff, I discovered that an administration officer from the Department of Corrections and an employee from Arohata Prison in Wellington had also gone over to take a look at this programme, and there may have been others.

It *was* a long day, and the tall, gracious African-American executive director could not have been more proud of his facility — and justifiably so — than if he had been conducting me on a tour of Washington's Capitol. I was astonished at the efficiency of the whole centre. All the guards I came in contact with had previously been prison inmates, had graduated from Stay'n Out in New York, Ohio, Alabama, or Hawaii, to name a few, and had been trained to fill positions within the programme.

The place was run like a boot camp: beds could have had a coin bounced on them and every one had been made with hospital corners, shoes were in neat lines under the bed, the floors were polished and the window sills dusted. When I was introduced to the group to whom I was to speak, I *really* understood what facing a gang of criminals was all about. Even in Paremoremo's maximum-security areas, I had been dealing with a bunch of primary-school youngsters compared with what was in front of me now. These men had seen life that only a horror movie writer could have dreamed up.

'So, Ma'am,' (they were genuinely polite), 'why do you do what you're doing?' The speaker could have been Haitian, Puerto Rican or Cuban, or maybe he was a mixture. A scar ran from his right eye to the bottom of his nose. His face was pock-marked, and he had a front tooth missing; I noticed a heart tattooed on his neck with 'Jesus' ribboned across it.

I had learnt to take a few seconds to think about answers to questions such as these from people such as this. I told parts of my story relevant to how I ended up in Paremoremo, and finished by saying: 'Perhaps I can explain in a story. It's the story of the holy man who asked God if he could see Heaven and Hell. God was most obliging and said, "Yes, by all means." He took the holy man to a room that had a large, round table, in the middle of which was a pot of steaming stew smelling of meat, herbs, spices — absolutely delicious. Around the table sat a number of people clutching long-handled spoons that were fashioned in such a way that they could not reach into the stew and then up to their mouths. They were skinny, bad tempered, angry, and fighting amongst themselves, jostling each other and spilling the food all over the table. "What is this?" asked the holy man. "This is Hell," answered God. He then took the man to another room which contained another round table, another pot of steaming stew in the middle, and more people with the same long-handled spoons — but these people were different. They were well fed and joking and laughing amongst themselves. "What is this?" enquired the holy man. "This is Heaven," answered God. "But I don't understand," exclaimed the holy man. "Why is there such a difference?" "Well, it's like this," said God. "These men are not trying to feed themselves, they have learnt to feed each other."'

I never saw those men again, but perhaps in the sands of time I left a footprint for them.

When I left, my new African-American friend assured me he would be only too delighted to come to New Zealand, asking only for his travel and accommodation expenses to be paid. He would waive the honorarium that was customary for American speakers. Sadly, no one took him up on this offer; it would have saved New Zealand a lot of money to have had him tour the country, rather than keep sending people over to New York!

Back home, there was no letter of acknowledgement for my report, but I was used to that, so I pursued my own course of action, realizing I could become too much of a nuisance if I did not quieten down. There were two areas that I had not previously pursued, although after the visit to New York I realized how important they were. First, more and more of the class participants were asking about follow-up groups; and secondly, the programme manager at Paremoremo, Murray Sweet, wanted to know whether I knew of any way in which an Alcoholics Anonymous (AA) group could be established there. He had been in touch with the Auckland Central Office of AA, so I suggested that we both go in and talk with the secretary there about how we might do this.

Ted, at Central Office in Mayoral Drive (incongruously enough in rooms above a wine shop), could not have been more helpful. He explained to Murray that under no circumstances would AA accept any payment, as the fellowship was entirely self-supporting and declined outside contributions because it could not afford to be seen to be allied to any institution or cause. He went on to say that all members gave their time voluntarily to help others who had a desire to stop drinking, and that there were only two problems he could foresee: one was finding members that the men inside could relate to, and the other was overcoming the issue of security clearance, because members lived with a tradition of remaining anonymous. However, the procedure was not as complicated as Murray and I had anticipated, as other prisons in the country had already held AA meetings and so had set precedents.

The amazing recovered-alcoholic members of AA are just a handful of the people who go quietly about the business of helping suffering alcoholics to achieve sobriety, simply by offering strength and hope through sharing their own experience of what it was like, what happened, and what it is like now for them. There are no membership lists, no dues or fees (although one could say that the entrance fee, paid in the cost of liquor consumption, is phenomenal). A person decides to join simply by saying so. For the men inside who chose to come to the weekly meetings, this was a *very* different experience. The majority of the volunteers, who would drive from one side of Auckland to the other in rush-hour traffic, came from the less-than-salubrious south side. They would not dream of taking money for their time ('I never paid anyone in this outfit to help me,' said one, 'so why would I ask for money from you?').

When there were challenges in the group, these visitors knew how to handle them. A good many had been where the inmates were, and, as they pointed out, 'Even if you think I'm an egg or a wanker, at seven o'clock this evening *I'm* the one who is going to be walking out of here!' They had a powerful message, and the inmates came back for more.

The follow-up group consisted of participants selected from four of my classes, and was run by Tim and his wife like a boot camp. Tim had gained enormous respect from the inmates during the time he had been accompanying me for the final sessions of the course. Those who knew him from his drug-using and drug-dealing days *knew* he was different; he even *looked* different. Tim had now graduated from painting houses to establishing his own rehabilitation house in South Auckland. He was still not a man you messed with, but now he had broken the shell of anger, aggression, hostility and violence and replaced it with honesty, assertiveness, forthrightness and, as he termed it, 'getting real'.

His wife, Faye, was as formidable as he was. A strong, proud Maori woman with a mane of flowing hair, she had been through her own Hell and out the other side; she knew how close she had come to a possible life sentence herself. Her X-ray eyes could bore through a steel door. Understanding, empathy, and the most precious gift of all — time — was what she was prepared to give the men in the group, but they knew immediately that she was not there to mess around and listen to excuses or stories of self-pity. Frank, honest and open, she too gained enormous respect.

In a report published in 1992 by the Department of Justice, titled 'Substance Abuse Survey', it was noted that 'it was evident from the interviews, that inmates appreciated programs where counsellors were open, honest, frank, direct and to the point . . . they recognized the value, as did prisons, of working both with people who had first-hand substance abuse experience, and with people who had professional training.' Of course. This does not mean that *every* ex-prison inmate who has had a drug and/or alcohol problem is appropriate in such circumstances, but Tim and Faye could not have been better qualified.

At the conclusion of both my course and Tim's follow-up course, the participants were asked to complete evaluation forms. Almost without exception they were positive; so the next step for them was to continue into anger management, a lifestyle course and/or Alcoholics Anonymous or Narcotic Anonymous meetings where they could form a support system as part of their release plan. This was along similar lines to the programme Stay'n Out.

Finally, our balloon of hope mingled with excitement was burst. The letter came, in March 2002: 'The Department of Corrections are currently reviewing the running of all programmes throughout the Prison Services under the new Integrated Offender Management System. At this stage I am unable to give any clear direction as to the volumes of programme hours that might be required from external providers.' The last course I was to conduct at Paremoremo was early in 2004, at the request of a group of inmates and supported by their unit manager. External providers such as ourselves were pulled from the system to be replaced by the new system, IOMS.

This new system was heralded as the answer to the hugely expensive problem of released prisoners reoffending, which would provide rehabilitation programmes targeted to those who were motivated to change. Yet it was basically just a computer system designed to gather data on offenders, measure the risk of them re-offending, and design individualized rehabilitiation programmes. Commentators in the media identified a number of problems, including the difficulty of assessing which offenders were truly motivated to change, the lack of habitation centres to help inmates prepare for life outside prison, and the fact that so many prisoners are released back into the very environment in which they started offending in the first place. At the same time, it was noted that the stricter sentencing and parole laws enacted in 2002 had meant a big jump in the prison population. Problems were predicted — and soon emerged.

In September 2004, *The New Zealand Herald* got hold of Corrections Department reports under the Official Information Act, and these stated that the database was so hard to operate that staff often didn't use it. In particular, the *Herald* reported that 'staff have trouble with the new system's complicated and lengthy assessment requirements, and do not complete them'. A significant number of records were still on paper rather than in the database, severely affecting its effectiveness, and it was suggested that inmates and probationers were placed on programmes that they did not need and were not placed on programmes that they *did* need because of a lack of availability of those programmes. The Corrections Department responded by spending more money on additional staff training.

In August 2008, I spoke with someone still actively involved in the justice system, and they confirmed my suspicion that this entire programme was a cost-cutting exercise, that Corrections Department staff (who were cheaper to employ than outside providers) could and did apply for training to facilitate the courses, and that to this person's knowledge the inmates did not have the opportunity to enter the course a second time. One of the advantages of the programme our Trust provided was that an inmate had a chance to repeat the course if he was not taking the space of a first-time participant. This meant that the men had time to process the information and return for reinforcement if they chose to, and many of them did. A good example of this was the Mongrel Mob leader repeating the special course I ran for his chapter of the Mob.

Canterbury University criminologist Dr Greg Newbold, who

served a seven-and-a-half-year prison term as an inmate in Paremoremo in the 1970s, was one of those who had predicted problems with the IOMS system. In a December 2007 *New Zealand Herald* article entitled '$40m to stop crims reoffending "a failure"', he went on to say that he believed prisons should provide rehabilitative services such as education and drug and alcohol counselling to make prisoners better parents and neighbours after release. 'Identify the small number of inmates who want to do something, give them programmes, but give them no early release. Do their lag. Their reward will come when they get out of jail and they don't go back.'

The Corrections Department's director of psychological services responded to Dr Newbold's statements by saying international evidence showed that programmes could reduce reoffending if properly implemented. 'It's a new ball game now. We are recruiting people who have attributes such as a social science background or experience in occupational therapy, psychiatric nursing and education.' This statement raises several issues in my mind. What backgrounds do these academic people come from and how relevant are their experiences? Did the 'international evidence' include examining the Stay'n Out programme, visited by three people (apparently at the country's expense), endorsed by Phil Goff as well as in my own report, and having a proven success rate over the years? There is little evidence to show that it was indeed considered. And — most importantly — where are the people with *real life experience* in all this? The recovered alcoholics and marijuana smokers; the ex-prison inmates who are 'stay'n out'?

One of the first questions I was asked by course participants in the early years was who I worked for. The fact that this was a non-government charitable trust was an immediate credential with the men, as was also the fact that I worked with schoolchildren, too. If I had said that I worked for a government department the inmates would have shut down on me. Life experience was ultimately what they related to — not some 'academic fucking bullshit', as they called it. Changes away from programmes being delivered by people who had 'been there, done that' to those who had simply learnt about the problems worried me then and worries me now. Of course providing accurate information on drug and alcohol use is important, but it is the shared life experience that often leads to the listener finding a connection and actually taking that information on board.

Under the IOMS reforms, not only were many of the previously separate, targeted programmes lumped together into one general one, but current Corrections Department personnel could apply for training to become facilitators. In the pilot stages of the new system, I saw some classes being taught by ex-prison guards; and this at a time when there was a long history of tension between guards and inmates. There was no way that inmates were going to identify with Department personnel (or academics) in the same way that they could with the ex-inmates who were demonstrating how they had turned their lives around.

Ex-inmates often wrote to me, and one letter in particular sticks in my mind: 'Forgive me if it seemed I wasn't listening at times, but I was, and I'm living proof that your course works. I am and have been made aware that drugs and alcohol and tobacco have ruled my life instead of it being ruled by me . . . but now I am even more aware of things I can do to change my attitude too . . . I hope to keep in contact on my progress as I go on, so I hope that will be OK with you. Please give my regards to the guys [Mohi, Clem and Colin] about their progress and the excellent help they gave me in making it easier for me to make my mind up about being clean.'

Since 2004, SAET has not been asked to come back into the prisons to deliver any programmes, and I am not aware of any other external provider who has been invited back. It is a sad fact that in so many government departments there is an unwillingness to use outside agencies and people like myself in the area of drug and alcohol education. Instead of using these people as assets, they often treat them as a threat, probably because they could very likely expose some of the departments' incompetencies. This particular problem is clearly demonstrated in the history of how the government education people have dealt with the many individuals and organizations who have been available in this area, by failing to publicly support them or to integrate them with their own programmes.

Of course, government agencies do have to be cautious of bringing in outsiders, as some have hidden agendas. But in our case, it was simply a matter of delivering something that worked. As a 1993 letter addressed to me from a custody manager in Auckland Prison put it:

> I wish to place on record to your organisation my appreciation for the input from yourself in the programmes you have delivered at this Prison.
>
> In discussing the results from your presentations, it is obvious that this is without doubt the most sought after and well received programme at this division. Inmates laud it as the most positive step they have taken on the path to finding a better way in life, and as a flow-on this can only make our job so much easier.
>
> When an inmate appears before the District Prisons Board after having completed a Substance Abuse Course run by yourself he knows two things:
>
> 1 That a positive step has been taken by himself for the future.
> 2 That your written assessment will carry weight if it is positive, and they also know that they have to earn that positive assessment.
>
> From the Board's perspective, we are grateful for the accommodations that you have made in allowing inmates to commence your Course at our request.
>
> In closing I wish you and your organisation well and anticipate hopefully a continued mutually beneficial future.

By 2004, I had been teaching these courses for nearly fourteen years.

Before I left prisons, however, I experienced one of the most moving events of my life. I will never defend the actions that led the men I worked with into the prison system, nor will I argue against the fact that there are some who should never be released as they are incorrigible, evil, criminally insane, and a danger to society. The ones I *will* argue for are those who can be helped back into the mainstream of life. Many have extraordinary talents, particularly in the area of the arts, and my collection of bone carvings bears that out.

I came to know one particularly talented wood carver, who had done time in maximum- and medium-security for a crime that, while still serious, could perhaps be understood by the average member of the public. When an innocent family member is hurt, then utu (revenge) is acceptable in some cultures; this man was prepared to accept the consequences that he *knew* would follow. He had carved a piece of kauri wood for me (I had been granted permission for him to do so at a mutually arranged price), and he requested that we have a presentation ceremony in the chapel.

Any place that has been blessed or cleansed through ritual possesses an aura of calmness, serenity and peacefulness that all but the most stone-hearted can sense when they envelop themselves in its silence for even a few moments. I had experienced this atmosphere in the prison chapel several times. Classes that I had held there appeared to have a completely different dynamic than ones held in the other rooms around the institution.

Colin and I waited as Ben, the carver, and six others were released through the clanging gates and entered the chapel. There was a solemnity in their demeanour as Ben, carrying the carving and a tokotoko (Maori healing stick which also denotes respect for knowledge), and his friends took their places opposite us.

I wondered, again, at the sheer presence emanating from these men. Their physical scars were minuscule in comparison with the mental and emotional ones, hidden from all except those who had trodden similar paths, and survived. To some their sheer energy would have been intimidating, but I saw a proud strength that I had come to recognize was only threatening to those who lacked integrity and who condemned prior to investigation.

Colin performed the waiata for us, as I am tone deaf so cannot sing a note in tune — and anyway the lump in my throat was close to choking me. The plaque of kauri wood had been stripped and polished, and two heron birds had emerged. I had asked Ben to release whatever he felt was in the old panel I had brought him. It was beautiful.

Ben was still standing in front of me. The dam burst, and my tears could be contained no longer: this tall, tattooed, proud, young Maori man in the prime of his life, who had survived God alone knew what, was holding out the tokotoko to me, one of the greatest honours his culture can bestow, and seldom given to a woman. Unsolicited, he had carved it for me as a sign of respect and appreciation for my years of work with so many Maori. The stick was carved with images relating to the Three Baskets of Knowledge, Nga Kete Matauranga.

According to Maori legend, there were three stages of being before the world as it is now, formed by the creator Io: Te Kore, the time of nothingness; Te Po, the time of darkness and doubt; and Te Ao Marama, the dawning of physical and spiritual knowledge. Having completed his formation of the physical world, Io sent a message to Earth asking for one of the children of Ranginui and Papatuanuku, the Sky Father and the Earth Mother, to be sent to him. Tane was chosen, and he ascended the Twelve Heavens to Rangiatea, the dwelling of Io. Io handed Tane three ketes, each containing knowledge. The baskets were:

- Te Kete Tuauri, containing knowledge of the philosophy of the humanities; love, peace and goodness.

- Te Kete Tuaatea, containing the knowledge of history and tradition, and the incantations of ritual.
- Te Kete Aronui, containing knowledge of the arts, war, agriculture, building and carving.

No dinner with the Governor General, ball at Government House, or Humanitarian Award from the United States Navy could have surpassed this simple ceremony in a prison chapel. I experienced the true meaning of the word 'humble'.

Chapter 21

The teenage epidemic

You can release a man from prison, but never prison from the man. Mohi, Colin, James and Tim (three Maori and one Samoan; Clem the European had moved from Auckland) were despondent when I explained that our services were no longer required at Paremoremo. Even the AA meeting had to close. The prison had brought back lockdown time to 5 p.m., and there was no way that any of the outside AA members could be at the jail by 4 p.m. One important aspect of the outside role models was demonstrating that their lives had changed, and this meant being employed: no chance of getting time off to talk to a bunch of prison inmates!

In hindsight, it was the right time for us to leave prisons. Methamphetamine, the drug that had been causing mayhem in the States (particularly Hawaii), had begun to rear its ugly head here, and I realized that there were safety issues emerging in our groups. Teeth-grinding and skin-scratching were becoming more apparent in some of the participants, as was their inability to sit still for any period of time. Relaxation exercises were virtually impossible, emotional mood-swings were increasing dramatically, and some participants were panicking in the enclosed environment with the number of people in the room. In one class I even asked for a participant to be removed, as I sensed that a plastic chair could be put to a use other than being sat on! I was rapidly moving towards the stage of being forced to have a guard in the room, which would have stifled class participation and defeated the purpose of the course.

Considering that statistic after statistic shows anywhere between 80 and 85 per cent of crimes committed are under the influence of drugs and/or alcohol, or are related to procuring these — and this was confirmed verbally to me by inmates — it makes sense to put the subject at the top of any list. But prison cells are at the bottom of the cliff: attention needs to be focused further back, in numerous areas but above all in the schools. As Murray Deaker with FADE had realized in the early 1980s, as I had realized from training in an environment that was already confronting the problem, and as Barbara Divehall realized when she proposed PRYDE, *parents* had to be part of the equation as well — moving away from prisons at least meant that I could increase my availability to schools and young people.

We left the prisons, but we did not leave the field of education. The men went their separate ways, but we did not leave each other's lives. Mohi, Colin and Tony, a recovered marijuana addict, were happy to have me advise schools of their availability to accompany me to presentations. This was of enormous value. In the field of alcohol and drug education, certain attributes in an individual can make their message extremely powerful: it is not just *what* is said, but *how* it is said and *who* says it. These three men had all done time; they neither condoned nor condemned any particular substances, but simply spoke about what had happened to them. Prison is not a holiday camp, despite what some television shows may convey, and the students needed to hear this — and they heard it so much better from those men than from me. They left no doubt in the minds of their listeners that using drugs and alcohol was 'not a great place to go', and that the consequences to both their health and their lives were sometimes irreparable.

Mohi's flexible working hours had always allowed him to be more available than the others to accompany me on my out-of-town trips, and there was many a time when he assisted my own presentations by settling unruly classes down. When Mohi believed the pupils were behaving disrespectfully to me, he let them know. There is at least one school where neither the staff nor the pupils will forget us. Ngaruawahia is several kilometres out of Auckland,

and I had been dubious about accepting a request to spend the day with the pupils and the evening with the parents. Ninety-five per cent of the population of this small town was Maori, and I was not entirely comfortable, given my background. However, Mohi decided that we *had* to go!

Ten minutes into my first presentation for the day, I thought: 'I've lost them, and I don't believe they want to come back.' A group of Year 11 or Year 12 boys at the back of the room were holding their own meeting, totally ignoring me but making sure I *knew* they were ignoring me. Others were whispering in pairs or small groups, clicking biro pens and rustling papers. Mohi, behind me on the raised platform, leaned forward and whispered loudly at me: 'Siddown, Liz, I'll deal with these *little shits.*'

If he had fired a machine-gun at the ceiling, he could not have had a greater impact on them. More than a hundred pairs of eyes became glued to him, and a leaf could have been heard to fall in the hall. He was angry, and they felt it. He spoke about respect, knowledge, wisdom and arrogance. He told the story of how we had met, the relationship we now had, and where the bone carving around my neck had come from (D Block). He spoke of whakapapa, walking tall, and prejudice. He spoke of destruction — of themselves and their culture — through the use of alcohol and drugs, and how they held the key to the future. Finally, he told them to 'shut the *fuck* up' and to listen to me.

Word went home, I am positive — and not about me! — but the parents packed the library that night. One does not educate children, parents and communities by having the geography teacher (with all due respect to geography teachers) educate on mind-changing and mood-altering chemicals, *nor* (with all due respect to academia) do children learn about these issues from listening to an academic presentation. If you do not live in their world, then how do you know what is happening? You have to read *Dolly* magazine, not *Time*.

☙

Rosemary had had a chequered career at a private girls' school in Auckland. Intelligent, athletic, a tomboy and a rebel, her parents had been concerned when her school grades dropped, and her moods began wild swings from explosions to depression; she was unable to concentrate, needed to keep the light on in her room all night because of nightmares, and was losing interest in sport — all of these becoming more and more evident. The crunch came when the school rang to ask if her mother could inform them whether Rosemary would be there later in the day. No, it was not a mufti day. Yes, there were other girls in her class not there as well.

I knew where they were going after the hour I spent with them in a Remuera sitting room straight out of *House and Garden*. All five of them thought it was a huge joke that I was there. The fact that I'd worked in Paremoremo did gain their attention initially, as did my non-moralistic attitude and the fact that I came from a similar background to their own — but I knew that after I left, two of them at least would be consuming some mind-altering chemical before heading for their jobs at the supermarket checkouts.

Three years later, Rosemary confirmed this when she sat in front of me asking for help. What she *also* confirmed was that the reason she was sitting there now was because she was frightened, and she knew that I knew more than she did about what was happening to her. She had had a massive panic attack while driving over the harbour bridge. Having progressed from cigarettes to alcohol and marijuana, she was now using cocaine and had been experimenting with P. She did not remember much of what I had said that afternoon in her parents' sitting room, but she did remember how she had felt. *Someone* knew and understood things that she didn't, and although that was scary it was also comforting.

Any drugs were easy to get, she told me. Every school had dealers, and anyway you could always go to another local school during the day and find them. All you had to do was dress in mufti on the mufti day of another school, and then just blend in with the other students. She and her friends had often done that at a neighbouring school; no one ever asked who they were. They found the dealers, and then 'got out of it for the day'. Booze and weed was available at all the parties (*Booze and grass, you're on your arse. Grass and booze, you've nothing to lose* — they knew the order in which to consume the substances). Sometimes there would be competitions to see who could projectile-vomit the farthest. Then there were the competitions for who could get drunk and 'laid' first. (Today, it's oral sex so as not to catch various diseases.) Now the fun had gone. She'd been raped twice — that she remembered — although she had never told anyone, an all-too-frequent occurrence with teenage girls. She thought she was going crazy, and needed to do something.

The tears started and I was right there with her. This pretty nineteen-year-old, skinny because of anorexia and bulimia, was me — but worse. She had been caught up in the relentless progression of drug traders preying on the young, ignorant and moneyed section of society, where the 'have nots' sold to the 'haves', who were then selling to the 'haves' at a younger and younger age. Those of us at the coalface had been watching the ever-creeping tentacles of this epidemic, feeling powerless to do more to prevent it.

Rosemary had a long recovery ahead of her, but today she is about to complete a successful course of higher education; her value to society will be priceless.

Children are naturally curious, and have an inherent internal wisdom. Whether we like it or not, every single one of them in the pharmaceutical society of today will be faced with decisions around drugs and alcohol. We can teach them all the stress management, communications and how-to-say-no skills in the world, but this has no real significance if we do not also give them facts as to *why* these substances are harmful, a danger to their health and safety. Many of them have extremely distorted belief systems in this area, fed by unsubstantiated 'facts' from those interested in creating new consumers. We cannot change a person's belief system for them, but we *can* influence them to change their own belief system by giving them information that their own internal wisdom will comprehend.

This is borne out in one of the many letters I have received from students attending my presentations on smoking, marijuana and alcohol:

> The 45 minutes you came to talk really made me think and wonder. It gave me the details behind all the reasons not to use these substances by getting right into the depth. Plus all the things that would happen to you.
>
> I have many friends that use all these substances, now I can pass on the message to them and give them the scientific reason to stop using marijuana. I am glad you came to talk to us before we left school and it would be a great idea to try to get to every school. Your speech related to me and I am sure it would to other students. You were different from any other speaker because you related to us and got into great depth about each drug.

We also need to *not* give our children the wrong messages. De-criminalization? All our young people will hear is that 'it's OK to use'. Teenagers seldom read the daily papers. I do; and am always grateful to the reporters who pick up on and *print* the facts about how large a part marijuana plays in many crimes. The ignorance around this substance, fed by myth and misinformation, still astounds me. I am not discounting the damage that abuse of alcohol causes, but until a focus is placed on the influence of cannabis, particularly, in the lives of the many young people that it cripples, we will continue not only to dumb-down a whole generation, but to produce a society that will have massive social and economic problems as a result.

On 18 July 1992, the *Listener* published an article by me entitled 'Marijuana — The Hidden Teenage Epidemic'. In this I stated that 'we face an epidemic with our teenagers that if it were measles, meningitis, or polio would cause a public outcry. It is an epidemic that is not killing our young people but crippling them. Thousands of scientific papers have been published that give conclusive evidence of the harmful effects — information that was not available in the 1960s and early 1970s.' In the 1940s, various brands of cigarettes were advertized as 'good for the throat' — a statement which is now incomprehensible. Young people are endowed with logic and common sense; and since they are now perfectly aware of the harmful effects of cigarette smoking, they understand (given enough logical facts) how the smoking of *any* substance is damaging to their physical and/or mental and emotional health.

Children can be taught to think critically and need to do so, rather than being spoon-fed from television, videos and statements incorporating lies of omission as well as commission. How can they learn if their brains are taken over by a chemical that impairs the brain cells responsible for thought, memory, learning, speech, and the controlling of emotions? And many people are not aware that marijuana has changed. I am not talking about the marijuana of the 1960s, '70s or even '80s. Today's increase in potency of the psychoactive chemical THC found in marijuana can be validated not only by the Institute of Environmental Science and Research but — for what it's worth — the growers who use hydroponics, special lighting conditions, and additional chemicals.

The majority of adults have no comprehension of the dangers involved in the chemical world in which our teenagers live now. And, again with all due respect to the teaching profession, when introduced to the staff of one school with an explanation of why I was there, I only had to send a swift glance around the room to discover some who were not at all comfortable with my presence. Of course marijuana is smoked throughout our teacher-training establishments. Ask any teacher who does *not* smoke it, and they will endorse that statement. So what are they telling our children?

And the politicians don't help. On 4 May 2000, *The New Zealand Herald* headlined an article 'Coroner Savages Pro-drug Leaders'. Coroner Mate Frankovic was commenting on the death of a twenty-four-year-old on Pakatoa Island after it was found that he had five times as much Ecstasy in his blood as the country's first E victim, Ngaire O'Neill in 1988.

> 'I feel sure that some of our parliamentarians might revise their thinking towards the decriminalisation of the use of marijuana . . . if they were to attend a few inquests,' he said.
>
> Last night Prime Minister Helen Clark said the coroner's comments were illogical and unhelpful in the cannabis debate.
>
> 'It's drawing a very long bow from an inquest into a tragic death from Ecstasy to lambasting those saying the legal status of cannabis needs a second look.'
>
> Pro-cannabis Green MP Nandor Tanczos rejected the coroner's comments as 'weird logic' [and] said he could not understand why Mr Frankovich was linking cannabis reform with an Ecstasy death.

It was the third-to-last paragraph of the article that caught my eye: 'Sergeant Lance Burdett told the inquest Mr Langridge *had a predisposition towards cannabis use*' (my italics). I was — and am — incensed at the sheer ignorance and stupidity of Helen Clark, Nandor Tanczos, and all the others out there who make these ridiculous statements which simply display their arrogance and ignorance of a field they know little about. They not only endanger our children's lives, but they feed nonsense to an unsuspecting public.

Mr Langridge was a cannabis user. When a person smokes cannabis, time and depth perception become distorted. The user will often think that five minutes has passed when in reality it is possibly two. The slowest way to get any chemical to the brain is via the stomach (ask any medical professional); depending on what the substance is, it can take fifteen to twenty minutes. So — Mr Langridge, a cannabis smoker, drops a tablet of E. Nothing happens. So he takes another, and then another . . . The first one finally hits the brain, and there are another how many more to go? In all my twenty-two years of working with schools, thousands of schoolchildren and parents, I have never met one government academic who understood the above equation, and we are leaving our children's drug and alcohol education to them? Spare me.

There have been times when my indignation, as well as my physical, mental and emotional energy, have started to wane — generally about November each year! However, by the following February, as requests for our programme started to flood back from schools in answer to our annual letter letting them know our services were still available (and at no charge to the school), I was always revitalized to go back — to another group of sadly ignorant teenagers. Winning the war? I was asked. No, we try to reduce the casualties.

Incident after incident over the years has inspired me, and others like me, to continue. A call from the head of health at Newlands College in Wellington, inviting me to spend time with the students, was extraordinarily gratifying. I had spoken to her when she was a Year 13 student, had made a difference to her life, and now she wanted me to talk to her classes. The father of a girl at Auckland's Diocesan School for Girls spoke at the conclusion of a parents' evening, and encouraged me to continue doing what I was doing for as long as I could. He concluded by saying that I knew more than he did in this area — and he was a doctor! Henceforth he would take a urine sample from *every* teenager who came to his surgery, whether or not they complained about some of the withdrawal symptoms that I had explained frequently occurred with discontinuing marijuana use.

Rutherford High School was where John Fauvel, the first-ever person to be appointed President of Toastmasters International outside of America, heard me speak. Weeks later, he informed me that Auckland Toastmasters wished to present me with their annual Toastmaster of the Year award, and at our request he agreed to become another trustee of SAET. An Auckland businessman, Murray Cruickshank, with daughters at St Cuthbert's College, later joined the Trust board, flabbergasted at how little he knew about the whole teenage drug and alcohol scene.

Twenty-seven staff members of St Peter's School in Cambridge were outraged enough at a letter received from Green Party Co-leader Rod Donald, MP, attempting to justify the party's campaign for the decriminalization of cannabis in 2000 that they were prepared to put their signatures on a letter back to him. 'We find your reasoning facile and ill informed,' they wrote. 'Your colleague Nandor Tanczos clearly *does* promote the use of cannabis to our nation's children through his public pronouncements about his own drug habit . . . Current drug laws do nothing to undermine effective drug education. Instead they provide a sound legal homework to emphasize the messages taught in this school . . . We suggest that you spend an extended period of time in a classroom attempting to teach and control pupils who are drug users. We are certain that any teacher would willingly swap places with you . . . Your current position grossly undermines them and will drive many fine teachers out of the profession. If you are successful, our nation's children will pay a terrible price.'

Ian McKinnon, headmaster of Scots College in Wellington and a gentleman and a wordsmith, was one of the Trust's greatest supporters, and my annual visit to his school was a trip I always found enjoyable. Not only did he emphasize, loudly and clearly, how important the information was that I would present to the students, but he reiterated the strong stance that the school took and the zero tolerance that it maintained on drug use.

I felt rather like a naughty schoolgirl when, in 1997, he invited me to his office as I was about to return to Auckland. It was, for me, a typical headmaster's office. Had I been a thirteen-year-old boy, the heavy, imposing furniture, book-lined walls and thick, dense carpet would have seemed a never-ending sea of terror that would need to be crossed to find the consequences for the summons. Ian McKinnon was by no means a harsh or unfair man; to the contrary, I found him to be a compassionate disciplinarian with a genuine concern for the welfare of all his pupils, and with unfailing regularity I would hear him encouraging them to strive for excellence. No — it was my own interpretation of the situation that initiated my feeling of apprehension.

He gestured to the chair opposite him across the desk, and, glancing at the blotter pad in front of him, I saw a copy of my curriculum vitae. His eyes skimmed each of the five pages as he flicked through them, and then — fixing me with that sagacious look peculiarly prevalent in the headmasters of a rapidly declining era — he smiled. 'I believe you should be recognized for this.' He jabbed at the pages in front of him. 'Over the years I have proposed a number of people for New Year and Queen's Birthday Honours. Would you be willing to have me put your name forward?'

Of all the situations I had anticipated as my steps sank through the carpet from the door to the desk, this had obviously not been one of them; and as I left for Auckland, I had no inkling of what the following year would bring as a consequence of my saying the simple word 'yes'. On 31 December, the man who had been in my life for the past eleven years in varying capacities plumped the pillows at my back, kissed me good morning, and settled himself with Hobart's newspaper, after placing cups of tea on either side of the bed. We were at Wrest Point Casino for their New Year's Eve party. Gingerly, I reached for the sheet of paper that was acting as my bookmark: a photocopy of the one from the Governor General, part of which read: 'The Honour will be included in the New Year Honours 1998 which will be announced at 6.00am, Wednesday 31st December 1997. I would be grateful if this information could remain confidential until then.'

His face was a picture — unusual for a man who, for over thirty years of his life, had learnt to maintain a certain degree of control over his facial expressions. 'Do you know what this means?' he managed to splutter.

'What?' I feigned ignorance.

'A Companion of the New Zealand Order of Merit is equivalent to what used to be called Companion of the British Empire — CBE. This means you are half a Dame. You can't be my mistress any more: you'll *have* to marry me.'

Chapter 22

A cop, a concubine and casinos

His energy could have opened the door for him — no wonder some introduced him with 'Hurricane' added to the beginning of his first name. I had been surprised when he had agreed to meet me in my office at FADE rather than his own at Auckland Central Police Station, as I had labelled him as arrogant, but I was being unfair: I believe he felt slightly off-balance and was not sure how to handle me. Four years with the US Navy can certainly *sound* intimidating!

As Ian Hastings slid his wiry frame down in the chair, legs straight and ankles crossed, his eyes held mine in a steady gaze. *Don't start trying to interrogate me*, my eyes shot back at him. I'd dealt with more than one four-striper who'd looked at me like that. We smiled. *This is going to be an interesting relationship*, I thought. 'Tell me, how did you become involved in FADE?' I asked.

I learnt that a great part of Ian's career in the Criminal Investigation Branch of the police had been spent in the vice and drugs law enforcement area. He had risen through the ranks to eventually become Detective Inspector in charge of the Auckland Drug Squad. After his return from his Woolf Fisher Scholarship trip, Murray Deaker had had an unpleasant incident because of his outspoken views on the drug scene, and as a result had decided that the head of the Drug Squad would be a useful trustee for FADE.

That meeting was the first of many over the following weeks and months. It was inevitable that more and more time would be spent in each other's company, as he eventually became an integral part of the parent evenings at which I spoke. I presented the facts, consequences and harmful effects on young people during their developing years; Ian followed with descriptions of the available drugs circulating in the community and the legal consequences for people using and supplying. If we were fortunate to have Barbara Divehall available to share her experiences with parent support groups, then we made an impressive and knowledgeable trio. It was not long before I had learnt how to deal roulette at the numerous fundraising casino evenings that Ian conducted, perfectly legitimately. He had started raising money for the Combined Services Men's Basketball Team, which he captained for a number of years, but then switched to fundraising for FADE and ultimately for SAET.

More often than not, it was practical for Ian to remain in town rather than travel through peak-hour traffic to Howick and then retrace his steps for a seven o'clock parent meeting on the North Shore or in West Auckland. So we would eat together, exchanging information and updates on the progressive availability of substances in schools and what Ian had gleaned from his informants and members of the Drug Squad. He quickly discovered — and was taken aback by — how little he knew about the harmful effects of marijuana in particular, confessing that so far as he was concerned, as a law enforcement officer, he busted them, locked them up, and went after the next one. He soon became adamant that we had to start using some of the recovered marijuana addicts, members of Marijuana Anonymous, in our parent evenings.

Months earlier, I had helped two members of Narcotics Anonymous set up meetings in Auckland for marijuana addicts, using the same principles as the AA and NA programmes. They had discovered an obscure article in a magazine that had a contact address in Van Nuys, California; from them, we received pamphlets and an encouraging letter that ultimately enabled these enthusiastic recovered users to establish groups in Thames, Tauranga and Christchurch. Not every school was agreeable to them accompanying us, but for the parents with whom they came in contact they were an invaluable source of information and were able to answer an avalanche of questions from their own experience.

Soon, the half-empty garage at my house started to accumulate casino equipment. Now it was not only the parent and casino evenings that were throwing us together, but the constant trafficking to and from the house for the equipment. As a senior officer, he drove an unmarked police car; just as well, or the little old ladies in Caughey Preston retirement home opposite would have had the Remuera gossipmongers operating on overtime.

There was no mistaking his eldest daughter. Debbie had her father's eyes and same set of chin, and I could not miss her as I skimmed the faces of the Howick College students in front of me. I needed no cross-examination to realize she'd been primed to assess me and my presentation. Obviously, the family were curious about me: their father was spending an inordinate amount of time with me at parent evenings and casino events, and it was not long before I was around the household for a number of reasons. Trudie, the second daughter, was always involved in one project or another, whether ice-skating or church activities; Robbie was following in his father's footsteps as a basketballer; and his wife's life obviously revolved around Ian and the children.

Relationships of any type are always in a constant state of change. Incidents occur, environments alter, individual characteristics become more pronounced; some tolerable, some less so. People enter and exit our lives, some of them leaving indelible footprints that contribute to changes and spurts of growth, altering our attitudes and belief systems to continually propel us forward on paths we had never envisaged in our early years. People grow emotionally, or remain stuck; take risks, or shut themselves away; are curious and explore, or become fixed on what has always been, or what might have been — a Miss Haversham life of their own. It was inevitable, as Ian and I spent more and more time together, that the intense physical attraction we both felt but never discussed would reach a point where a decision would need to be made: whether we would yield to the electrifying, vibrating sexual passion that was ticking like a time-bomb in both of us or be rational about circumstances and decide to intellectually defuse it.

One night over dinner, during a pause in the conversation, Ian in his forthright way brought my fork full of food to a screeching halt in mid-air: 'Would you be my mistress?' My gaze became glued to the red-and-white checked tablecloth. It reminded me of a chess board, and we were the players — but this was a dangerous game. I knew, and if every woman is honest *she* knows, that an answer of yes meant no going back. It was a life-changing decision in what seemed a simple situation. I knew that if I succumbed to the sexual cauldron on the edge of which we sat, my life would be journeying into unknown and unpredictable territory. I also knew that the adventuress I had become was going to go there anyway! I believed (rashly) that no matter what eventuated, I could handle it.

I failed to consider that time had proved this was not some teenage infatuation, not just immediate sexual gratification for either of us. Something considerably more complex had occurred, and the sexual act was to only enhance the mutual understanding and connectedness that had grown between us. Knowledge such as this develops in hindsight, not foresight. I was no desperate, needy forty-four-year-old woman searching for emotional and financial security and willing to gain both at any cost. No, there was something different, yet familiar, in what was happening to me; something, some experience that, try as I might, I could not extract from my memory bank.

Eventually, the ensuing years brought to light the realization that 'it' had occurred once before. *Love never dies*: the container in which one experiences it often does, but it will awaken again, at the most unexpected time, in an unexpected way, when one is going about doing other things. Lust and infatuation are not based on a mutual understanding or a meeting of two compatible souls; there is no spiritual base to them, and they will often die a natural death or become destructive as time passes. Love may include sexual passion, but it is vastly more than that; it is something that one *grows* into rather than *falls* into. Its base is a mutual understanding, belonging and caring, and although it can go through crises, these lead to growth rather than a need to escape from them. Love will survive disagreements, physical separations and even temporary infidelities, which lust and infatuation do not have the emotional maturity to overcome.

For me, the crisis came five years later. The pain of the mental and emotional deceit, the pretence, the hiding, and the justifications and rationalizations became too acute. One Thursday afternoon, my longtime friend and psychotherapist helped me make the decision I knew I needed to make. Ian's life was comfortable — secure job, ideal family, house, car, boat, and a pension on retirement. What was I facing? At forty-nine years of age I did not want to be someone's mistress for the remainder of my life, and Ian had made it clear to me that there was no way he was going to change his circumstances. The three-year relationship terminated by his previous mistress was proof enough of that.

The casino evening that Friday night finished at nine o'clock, and after the equipment was stored in the garage and we were sipping our mugs of tea in the living room, he turned and confronted me. 'Something's not right with you, Liz. What is it? You've not been yourself all evening.' He later told me that he had had a premonition as to what would follow — he knew that at some stage the relationship would need to end and that I would be the one to end it.

I told him I could not go on with how we were. For me it was a dead-end street. As long as we were a couple, so to speak, there was no chance of my allowing anyone else into my life and he was not going to leave his wife, so we needed to contemplate what to do. With both of us in tears, he headed for the back door with the words 'I knew this had to happen. I don't think we should see each other for two weeks.' I watched the car crawl out of the driveway like a tired dog dragging its hind legs.

I woke Anita, one of my confidantes, in San Diego at three o'clock in the morning her time, and blubbering, with lungs heaving for air, I dumped on her until she had no more to say to me. I called my New Zealand mentor and blubbered down the telephone to her. I had a mental and emotional hangover, drinking cup after cup of coffee until I was wired like a guitar string and could only doze fitfully on the couch where he used to lounge every evening that we spent together. I felt physically sick, my throat ached and there was a tight band squeezing my chest. I had no idea what decisions to make, except to spend the next day with my mentor and remember that — *no matter what* — I must not anaesthetize the pain with any chemical: no alcohol, no tranquillizers, no antidepressants. I *could* survive, one day at a time. I was *not* going to die. I had to leave on Sunday for two schools out of town, and that was *all* on which I must concentrate for that day.

I turned to my three stalwarts in life: books, people, and a Power that had somehow brought me this far in life, and, as the story 'Footsteps' describes, will metaphorically carry me until I can discover the strength to walk again. The lessons learnt from all of the pains of the past only strengthened me to cope with living through the next few days — nothing comes to stay, it comes to pass. I had work to do, children to teach, parents to help. My life had to continue, irrespective of whether Ian was included in it or not.

There were eight messages awaiting my return, and it took a herculean effort to listen through to the final one. The fifth voice simply stated: 'Ian's in a bad state; you need to call me.' Jan and Dave had known Ian for some time, with Jan organizing all his casino staff and being perfectly aware of the changes in his relationship with me over the years. 'Ian called in on his way to work yesterday in floods of tears,' she replied in answer to my query. 'He's not in a good place — can't sleep, hopes it's you whenever the phone rings, has his door at the office closed most of the time, and is abandoning everything in his in-tray.'

Two prison classes the next day kept my thoughts occupied, and several caffeine fixes sustained me until he snailed his way up the back steps around 5.30. 'I can't live without you,' he blurted as he crossed the door's threshold into the living room, crashing through the vibrating silence that smothered the walls and ceiling. 'I'm in love with you—' and the rest was lost among the sobs and gasps for air as he desperately attempted to maintain control of the emotions that appeared to have been engulfing him for days.

I could not move. Not a finger, not a foot, not a muscle in my system was mobile except my heart — which was pounding until I was sure the windows would rattle. I suddenly realized that I had even stopped breathing. *Breathe!* I silently shouted. *Breathe, breathe,* replied the large purple and red poppies on the curtains. I did not know what to say, so I said nothing. I just knelt on the sheepskin rug in front of him and held his hands. His eyes were streaming, his nose was running, and when I left and returned with a roll of toilet paper all he could do was hold me and sob. 'Oh my God,' I thought, 'what if he is having some kind of psychotic breakdown?' (*Always anticipate the worst — then work backwards!*) 'What if . . . what if . . . ?' and I started to tear through the US Navy Reference Manual in my head. 'Make sure they breathe' — the gasps for air told me that; 'Keep them from harming themselves' — I was holding him. *It will pass, it will pass,* kept echoing through the space between my ears — and it did. But then came the next torpedo: 'I'll have to leave her.'

I could hear my mentor's deep breath in at the other end of the telephone line. 'You truly are having an unusual life, my dear. This would be what in the old days my mother would call "being in a pickle".' I could smile a little, but the smile faded as an image of my own mother flashed into my head. 'Oh Lord, I'm going to have to tell her now, because she's going to *know* one way or another' — as if she didn't already suspect, as if a *number* of people didn't already suspect! — that something has been going on between the two of us. I had already heard my poor father turning in his grave.

Mother never altered the pace of her lifted and lowered teacup as I told her of the decision I needed to make. Yet again, I realized what an extraordinary woman she was. She had neither condemned nor condoned any decision or action I'd taken in my life over the twenty-one years since I had ceased drinking. I knew she was proud of me — her friends told me so. She had *adored* John, and in her own way had gone through her own grief at his death. They had shared a common intellect and sense of humour. I knew how much she had enjoyed Ian's company on the occasions they had met. She had great respect and admiration for all areas of the legal and law-enforcing sections of society, and Ian, like John, made her laugh. Her reply was true to type: 'It's your life, Elizabeth. I cannot make decisions for you.'

Although in my past I had resented the fact that I had felt abandoned by her to nannies and boarding school, I had grown older and hopefully wiser through my experiences, and now viewed our relationship with a sense of gratitude. Unlike many other mothers I had encountered, she had not suffocated me with daily telephone calls of inconsequential conversations, guilt-enhanced criticisms of any of my friends, or yearnings for grandchildren that carried underlying messages of comparisons with others in her age group. Her wisdom, sought but never imposed, had always guided me, particularly in the years since John's death. I did not ask for any of her thoughts over that teapot: I knew I had to take my own action and accept whatever consequences came as a result.

My problem was that I had never anticipated that Ian would leave his wife. She raised their children, took care of him, had done nothing wrong; but he told me he had come to realize that there was no longer an emotional connection for him with her. He left a few days before her forty-sixth birthday and the emotional volcanic eruption for which I had prepared myself then blasted forth. His mother-in-law wrote me a vitriolic two-page letter (mothers-in-law!), of which I took not the slightest notice and promptly burnt; his own mother voiced her disapproval, but in the same breath said she understood; his wife never sent a whisper. Then there were his three children, scattered around the globe. I knew they would all be stunned, hurt, furious, frightened, confused, and condemning in their own individual ways. I metaphorically roped myself to the largest tree and waited for the tsunami to arrive.

Debbie was (is) the feisty one of the three. I recognized her handwriting immediately the letter was in my hand. I think she had thumbed her way through a thesaurus, discovering words that finally sent me to both Oxford and Chambers dictionaries. If I thought I could have used them in the future, I would have copied them into a notebook! She was, understandably, *beside* herself. She was in England, engaged to be married there, and would be facing a father giving her away who was no longer in such a relationship himself! I would *never* be allowed *near* her children, she would never *speak* to me again . . . The ashes were disposed of in the following week's rubbish. Keep the letter? What for? To use as evidence? When? Where? With whom? I never even contemplated a reply. It would have been like chasing a tsunami wave back into the ocean. Forget it. The least-expected form of behaviour on my part in such a situation would have the most positive consequences; I did nothing.

Robbie returned from his work experience in a youth camp in America to inform Ian that if his father ever put the two of us to work at one of his casino evenings, even if we were at opposite ends of the room, he would kill me!

Trudie asked if we could have lunch and talk. I listened; she talked. The situation was difficult for her, as she was living at home and did not know how to cope with her mother, but at least she had the courage to try to clear the air between us as best she could. I knew, but could never say so, that the passing of time could change situations, attitudes and beliefs, and that excuses, reasons, shifting blame and attempting to justify the situation was futile; my side of the story would be falling on stony ground. The fact that I had never dreamt that Ian would leave was a useless statement, not to be believed — I was the Wicked Witch from the West who had stolen their father and destroyed the happy family.

Ian had moved in with a friend to start with, but after six weeks we decided that living apart was slightly ludicrous. We were both in our late forties, had friends who had succumbed to cancer or heart attacks, and what were we trying to prove by living separately when we intended to be together? Over the ensuing months, Ian and I settled into our respective routines, aware that there would be condemnation of our situation from some people; but we found that we could live without the few who did condemn us.

My fiftieth birthday was spent quietly with our two mothers and my sister Jenny, who was on a visit from England. Ian was promoted to Detective Superintendent, and schools asking for presentations increased in number; as did the demands for our classes in the prison. Although he accepted it, Ian understandably found difficult the emotional distancing and anger that his children imposed on him through silence, and also found it difficult to believe me when I said that time would somehow heal it all. I found pleasure in my mother's obvious enjoyment of Ian's company, and was glad that, for the next eight or ten years at least, she would be able to feel a certain security of a man around the family. She was physical health personified, walked where she could, practised yoga, played bridge and had been a vegetarian for years, so when my cell phone rang on that fateful Thursday I could not believe Phil Cook's voice on the other end: 'You need to go to Auckland Hospital Accident and Emergency, Elizabeth. Your mother had a stroke while we were drinking coffee this morning.'

I had spoken to Mother at eight o'clock that morning when she had told me of her plans for the day, and that, yes, it would be nice to see me for a cup of tea around 5.30 when I was on my way home, five minutes drive from where she lived. I was never to speak with my mother again.

Chapter 23

Two weddings, a funeral, and half a dame

Whether or not I was aware of it at the time, my mother influenced my life both by her presence and her absence. At varying stages I loved her and hated her, but I could never ignore her. I sought her advice and opinion, wanted her praise and acceptance, and would live for days grappling with the overwhelming guilt that would envelop me after her tight-lipped disapproval. I was desperate to please her, yet ultimately rebelled against her conventional lifestyle. I wanted her dignity and elegance, but not her emotional unavailability. I was in awe of her verbal agility, her rubbish-bin mind that could recite the dates of English monarchs by heart and also believe in Rachel Carson. I coveted her Raynes shoes, yet was incredibly embarrassed by her 1940s cherry-pink swimsuit!

She was predictable, and yet often an enigma. Her upper-middle-class background, allied not only with the experience of spending the war years as a cipher officer in the British Navy but also with the cultural shock of ending up in one of the more primitive recesses of the Empire, meant that ultimately she fitted in nowhere. To the day she died, she devoured the Sunday editions of four English newspapers and a conglomeration of magazines from *Country Life* to *Tatler*. She never lost her cultured English accent, always changed for dinner, and would not dream of being seen outside the house without her gloves. Remuera shopping centre was her village, where every Christmas she would religiously bake and deliver shortbread to staff in selected shops and the bank.

Yet she could be incredibly risqué — a familiar figure striding up Victoria Avenue, parasol bobbing, gloved hands clutching the home-baked Christmas parcels, sensible shoes clipping the asphalt . . . and no knickers on under the knee-length skirt! 'One should let every orifice *breathe*, Elizabeth.' As a result, I have never worn a tampon in my life!

As Father's drinking became more of a problem over the years, she tolerated his behaviour because it was her 'duty' to remain in what I ultimately saw as a loveless marriage; yet when he died, although there was relief for her, I believe that after forty-five years together she felt a certain loneliness. She was never demanding of me, but was grateful for my insistence that I call her to ensure she was coping with the day-to-day irritations that would often arise. I firmly believe she saw all my strengths and weaknesses and the limitations that society imposed on me as a woman, deep down seeking for me what she had never had for herself. By the time she had convinced Father that the law of primogeniture in the family business could be applied to me, however, it was too late. I was on another path. The pain and heartache she must have felt through my years of turbulence I can only imagine, but, with her amazing ability to find a reason for any of life's vicissitudes, I am sure she ultimately accepted (without understanding) that I had found my own meaning to my life.

Twice she pulled the feeding tubes from her nose, and on the second time the sympathetic doctor agreed with my sisters and me that this was an indication she no longer wanted to be fed. Mother had had a constant fear for years that she would end up a cabbage in an old people's home. She would plead with anyone, anywhere, whom she thought would have a modicum of influence to 'turn the tap off on me', 'pull the plug'; her last desperate plea would be 'Shoot me!' Her motto was that when her time was up, she wanted to go and leave room for someone else.

As Jenny, Georgina and I followed our mother's coffin down the aisle of St Mark's Anglican Church in Remuera, my blurred vision could do no more than scan the familiar faces in the pews. When we reached the font at the back of the church, a single figure caught my eye. With a superhuman effort I cleared the teardrops to make sure I was not imaging what I saw: a brown face with a halo of black curls, a tooth missing in his smile, and a tattooed hand raised in acknowledgement. James, my Samoan, ex-junkie prison-inmate friend had come to pay his respects. The only brown face among the élite Europeans of Remuera, he had found the courage to support me in my loss. I knew without a shadow of a doubt that it would have touched mother's heart as it did mine.

I missed Mother in the following years. I had detached myself from her in myriad ways, and will be forever grateful that she had let me go, but her abundance of experience, wisdom and foresightedness were treasures that I still wanted to gather to me. However, today I am grateful for the legacy, certainly for her foresight, that she left with me. She had envisaged both the spread of Islam and the approaching fresh-water shortage in the world twenty years previously, and was an avid environmentalist (without joining the Greenie clan). I like to believe I have inherited some of what many at the time would have called her 'eccentricities'; they seldom carry that label today.

The following four years brought my sisters and me closer together through yet more interesting events in my life; the first causing frantic telephone calls between them across the high seas. I had been whisked into hospital with a growth on my colon. Georgina, as a nurse, was well aware of the implications of such a diagnosis for the intermittent bouts of internal pain I had been suffering. She was relieved to hear, however, that I was under the care of a specialist for whom she had the utmost regard — David Morris.

David had chosen medicine as his career, finally specializing in general surgery and colonoscopy. He was following a long line of significant medical practitioners in his family. His grandmother,

Alice Horsley, was the first woman doctor in Auckland and the first woman medical practitioner employed by the Hospital Board. His father, Selwyn, treated many wounded during World War II who were shipped to Auckland from battles in the Pacific; and his elder brother, John, was a well-known orthopaedic surgeon. David continued this tradition, treating the casualties of war both in Vietnam and later Afghanistan, and he married the theatre nurse with whom he worked in Vietnam. In the early 'nineties, David and his wife Lien were prime movers in establishing the New Zealand Vietnam Health Trust to provide training and equipment for the hospital in Quy Nhon where they had previously worked. Today they are supported by NZAID in Wellington in their continuing work with those in the Quy Nhon hospital who cannot afford the medical treatment they need. On meeting David, no one would be aware of these unselfish and humane contributions that he makes to others' lives. His quiet, unassuming exterior belies what I later discovered was a man who had no tolerance for unethical or arrogant behaviour. This man saved my life.

I had no need to request the plain facts revealed by the photographs obtained from an internal examination. The growth on my rectum would need to be removed. I would also have to undergo a hysterectomy, as there was no other way to approach the lump. Whether it was benign or malignant could not be discovered until laboratory examinations had been done, and there was the possibility that I would need to wear a stoma (bag) over the opening indefinitely.

Well, having graduated through anorexia, bulimia and alcoholism, nursed a husband with cancer, trained with the US Navy, worked with teenagers and prison inmates, and buried a father and now a mother, how was a growth on the rectum anything to worry about? Acceptance, resignation, desensitization, or just an incredibly high tolerance for life's adventures allowed me to simply blink. In quick succession I thought: 'What about Ian? What about my prison classes and the schools? Is my will up to date?' This last was the least of my worries. My lawyer, Greg Towers, could set his calendar by my regularity: every three years I would be on his doorstep with a tweak here and there, John having emphatically instilled in me the necessity to keep my last wishes up to date. The other concerns were dealt with within forty-eight hours.

I obviously lived to tell the tale, but for four months I was accompanied by a plastic bag, of sorts, attached to my side. An embarrassing and extremely frustrating experience. I was forced to find handicapped loos, could wear no figure-hugging clothes, and often needed to leave the table halfway through a meal as my internal involuntary muscles unexpectedly announced: 'Here we go for your next sprint training!' However, I was determined that if I had to live with an unanticipated addition to my frame, then live I would. On a holiday to the Cook Islands, I learnt to swim *before* a meal, never after; to avoid spices at all costs, or the ancient torture rack would have nothing on the agony of vice-like side cramps that could last for an hour; and to be grateful for an event that I knew I would eventually be able to share with others who would be confronting a similar experience.

David reconnected my insides, leaving me with yet another addition to the road map on my stomach. I now had a valuable collection of external as well as internal scars, all telling their stories. If and when I reach the Pearly Gates and am asked how I found life, I already know how I will reply: 'Yup — I had a good time!'

The first proposal of marriage came on the Saturday morning I broke the yolk of his poached egg (he *hated* the yolk breaking before he was ready to poke it with his knife); the second as I slipped alighting from a Melbourne tram; and the third over a meal of Japanese teppanyaki in Bangkok. As he completed the question for the third time, I put down my chopsticks and removed his from the plate in front of him.

'Do you realize how many times you have asked me that question?' I enquired.

His look was one of total surprise. 'No,' he replied in all innocence.

'Three times' — I slowly rolled the 'r' and clicked the 't'.

His eyes widened and the eyebrows elevated: 'Oh well, I guess I was just making sure.'

'Sure of what?'

'That you wanted to marry me.'

'How do you know I've said "yes"?'

'Well, if you had said "no", you would not have my chopsticks on your plate, would you?' That was his *touché!* moment of the year.

By December 1997, in Hobart, we were making a list of invitees. The International Gossipmongers Society, based in Auckland, leapt onto its telephones and faxes. With barely three months to go to The Day, we never even contemplated arranging the whole ceremony in any other way except by ourselves. As the news spread, in came the invitations of help. Christine (Fletcher) would not let us set foot in any other venue except her own garden once she heard we wanted the occasion to take place outdoors: 'Leave it to me, Liz. I'll take care of that part.' Bryan and Robyn Jackson of Jackson's Antique Museum offered us one of their vintage cars; friends Dale and Mindy insisted on decorating the reception venue; and a longtime dressmaking friend surveyed my bolt of gold lamé with drooling lips.

Finally the day arrived, but not before panic stations at ten o'clock the previous evening. We had no Master of Ceremonies! Who did we know who was articulate, funny, cynical, and knew us both reasonably well? In unison: 'Murray Deaker!' I don't think Murray slept a wink that night.

As the red-and-white 1933 Studebaker limousine festooned with white ribbons backed into the driveway, we could see the little old ladies in the home opposite almost jockeying their wheelchairs for a position at the windows! Out of over 200 very collectable cars, Bryan had chosen his favourite (and most reliable) vehicle, the one with a track record of the least number of breakdowns. In my backless, long-trained, gold lamé gown, with my two fair-haired nieces in gold satin, we must have been an impressive sight as we headed slowly along Remuera Road for the twenty-minute ride to Mt Eden. Following us was a nondescript Toyota which needed a coat of paint, with my three male supporters inside.

As we started up the barely discernable incline towards the Remuera shops, there was an ominous coughing and sneezing from the bonnet of our car. Gradually, like an old, tired dog being taken for a stroll and resisting continuing for the specified distance, the limo shuddered to a halt slap-bang in the middle of Remuera Road! As the traffic piled up behind us, I thought Robyn would either be run over or do herself an injury. She was dancing up and down beside Bryan, who had his head under the bonnet, prodding and pulling at the engine's innards, with no co-operation from the motor as regards starting. Out leapt my three supporters from the Toyota: two brown faces waving tattooed hands and one white face looking like he belonged to the Hell's Angels (which he had) — Mohi, Colin and Clem, coming to the rescue. Remuera Road cannot have witnessed a scene such as the one presented that day. I was on the road resplendent in my lamé, Robyn still cavorting in her stilettos, with diamonds flashing in the sunlight and her string of pearls bobbing around her neck, pleading with Bryan to 'do *something*', and three men in dinner suits who looked suspiciously like prison escapees had their heads under the car bonnet while cars were backed up on either side, horns hooting in either total frustration or applauding the free entertainment.

There was only one solution. We were already fashionably late and the car was refusing to budge, so into the beat-up Toyota piled the six of us — the future bride, two bridesmaids and three 'dickey suited' supporters, leaving behind a dancing Robyn and a swearing Bryan.

Naturally, nobody was expecting us in anything other than the art deco transport they had heard about. Fortunately Alec, our bouncer at the gate, recognized us, although his eyes widened into the size of ship portholes as we clunked and farted past him, finally arriving with a *phut, phut, shudder* at the top of the driveway. The passenger side faced the assembled guests, so that the first person who became visible was Colin, his white-banded gangster hat at a rakish angle. Leaning into the car, he called to Mohi and Clem, 'Don't forget your guns!'

The guests froze as if they had been doused in a truckload of instant concrete. Some managed to grab onto the family heirlooms around their necks, others had their hands over their wallet pockets. They gaped in disbelief as I calmly walked around the car, my nieces following, adjusted my gold train, and, in a voice which quietly announced that I was in control of the whole situation, said, 'OK guys — are we ready?'

Ian's laugh cracked the thundering silence as the ripples started: 'They're Liz's friends. It's OK.' Everyone took their seats then, as our party arranged ourselves for the walk up the grass to the 'altar' table. My nieces, Bo and Josephine, looked like little golden angels, but could hardly contain their excitement at walking next to Mohi, Colin and Clem dressed in their gangster outfits, plastic machine guns at the ready.

Halfway up the 'aisle', I felt something happening behind me; years in Paremoremo had given me a sixth sense.

'Cops,' whispered Clem. 'A whole lot of the fuckers.'

'Of course,' whispered back Colin. 'Ian's friends, you egg.'

'Shut the fuck up,' hissed Mohi. 'This is Liz's fucking wedding.' I was sure I could hear the hairs slowly descending on the backs of their necks.

Ian's brother, David, married us. Ian's second daughter, Trudie, attended the wedding, and Debbie and Robbie arrived for the reception. A crack in the ice had appeared, perhaps helped by the fact that their mother had a new man in her life.

There was no shortage of transport to the reception at the Ellerslie War Memorial Hall, and an amazing sight met our eyes as we pulled up in front of the building. There stood Bryan and Robyn, smiling like Cheshire cats, leaning against the door of the red-and-white Studebaker. They had found some helpful Remuera-ite who had towed the reluctant vehicle all the way to the reception. Bryan was in his element: everyone wanted their photos taken inside and out — including the 'gangsters'!

The last thing Ian and I had wanted was a white-tablecloth function. The tables were wooden trestles, the seating arrangements were unorganized, and the noise was deafening. There was a smorgasbord of society discovering where they each fitted into our lives — gamblers, police officers, ex-drug addicts, recovered alcoholics, gardeners, plumbers, builders, bank managers, lawyers and stock-brokers, topped up with ex-prison inmates. Murray excelled himself, and Ian clinched the proceedings before the dancing commenced by thanking the Corrections Department 'for allowing Liz's bodyguards a day's leave from Paremoremo'. There are guests who to this day still believe that Mohi, Colin and Clem were out on special leave!

A month later, both Ian and I were thankful that, although the wedding had been pulled together in haste, at least we could attend Government House in Wellington as man and wife. We were there with his mother, my sisters and Emily, my niece from England who was on her gap year. As the Companion of the New Zealand Order of Merit was pinned to my chest in recognition of my work in the field of substance abuse education, I silently accepted the white cross on the crimson ribbon on behalf of all the hundreds of people who had played a part in my life. It was not mine, it was *ours* — a recognition for all of us who continue to work to reduce the casualties of the universal epidemic of drug use and, increasingly, the major underlying cause of our social malaise.

From a gold-laméd bride to Mistress of Ceremonies at an ex-mobster's wedding was the next Shakespearean part that I was invited to play on the stage of life. My own wedding had created a virus amongst my 'gangster' friends! Clem married his long-time partner, and Mohi decided it was time he placed a ring on the finger of Sandra, his Welsh girlfriend.

The tiny church at Ohinemutu on the shores of Lake Rotorua was a fairytale setting for the simple ceremony. Across the lake stood Mokoia Island, the scene of the Maori love story of Hinemoa and Tutanekai. Hinemoa was the daughter of a Maori chief, and against her father's wishes swam across the lake one night, buoyed by calabashes to keep her afloat, to meet her lover Tutanekai, who guided her with music from his flute. Wrapping her in his cloak, he carried her to a thermal hot pool to warm her. Eventually her father forgave her, and they 'married and lived happily ever after'.

Ninety-eight per cent of the attendees at the wedding reception were Maori, many with life stories that would have been as interesting as Mohi's, and all wondering why *I* was in charge of the proceedings — from a cultural perspective this was not a role for a female, but my tokotoko obviously intrigued them. At the end of Mohi's speech they had their explanation, but a ripple of unease had started to swell by the time he had concluded. The assembled mob had been left in no doubt as to *which* government department Ian had recently retired from. Some of the storytelling had been fairly specific, one man describing how he and Mohi had once stolen two pairs of trousers from a department store in Whangarei.

Ian gave the final speech, breaking the thundering silence, and leaving them with a vision of a police officer that few of them would have imagined. Rotorua has never been an area of the country that has been particularly enamoured of the police force.

He explained how he had met Mohi through me, the immense amount of admiration he had for Mohi and others like him who had turned their lives around since they had discarded their substance use and abuse. He described his retired life as 'the gambling policeman', running casinos as entertainment and to raise money for drug education, and how his most loyal and trustworthy workers were now people such as Mohi. The guests' eyes grew wider by the sentence as Ian continued; Mohi had access to his credit card, was sometimes given hundreds of dollars in cash to pay the croupiers' wages, and often had the use of his car for out-of-Auckland functions. His closing story almost brought on a standing ovation.

'Finally,' he chuckled, 'there was only one crime in all my thirty-three years in the police that we were unable to solve — and that was what happened to two pairs of trousers that were stolen from a department store in Whangarei.'

Chapter 24

Understanding metamorphoses

As he stopped the car at the gate for me to collect the mail, I heard the engine die. 'I can't live here any more. It's your place, not ours' — and I knew he was serious. There was John's ghost in every room, Mother's antiques waiting to be tripped over or knocked to the floor at a wrong turning, and, although I had tried my best to stamp every room with an 'ours' rather than a 'mine' feeling, there were walls that seemed to whisper to him 'Who are you?' He was surrounded by a musty sense of old, worn-out lives hovering like a silent, curling mist, its fingers poking into any nook or cranny that was unsealed. While I could sense the need to move, I could think of nothing more daunting.

The accumulation of shoes, clothes, knick-knacks, manuals and books, not to mention much of Mother's furniture, pictures and several ancient dead animals that had belonged to my grand-mother, looked like a Steptoe and Son's junkyard or an antique/art deco collector's paradise, depending on your taste. Decisions were not hard: Waiheke Island was not the place for most of these objects, but my toes were firmly dug into concrete over two items — my books and eight book cases, including the custom-built glass-fronted one that stretched from floor to ceiling in the sitting room.

Three months later, I was in the grip of a depression never before experienced. Not only had I vacated a home of twenty-five years in which I knew every creak and rattle and groan of the woodwork, but familiar furniture and pictures were no longer with me. I was separated from my friends by a thirty-five-minute ferry ride, and I had left far behind the environment in which I had grown up; where I had drunk myself into its gutters, walked its pavements again with my head held high, the place I had called home for the majority of my life. I had left the '*House and Garden*' home for a kitset Lockwood beach house on a 4000-person island with a garden like an Amazon jungle of convolvulus and honeysuckle, a dirt-track driveway, and a washing machine that leered at me when I entered the 'front door'. It had seemed like a great adventure to move to the beach house, the outlook reminding Ian of Island Bay in Wellington where he grew up, but for me the timber walls, low-stud ceiling and isolation gave me a sense of suffocating abandonment. I was grateful for my school work, that I could forget my circumstances amongst my prison classes, that I could lean on my recovered-alcoholic friends — and that Ian was in total agreement that we should contact Dick, our 'pet' builder, to help us create something in which I could live.

We commenced the changes to the house, and while that was stimulating, I was still miserable. Life is full of what are so often seen as impossible situations, but are actually tremendous opportunities. In retrospect, our relocation to Waiheke was an unexpected opportunity for me to yet again take stock of my 'store cupboard'. This time, it was not making the moral inventory that had been necessary at the termination of my active alcoholic career, but instead reassessing a new and different chapter in my life that could progress only if I disentangled myself from many of the invisible restraints of the past. The shock at the time could not be seen from such a perspective — of course not; I was experiencing it subjectively. However, there were dark clouds looming for the family; clouds that when they became visible allowed me to forget my lack of gratitude for all I had, and brought about the 'cure' for my depression — focusing on helping someone else.

There is nothing that will connect a group more quickly than a crisis (the Chinese consider this to also be an opportunity), and every family faces at least one. Ian's came with his son, Robbie, in such a way that it was impossible for me not to be involved. The situation was a climax to Robbie's drug-using, and his story is a classic example of what happens to many of our young people today.

By the time Robbie was involved in the party circuit at seventeen, he believed that everyone drank alcohol and at least experimented with cannabis. He discovered that the latter's initial effect gave him a feeling of self-confidence, euphoria, relaxation and a humorous perspective on everything — whether it was funny or not. Despite his father's obsessional involvement in the subject, he believed marijuana was a harmless substance, and was soon using every weekend, as were all his friends. It never occurred to him that he was mixing primarily with those who smoked because of how important the substance had become to him; this just reinforced his belief that everyone used it. Before long his consumption increased, and occasional nights of use during the week were added to the regular weekend sessions, with LSD often thrown into the mix as well.

Training as a croupier in Christchurch removed him from the drug scene into which he had moved and also curtailed his usage; but on his return to Auckland, within a matter of days old acquaintances and a flatmate who smoked had immersed him in the culture again. From there it was a downward spiral. Taking a croupier's job at Melbourne Casino he was deprived of his friends and family, and, isolated and lonely, it was only a matter of time before he discovered the marijuana and peripheral drug culture in Australia. Within months he was a daily and nightly user, even buying his supply from one of the casino's supervisors. An operation on his shoulder incapacitated him, and his cannabis consumption increased, both in quantity and in strength. He abdicated all responsibilities to his girlfriend, Lucy, which ensured a life of hedonism.

No matter how well Robbie scrubbed himself up to see Ian and I on our trips to Melbourne, we both knew that there was something radically amiss. When his job at the casino ended, Ian agreed to bring him back to Auckland and enrol him at Whitecliffe Art School. A talented artist, Robbie's portfolio had him placed in the second-year stream, and we all breathed a sigh of relief as we knew that art was his passion. Two months later, having finished the relationship with Lucy (who had followed him to New Zealand), sold his car and graduated from marijuana smoking to LSD, magic mushrooms, GBH (liquid Ecstasy), nitrous oxide and E as a result of living in a druggie house, he was on a plane back to Melbourne. A precipitous descent into the darklands had started: work where he could find it, regular requests for money from members of the family, intimations of suicide, a continued association with his Ritalin-supplying, skateboarding sixteen-year-old friend who had conned his parents into believing he needed it, and trips to Adelaide to purchase marijuana to trade in Melbourne, hoping to make a quick dollar. Eventually, he ended up living in a flat with a paranoid, hallucinating alcoholic who made death threats to imaginary people over the telephone on a daily basis. There were hydroponically grown drugs in the bathroom, and magic mushroom cook-ups in the kitchen by the time we arrived in Melbourne for one of our regular visits.

Robbie slunk through the door of our hotel room, and burst into tears. I knew immediately, as I am sure Ian did, that he had finally hit the bottom of the barrel. However, when he requested a padded room to escape from all the people who were after him, I had a sinking feeling that perhaps we should have forced an intervention sooner; I was not sure that he hadn't developed paranoid schizophrenia. Only time would tell. After our reassurances that he could come home, enter treatment and start a different life, I was completely thrown off-balance when, as we entered the coffee shop for a well-earned caffeine fix, Robbie told his father that he wanted to talk to me alone. This was the boy, for he was emotionally around sixteen (that's what marijuana does to so many of our young people — stunts their emotional growth), who not many years previously had been threatening me with homicide!

I've conducted counselling sessions in stranger places than coffee shops, but one gratifying outcome from Robbie's trauma was that cement began to fill the cracks, or perhaps the crevasses, in the varying relationships within Ian's family. His ex-wife felt that Ian and I could be more helpful in this situation than she could, an attitude that I am not sure I would have been nearly so gracious to take had I been in her situation; Debbie helped her brother to detox in her home, with Trudie visiting on a regular basis full of encouragement. Somehow I knew that this was not enough, so I called Colin and explained the situation, and within a matter of hours he was knocking on Debbie's door. Yet again, one of life's incongruous situations: a Maori ex-prison inmate and recovered marijuana-addicted alcoholic, prepared to spend many of his evenings conveying a retired police officer's son to meetings of recovered alcoholics and drug addicts so that Robbie could understand that life without drugs was possible and meaningful.

After weeks in Higher Ground's Therapeutic Community Treatment Centre, Robbie found a plumber friend who employed him as a labourer. This triggered an interest in the trade and has resulted in our having a qualified plumber as a member of the family. *Never give up.* I wish all recoveries could be as straightforward as Robbie's; unfortunately, they are not.

The years have passed, and today there are birthdays and Christmases in which I participate; presents are exchanged and grandchildren do not differentiate between the laps on which they sit. Ian's wife has remarried, Robbie mends the pipes and clears the drains, Debbie types for me and signs emails with 'your loving stepdaughter', and Trudie prays for us all. Over the years I have lost touch with John's children, apart from his eldest, Mary Elizabeth, who followed in her father's footsteps to become a highly respected lawyer.

In families I have discovered a circle that an outsider can only be invited into and can never become a full part of. No matter what happens, as Grandma in Dodie Smith's play *Dear Octopus* comments, 'the family isn't what it was, *but* it is adaptable. It bends, it stretches but it never breaks.' Not all families today enjoy that type of connection, and at times members may feel either abandoned or suffocated; but when, like Canada geese, they can not only take care of each other but let others merge from the outskirts, then perhaps in this fragmented world of ours we can find a common purpose.

Canada geese head south for the winter, flying in a V formation. As each bird flaps its wings, it creates an uplift for those that follow; the whole flock together has a flying range about 70 per cent greater than if each bird flew on its own. When the leading goose at the head of the V tires, it falls back and another takes its place. Geese honk from behind, to encourage (not discourage!) those up front. If a goose gets sick or is wounded by gunshots, two other geese will follow it to the ground and stay with it until it is either able to fly or dies; only then will they continue with another formation, to catch up with their own group or remain with the new one. We could learn a lesson from these geese.

Years may have wrinkled my skin, but I hope I will never be devoid of enthusiasm as that would wrinkle my soul. I have had my adventures — painful and pleasurable, predictable and unexpected — and discovered that making a living is not the same as making a life: knowledge helps with the former, wisdom with the latter. I will forever be faced with opportunities from which to learn, for Nature does not demand perfection from us; only that we grow — moving from being smart, believing only half of what we hear, to being brilliant, knowing which half to believe. I have grown to learn how to *feel* a moment rather than make use of it; and in the final analysis, people may forget what I have said and even what I did, but they will never forget how I made them *feel*.

From being a self-centred, bitter, destructive, hedonistic piranha on society, I believe I have walked a million miles, beginning with that first step on a different road — the one less travelled. I have not travelled it alone, and I am eternally grateful to the hundreds who have journeyed beside me. Along the way I have discovered that what makes life so consumingly interesting is not what I know but what I don't know. When my life is through, please extract what you can from me, and dig the rest into the compost heap!

Epilogue

Early in 2006, with encouragement from Ian and help from a medical student friend, I enrolled at Auckland University to commence the fulfilment of a lifelong dream — the completion of a degree in History. In July that year I received a letter from Professor Reay, head of the History Department, congratulating me on my excellent results; stating that I obviously had a real talent in the subject and if I intended to complete a Major in History, he would urge me to consider Honours studies. I have a life now full of the most fantastic choices and opportunities.

If you were to ask me where I am today, I would tell you this.

Ian and I are on Waiheke Island, a paradise in the middle of the Hauraki Gulf, thirty-five minutes by ferry from Auckland. Few people find *one* soul mate in life — how fortunate I am that I have been blessed with a second. Our two seven-year-old adopted children are adorable: white fluffy coats, little white paws, and the most amazing blue eyes that contrast so unexpectedly with their creamy faces. We love them to bits and each is a challenge for me today — I am trying to become the person my cats think I am.

Our garden mirrors my life. From chaos and a wilderness of convolvulus, honeysuckle, thistles, gorse and moth plants, we now walk among orange trees, vegetables and native ferns, a scene of order and productivity, to our wooden seat which sleeps and then wakes to a view of the Pacific Ocean. The ocean reminds me of all our moods; the garden of life's seasons. So, as I pass through the autumn of my life, do I have regrets, resentments or remorse? No. I have learnt that these are useless wastes of energy. I have made my amends where possible.

Could my life have been different? Of course, but I have acquired beliefs, values and attitudes that allow me to say that it has been unbelievably rich and meaningful in a way I could never have dreamed possible. If I had lived the life I had planned for myself at seventeen, I would have sold myself short. All of the challenges through the years have brought me to an understanding that the only true freedom we have is within us; to choose our own attitude — to find serenity to accept what we cannot change, courage to change what we can, and with God's (as each of us understands that word) help and guidance to discover the wisdom to know the difference.

A long time ago, in the depths of the Chinese country-side, there lived a farmer with a son who was his pride and joy. Over the years, the man taught his son the value of the horse that together they had trained and which had become indispensable to their way of life. One day the horse escaped and the family was devastated. How were they to exist without the animal on which they had become so dependent? They had little money and no other form of transport and no other animal to help them plough the fields.

A few days later, the horse returned and the farmer was amazed. Accompanying his horse were six stallions which he and his son set about breaking in, excitedly anticipating what they could do with their new-found wealth. Then disaster overtook them. The son broke his leg while working with one of the horses. His father was grief-stricken. Here was his beloved son handicapped for life.

It was not long before fighting broke out amongst the various Chinese warlords, and the local lord appeared on the farm to claim all the young, able-bodied men to fight. When he saw the man with the limp, he left him behind; he wanted no cripple in his army. The old father died later a happy man.

Old Chinese folk tale

To accept the seemingly bad along with the apparently good becomes first a skill and then an art in life which only we can learn for ourselves. To know the glories of success and the devastations of pain in all their varying forms is to live a life with a richness few are privileged to experience. What we do with all of our life's happenings depends on whether we become bitter or better. The difference is in the *I*.

Warning signals of a drinking problem

- You are concerned about your drinking.
- Others are concerned about your drinking.
- There are family arguments over your drinking.
- You feel annoyed when others refer to your drinking.
- You make excuses for your drinking.
- You have stopped drinking for a period of time to prove to others you can stop drinking, but are looking forward to the day when you can start again.
- You have sneaked drinks, or lied or made excuses about a drink.
- You hide supplies of alcohol.
- You frequently drink alone or at inappropriate times.
- Frequent attempts to control your drinking fail.
- You have a preoccupation with drinking or not drinking.
- You have missed days from work/school due to drinking.
- You have drinking-driving convictions.
- You scull drinks down quickly.
- You are unable to have one drink without craving more.
- You have experienced loss of memory from drinking.
- You get tremors and have early-morning drinks.
- There is an onset of lengthy intoxications.
- You are afraid to stop drinking.

Experiencing any number of the above points will indicate that a drinking problem may be developing.

Saying yes to three or more of these points means that you and/or your family members need to seek help, or the consequences will compound for all involved in the drinker's life.

Where to find help

Below is a selection of agencies, current at time of publication, that may be useful to the reader. These are a guide only, and the reader is encouraged to check the Internet for further information and additional services.

12-Step Programmes —
these can be found on an international basis

✦ **Alcoholics Anonymous**

www.alcoholics-anonymous.org.nz

☎ 0800 229 6757

✦ **Narcotics Anonymous**

www.nzna.org

☎ 0800 628 632

✦ **Overeaters Anonymous**

www.oaregion10.org

☎ Auckland (09) 376 3068
    Hamilton (07) 839 1599
    Wellington (04) 384 8821
    Canterbury (03) 365 3812
    Dunedin (03) 477 2255

✦ **Al-Anon/Alateen**

www.al-anon.org.nz

☎ General Service Office (09) 309 4792

✦ **Sex and Love Addicts Anonymous, Auckland**

http://aucknz.localslaa.org

☎ (09) 377 1800

✤ **Sex and Love Addicts Anonymous, Christchurch**
   meet at the Christchurch Community House, 141 Hereford St
   ☎ (03) 365 3139

Some residential services available for alcohol and drug dependency (others can be found on the Internet)

✤ **Odyssey House, Auckland**
   www.odyssey.org.nz
   ☎ (09) 638 4957

✤ **Higher Ground Drug Rehabilitation Trust, Auckland**
   www.higherground.org.nz
   ☎ (09) 834 0017

✤ **Bridge Programme (run by the Salvation Army)**
   www.sab.org.nz
   ☎ National Office (09) 369 5143

✤ **Wings Trust, Auckland**
   www.wingstrust.co.nz
   ☎ (09) 815 1631

✤ **Capri Trust, Auckland (normally for over-eighteens only)**
   www.capritrust.co.nz
   ☎ (09) 527 6090

✤ **Harbour House (Care NZ)**
   www.harbourhouse.co.nz
   ☎ Head Office (04) 384 2058

✤ **Moana House, Dunedin (men only)**
   www.moanahouse.org.nz
   ☎ (03) 477 0842

✤ **Springhill Residential Centre**
   42 Morris St, Napier
   ☎ (06) 835 4496

Eating disorders

✣ **EDEN (Eating Difficulties Education Network), Auckland**

www.eden.org.nz

☎ 09 378 9039

✣ **Mercy Ministries, Auckland (for young women)**

www.mercyministries.org.nz

☎ (09) 443 7136

✣ your local hospital or district health board

Other services

✣ **Care NZ**

www.carenz.co.nz

☎ Head Office (04) 384 2058

✣ **Hanmer Clinic**

☎ Hamilton (07) 834 0949

Tauranga (07) 579 6470

✣ **CADS (Community Alcohol and Drug Services), Auckland, (including programmes targeted at specific groups of people)**

www.cads.org.nz

☎ (09) 845 1818

✣ **Tupu Pacific Peoples Service, Auckland**

www.cads.org.nz

☎ (09) 845 1818

✣ **Te Atea Marino, Auckland**

www.cads.org.nz

☎ (09) 845 1818

✣ **TRANX, Auckland**

http://homepages.ihug.co.nz/~tranx

☎ (09) 356 7305

❧ **Riverstone Counselling Ltd**
   1 Grange Road, Mt Eden, Auckland
   www.riverstonegroup.co.nz
   ☎ (09) 623 7100

❧ **Alcohol Drug Helpline**
   www.adanz.org.nz
   ☎ 0800 787 797

❧ **your local district health board**